Communications in Computer and Information Science 1203

Commenced Publication in 2007
Founding and Former Series Editors:
Phoebe Chen, Alfredo Cuzzocrea, Xiaoyong Du, Orhun Kara, Ting Liu,
Krishna M. Sivalingam, Dominik Ślęzak, Takashi Washio, Xiaokang Yang,
and Junsong Yuan

Editorial Board Members

More information about this series at http://www.springer.com/series/7899

Sabu M. Thampi · Ljiljana Trajkovic ·
Kuan-Ching Li · Swagatam Das ·
Michal Wozniak · Stefano Berretti (Eds.)

Machine Learning and Metaheuristics Algorithms, and Applications

First Symposium, SoMMA 2019
Trivandrum, India, December 18–21, 2019
Revised Selected Papers

Springer

Editors
Sabu M. Thampi
Indian Institute of Information Technology
and Management - Kerala (IIITM-K)
Trivandrum, India

Kuan-Ching Li
Providence University
Taichung, Taiwan

Michal Wozniak
Wrocław University of Technology
Wrocław, Poland

Ljiljana Trajkovic
Simon Fraser University
Burnaby, BC, Canada

Swagatam Das
Indian Statistical Institute
Kolkata, West Bengal, India

Stefano Berretti
Università degli Studi di Firenze
Florence, Italy

ISSN 1865-0929   ISSN 1865-0937   (electronic)
Communications in Computer and Information Science
ISBN 978-981-15-4300-5   ISBN 978-981-15-4301-2   (eBook)
https://doi.org/10.1007/978-981-15-4301-2

This Springer imprint is published by the registered company Springer Nature Singapore Pte Ltd.
The registered company address is: 152 Beach Road, #21-01/04 Gateway East, Singapore 189721, Singapore

Preface

The Symposium on Machine Learning and Metaheuristics Algorithms, and Applications (SoMMA 2019) provided a forum for scientists and researchers to present their latest results and a means to discuss the recent developments in machine learning, metaheuristics, and their applications. The symposium was held in Trivandrum, Kerala, India, during December 18–21, 2019. SoMMA 2019 was hosted by the Indian Institute of Information Technology and Management-Kerala (IIITM-K), Trivandrum.

We received 53 submissions this year, out of which 23 papers (17 regular papers and 6 short papers) were accepted. The papers were subjected to a double-blind peer review, where the Technical Program Committee considered the significance, novelty, and technical quality of submission. We thank the program chairs for their wise advice and brilliant suggestions in organizing the technical program. We would like to extend our deepest appreciation to the Advisory Committee members. Thanks to all members of the Technical Program Committee, and the external reviewers, for their hard work in evaluating and discussing papers. We wish to thank all the members of the Organizing Committee, whose work and commitment was invaluable. We sincerely thank all the keynote speakers who shared with us their expertise and knowledge. Moreover, our warm gratitude should be given to all the authors who submitted their work to SoMMA 2019. The EDAS conference system proved very helpful during the submission, review, and editing phases.

We thank IIITM-K for hosting the conference. Our sincere thanks go to Dr. Saji Gopinath, Director at IIITM-K, for his continued support and cooperation. Recognition should go to the Local Organizing Committee members who all worked extremely hard on the details of important aspects of the conference programs and social activities. We appreciate the contributions of all the faculty and staff of IIITM-K and the student volunteers who contributed their time to make the conference successful.

We wish to express our gratitude to the team at Springer for their help and cooperation.

December 2019

S. M. Thampi
L. Trajkovic
K. Li
S. Das
M. Wozniak
S. Berretti

Organization

Chief Patron

Madhavan Nambiar   IIITM-K, India
(IAS Rtd., Chairman)

Patron

Saji Gopinath (Director)   IIITM-K, India

General Chairs

Sankar Kumar Pal   IIITM-K, India
Ljiljana Trajkovic   Simon Fraser University, Canada
Kuan-Ching Li   Providence University, Taiwan

General Executive Chair

Sabu M. Thampi   IIITM-K, India

Organizing Chair

Asharaf S.   IIITM-K, India

Technical Program Chairs

Swagatam Das   IIITM-K, India
Michal Wozniak   Wroclaw University, Warsaw, Poland
Millie Pant   Indian Institute of Technology, Roorkee, India
Stefano Berretti   University of Florence, Italy

Technical Program Committee Members

Hemanth Venkateswara   Arizona State University, USA
Nasser Najibi   Cornell University, USA
John Strassner   Huawei, USA
Nitish Paliwal   Intel Corp., USA
Yi Gai   Intel Labs, USA
Dennis Franklin   Kennesaw State University at Marietta Campus, USA
Eduard Babulak   Liberty University, USA
Mohammed Kaabar   Moreno Valley College, USA
Ricardo Rodriguez   Raytheon, USA

Mohamad Forouzanfar	SRI International, USA
Ratheesh Kumar Meleppat	University of California, Davis, USA
Atif Khan	University of Chicago, USA
Sherali Zeadally	University of Kentucky, USA
Valerio Formicola	University of Naples, Italy
Cheryl Brown	University of North Carolina at Charlotte, USA
Amar Almasude	Walden University, USA
Shuvendu Rana	University of Strathclyde, UK
Mohammad Al-Shabi	University of Sharjah, UAE
Muhammed Cinsdikici	Manisa Celal Bayar University, Turkey
Seyed Sahand Mohammadi Ziabari	Vrije University of Amsterdam, The Netherlands
Grienggrai Rajchakit	Maejo University, Thailand
Lien-Wu Chen	Feng Chia University, Taiwan
Pratap Sahu	Foxconn, Taiwan
Jeng-Feng Weng	National United University, Taiwan
Antonio Cimmino	Lasting Dynamics, Switzerland
Sang-wook Han	Royal Institute of Technology (KTH), Sweden
Houcine Hassan	Universidad Politecnica de Valencia, Spain
Maria-Estrella Sousa-Vieira	University of Vigo, Spain
Chau Yuen	Singapore University of Technology and Design, Singapore
Jalal Al Muhtadi	King Saud University, Saudi Arabia
Andreea Vescan	Babes-Bolyai University, Romania
Azizul Mohamad	Universiti Malaysia Perlis, Malaysia
Syamsiah Mashohor	Universiti Putra Malaysia, Malaysia
Sim-Hui Tee	Xiamen University Malaysia, Malaysia
Abdel Mehsen Ahmad	Lebanese International University, Lebanon
Chady El Moucary	Notre Dame University, Lebanon
Dhananjay Singh	Hankuk University of Foreign Studies, South Korea
Philip Daely	Institut Teknologi Telkom Surabaya, South Korea
Bayu Adhi Tama	Pohang University of Science and Technology (POSTECH), South Korea
Byeong-jun Han	Soongsil University, South Korea
Prashant Jamwal	Nazarbayev University, Kazakhstan
Akihiro Fujihara	Chiba Institute of Technology, Japan
Mauro Gaggero	National Research Council of Italy, Italy
Salvatore Serrano	University of Messina, Italy
Ugo Fiore	University of Naples Federico II, Italy
Lucia Sacchi	University of Pavia, Italy
Giacomo Veneri	University of Siena, Italy
Hiyam Hatem Jabbar	University of Sumer, Iraq
Safanah Raafat	University of Technology Baghdad, Iraq
Makram Fakhry	University of Technology, Baghdad, Iraq
Sasan Yousefi	KN Toosi University of Technology, Iran
Supratman Zakir	IAIN Bukittinggi, Indonesia
Priya Ranjan	Amity University, India

Sumita Mishra	Amity University at Lucknow Campus, India
Chinmay Chakraborty	Birla Institute of Technology, Mesra, India
Ciza Thomas	College of Engineering Trivandrum, India
T. C. Manjunath	Dayananda Sagar College of Engineering, Karnataka, India
Amitava Mukherjee	Globsyn Business School, Kolkata, India
Uppu Ramachnadraiah	Hindustan University, India
Rama Garimella	IIIT Hyderabad, India
Deepak Mishra	IIST, India
Nithin George	IIT Gandhinagar, India
S. Sastry Challa	IIT Hyderabad, India
Radhakrishna Pillai	Indian Institute of Management Kozhikode, India
Chinmoy Saha	Indian Institute of Space Science and Technology, India
Ravibabu Mulaveesala	Indian Institute of Technology Ropar, India
Kaushal Shukla	Indian Institute of Technology, Banaras Hindu University, India
Rajnish Yadav	Indian Space Research Organization, India
Manish Godse	Infosys Limited, India
Nimushakavi Murti Sarma	JNT University Hyderabad, India
Shashi Mehrotra	KL University, Vaddeswaram, India
Pawan Bhandari	McAfee, India
Ganesh Sable	MIT BAMU Aurangabad, India
Kumaravel S.	National Institute of Technology Calicut, India
Dattatraya Gaonkar	National Institute of Technology Surathkal, India
Mayank Dave	National Institute of Technology Kurukshetra, India
Sanjay Biswash	NIIT University, India
Kandasamy Selvaradjou	Pondicherry Engineering College, India
Jaydip Sen	Praxis Business School, India
Dilip Krishnaswamy	Reliance Industries Ltd., India
Gajendra Pratap Singh	Jawaharlal Nehru University, India
Saikat Shome	CSIR Central Mechanical Engineering Research Institute, Durgapur, India
Shashikant Patil	SVKM NMIMS Mumbai India, India
Bhagesh Seraogi	Tata Consultancy Services Ltd., India
Mahalakshmi T.	University of Kerala, India
Tanaji Khadtare	University of Pune, India
Ravichandra Bagalatti	Visveshwaraya Technological University, Belgaum and India
Valsa B.	VSSC, India
Kam Po Wong	The Hong Kong Polytechnic University, Hong Kong
Haridimos Kondylakis	FORTH-ICS, Greece
Nikolaos Sofianos	Democritus University of Thrace, Greece
Panagiotis Vlamos	Ionian University, Greece
Vasileios Baousis	University of Athens, Greece
Kostas Berberidis	University of Patras, Greece
Mahdi Bohlouli	Institute for Advanced Studies in Basic Science, Germany

Roland Weiniger	PIAGET Research Foundation, Germany
Benoit Muth	Benoit Muth, France
Drissa Houatra	Orange Labs, France
Michel Aldanondo	Toulouse University, Mines Albi, CGI, France
Philippe Canalda	Université de Franche-Comté, France
Pascal Lorenz	University of Haute Alsace, France
Amgad Salama	Alexandria University, Egypt
Samy Ghoniemy	The British University in Egypt (BUE), Egypt
Amr Elmougy	German University in Cairo, Egypt
Sebastián Basterrech	VSB-Technical University of Ostrava, Czech Republic
Petr Hajek	University of Pardubice, Czech Republic
George Dekoulis	Mesoyios College, Cyprus
Chia-Hung Wang	Fujian University of Technology, China
Zhicheng Hou	Chinese Academy of Sciences, China
Bin Cao	Harbin Institute of Technology, Shenzhen, China
Wei Wei	Xi'an University of Technology, China
Liang Huang	Zhejiang University of Technology, China
Ronggong Song	DRDC-Ottawa, Canada
Ahmed Mahmood	University of Guelph, Canada
Edmar Gurjão	Federal University of Campina Grande, Brazil
Renato Ishii	Universidade Federal do Mato Grosso do Sul, Brazil
Sarah Al-Shareeda	University of Bahrain, Bahrain
Gustavo Fernández Domínguez	AIT Austrian Institute of Technology, Austria
Saeid Nahavandi	Deakin University, Australia
Mehdi Gaham	Advanced Technologies Develeopement Center (CDTA) Algies, Algeria

Organized by

IIITM-Kerala

Contents

Hybrid Duty Cycle Algorithm for Industrial WSNs Using Machine Learning

Charbel Nicolas[1(✉)], Abdel-Mehsen Ahmad[2], Jose Rubio Hernan[3], and Gilbert Habib[1]

[1] LaRRIS, Faculty of Sciences, Lebanese University, Fanar, Lebanon
{Charbel.Nicolas,Gilbert.Habib}@ul.edu.lb
[2] School of Engineering, Lebanese International University, Beirut, Lebanon
abdelmehsen.ahmad@liu.edu.lb
[3] Electronics and Physics, Télécom SudParis, Institut Polytechnique de Paris, Evry, France
rubio_he@telecom-sudparis.eu

Abstract. Wireless Sensor Networks (WSNs) are used to monitor physical or environmental conditions. Due to energy and bandwidth constraints, wireless sensors are prone to packet loss during communication. To overcome the physical constraints of WSNs, there is an extensive renewed interest in applying data-driven machine learning methods. In this paper, we present a mission-critical surveillance system model for industrial environments. In our proposed system, a decision tree algorithm is installed on a centralized server to predict the wireless channel quality of the wireless sensors. Based on the machine-learning algorithm directives, wireless sensor nodes can proactively adapt their duty cycle to mobility, interference and hidden terminal. Extensive simulation results validate our proposed system. The prediction algorithm shows a classification accuracy exceeding 73%, which allows the duty cycle adaptation algorithm to significantly minimize the delay and energy cost compared to using pure TDMA or CSMA/CA protocols.

Keywords: Machine learning · J48 decision tree · Prediction · PRR · LQI · TDMA · CSMA/CA

1 Introduction

Fully automated factories use various types of systems to monitor the different components and parts of the production chain. Specifically, WSN (Wireless Sensor Network) has many advantages in monitoring the mobile parts that are difficult to monitor using fixed sensors. However, due to its limited resources, WSN node's energy depletion and hardware malfunctions can lead to node failures to form a robust network. Furthermore, these malfunctions may cause the node to fail in conveying the information and metrics about the production systems to the management server. Moreover, the industrial environment can also affect the wireless communication channels, leading to network reliability problems [6]. Usually in such environment, the traffic load flowing through the WSN can be characterized as minimal, only conveying periodically measured metrics.

© Springer Nature Singapore Pte Ltd. 2020
S. M. Thampi et al. (Eds.): SoMMA 2019, CCIS 1203, pp. 1–15, 2020.
https://doi.org/10.1007/978-981-15-4301-2_1

There are different layers of protocols that manage the wireless module in the WSN nodes. In this paper, we focus on the data link layer. In this latter, different types of protocols can be used, mainly opportunistic protocols like CSMA/CA, non-opportunistic protocols like TDMA, and hybrid protocols that can get the best of both worlds. In our previous work [4], we adapted the link layer dynamically between TDMA and CSMA/CA protocol based on the topology change without looking at the channel quality. In [9], we proposed a cognitive radio that analyzes the channel quality and adapts the MAC layer accordingly. The weakness of this method was the delay needed for adaptation. These solutions can be effective in specific environments. In the case of the industrial environment, the main issue is to minimize delays and avoid packet loss to minimize energy consumption. Traditionally, to reduce the energy consumption in WSN, duty cycling is used for scheduling by the link layer [11, 12]. The use of duty cycling is very efficient as the node goes to sleep when not active. Although duty cycling minimizes the energy cost, it does not minimize delays or manage the channel quality. To determine the channel quality, many parameters and metrics have been considered. The most used to characterize communication link stability and reliability is the packet reception ratio (PRR) [13]. By definition, the PRR is the number of packet received divided by the number of packet transmitted. In [3], authors utilize the PRR as the probability of successfully receiving a packet between two neighbor nodes. If the PRR is high means that the link quality is high and vice versa. PRR model in [3] shows a direct link with transmission power, receiver sensitivity, and distance between nodes. The transmission power and receiver sensitivity are evaluated using the Link Quality Indicator (LQI) [14]. The LQI represents the magnitude of the error between ideal constellations and a number of symbols immediately following the sync word in a transmitted packet. Moreover, the LQI presents a good correlation with PRR, however, it needs to be averaged over many packets (about 120 packets) [8].

Recently, various techniques form the machine-learning (ML) research area have lightened the interest of the wireless communication community specifically to improve the cognitive radio in wireless communication [15] and more precisely to improve the link layer in WSN [5, 16]. The survey done in [16] shows that most of the existing protocols use ML for reactive decisions, not proactive decisions, and only proactive algorithms have been used to adapt the routing algorithm at the routing layer. In [5], the proposed frame work classifies and chooses statically between applying TDMA or CSMA/CA.

In this paper, we propose an algorithm that predicts the channel quality and dynamically adapts the link layer using a hybrid TDMA-CSMA-sleep protocol. The proposed proactive adaption for the link layer uses the predicted PRR to have the time to adapt the physical layer (RF) to a hybrid TDMA-CSMA/CA mechanism, i.e., the time slot selection and organization.

The remainder of this paper is structured as follows. Section 2 positions our work in the current literature. In Sect. 3, we describe the part of the system managed by the Machine Learning-based Hybrid Duty Cycle Algorithm (ML-HDCA). Section 4 presents the topology of the network and the simulation results. And Sect. 5 concludes and discusses future work.

2 Related Work

The authors in [5] proposed a model to use ML in decision-making at the link layer to choose between TDMA and CSMA/CA. They do not propose dynamic protocol adaption or channel quality prediction to adapt preemptively to traffic throughput change. In [17], a hybrid TDMA and CSMA protocol is designed. It tackles the fire monitoring issue in buildings and consequently, the autonomous switching from energy-efficient normal monitoring to emergency monitoring to cope with heavy traffic. However, this paper does not address the issue of critical information loss due to poor channel quality. We assume, due to the nature of the industrial environment, that every aspect of the environment is usually monitored and kept by a centralized server. These logged data are usually analyzed by the network administrators to correct anomalies or upgrade the system. In this work, we will use these data as the dataset to create a reliable dynamically adaptable WSN. Moreover, we assume that the traffic load in the industrial WSN is minimal, due to the nature of information exchanged, which eliminates the need to manage the situations where we have high amount of traffic in the network.

To the best of our knowledge, our contribution is the first to introduce ML into the industrial environment to predict the state of the communication channel, and proactively protect the WSN critical information from being lost. We introduce the use of time as parameter to predict the channel quality. We argue that the particularity of monitoring the industrial topology (cf. Fig. 1), which is characterized by specific mobility patterns, the periodical mobility patterns will create a predictable state of the communication channels. Moreover, by using the time factor as a feature for the prediction, we show that the proactive adaptation of the protocols is better than only using ML in reactive protocol selection.

In the literature [16, 17], some studies used the traffic load to model or adapt the link layer mechanisms to increase the throughput. In this paper, we propose a mechanism to predict the PRR and adapt proactively the link layer scheme accordingly to prevent packet loss due to interference, hidden terminal and mobility. To predict the PRR, we require different characteristics and criteria, like the mobility state of a node, the link quality indicator (LQI) as there are a correlation between LQI and PRR [7], and the historical PRR values logged by the system periodically with their timestamps.

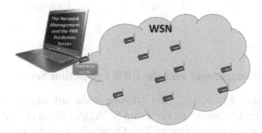

Fig. 1. A representation of the network management server, the gateway and the WSN.

3   System Description

Our system (cf. Fig. 1), called ML-HDCA, is composed of two parts. The first one is a centralized server containing the network management and the PRR prediction software. The second part is the hybrid duty cycle algorithm based on TDMA-CSMA/CA mechanisms. The sink node (gateway node) manages the newly arriving nodes by signaling and sending control messages from the server to the nodes. Usually, the server intervenes in two states of the nodes duty cycle: The initialization and the radio mechanism correction. During the initialization state, the new node arrives, and communicates to the server its mobility speed (fixed, low, high), the specific time where the predicted PRR is needed, and the LQI. The server, based on its ML algorithm (cf. Sect. 3.1), predicts the quality of the communication channel by calculating the predicted or estimated PRR. Then, the server replies to the sensor node by sending the predicted PRR for the specific requested time of day. Finally, the sensor adapts its data link layer accordingly. To classify the PRR, we use a terminology that is similar to the one used in [2]. The used PRR classes are *Bad* (<70%), *Good−* (70–80%), *Good+* (80–90%), and *Excellent* (>90%).

In the radio mechanism correction state, calculated PRR is sent periodically to the server and logged with the other data (cf. Table 1). Each hour, the node's radio adapts its configuration, either based on the predicted or the calculated PRR. In this paper, the scenario used focuses on only using the predicted PRR to update the radio configuration, and the calculated PRR to update the logging database on the ML server. Each sensor node selects the appropriate mode to communicate with its neighbors, depending on its neighborhood mode of configuration and its own configuration (cf. Sect. 3.2).

Table 1. Logged data (dataset) by the ML server.

Time of day	Mobility speed (High, Low, Fixed)	PRR classes (Bad, Gd−, Gd+, Excellent)	QoS of a TS (Excellent, Good, Bad) - LQI	PRR %
0:00	Fixed	Bad	Good	56,698%
1:00	Fixed	Excellent	Bad	0.8668%
...	...	...	...	...
23:00	Fixed	Excellent	Excellent	100%

3.1   The Network Management and the PRR Prediction Server

The server is composed of two parts. The first one is the software part that is composed of: (a) The Network management server using SCADA (Supervisory Control and Data Acquisition) technology in the system, or TinyOs platform with a server side application that can be used for data collection form the WSN, depending on the technology used. (b) The PRR prediction server (based on Weka [1] platform containing the data set and the prediction model). The second part is the hardware part that is composed of the computer server and the sink node (the gateway).

To build the classification model, we study and develop the relationship between the decision-making criterion (PRR) and the WSN features from the existing studies [3, 7]. Based on these studies, we conclude that, the most influential features that affect the classification criterion are the time, the LQI, the mobility status and the previous PRR values. All these features are logged on the server and form the dataset (cf. Table 1) used by the classification platform.

To generate the dataset, we create our own simulator to simulate the wireless sensor network and the radio behavior of each node. The data is transmitted in the header of each packet to the sink node then to the server. The simulator topology is further described in Sect. 4. We have trained and tested our classifier using the data generated by the simulator.

In order to validate the proposed model, we use two groups of datasets, one for training and another for evaluation. Afterwards, we import them into Weka for processing. Weka [1] is a java based platform that is composed of a collection of machine learning algorithms for data mining tasks; it processes the data set and generates the classification model. The classification model is validated by the second dataset. Then, Weka platform feeds the different features necessary for predicting the PRR from the requesting node. Finally, Weka generates the appropriate predicted PRR class to be used and the server sends it to the WSN node to adapt its physical layer. To do so, the channel quality forecast using the predicted PRR is used in different states of the WSN nodes: the initialization state and the steady state. During the WSN nodes state changes, the nodes update the information on the server by sending the LQI, the mobility state, the time of day, the existing PRR and the node ID to the server, and receive from the server the predicted PRR to use.

To choose the most suitable ML algorithm, we compared three classification algorithms: J48 decision tree, Sequential minimal optimization (SMO)-Support vector machine (SVM), and Random forest using our data set (cf. Table 1). To choose the best of the three classification algorithms we used the same data set of 5997 instances to test all the algorithms. The results showed that J48 decision tree is the best suited for our application (cf. Figs. 2, 3 and 4). It has the best delay to update the model (0.05 s), and the best time to apply classification (0.03 s), and a correct classification similar to the other algorithms with a percentage of 73.7%.

The resulting model and the confusion matrix of the Machine learning classification algorithm J48 decision tree that we chose to use by the server are shown in Fig. 5 and Table 2 respectively.

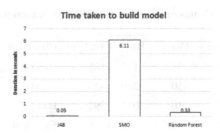

Fig. 2. Time taken to build the classification model.

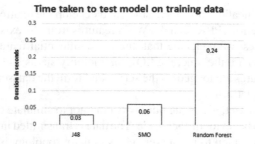

Fig. 3. Time taken to test the model on training data.

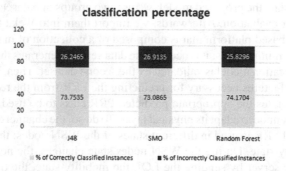

Fig. 4. Percentage of correctly classified instances.

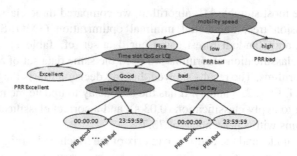

Fig. 5. The J48 decision tree model.

Table 2. Confusion matrix of the J48 classification model.

Good+	Good−	Bad	Excellent	Classifiers
21	63	145	165	Good+
0	150	249	429	Good−
0	110	3038	392	Bad
0	0	0	1235	Excellent

3.2 Hybrid TDMA-CSMA/CA Duty Cycle Algorithm Based on the PRR Classes

The standard CSMA/CA protocol is the initial state of the link layer mechanism for every new arriving node or any node that does not have any neighbor in TDMA mode. By receiving the predicted PRR from the server, as described earlier, the link layer of a sensor adapts to a specific configuration schema. Then, to calculate the actual PRR, the sensor node starts counting the number of correctly received packets from a neighbor. At the same time, this neighbor integrates in its packet header the total number of sent packets. This is done for all its neighbors. These numbers are used to calculate the real PRR value of the links, and then the PRR values for each node are averaged and sent to the server. This operation is done during the complete lifetime of a sensor and sent periodically through the header of the data packets to the server.

The node calculates the PRR and sends it to the server using this formula:

$PRR = \frac{\sum_{i=1}^{N} \frac{x_i}{X_i}}{N}$, where N is the total number of neighbors, X_i is the total number of packet sent by the neighbor i, x_i is the number of packets correctly received from the ith neighbor.

The server predicts the PRR using the model shown in Fig. 6 and sends it to the node. The sensor nodes only use the predicted PRR to proactively adapt their duty cycle as the link layer adaptation takes time.

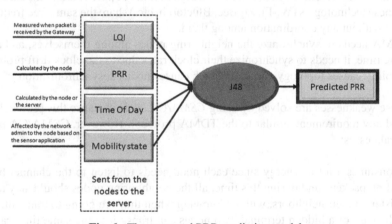

Fig. 6. The proposed PRR prediction model

3.3 Hybrid TDMA-CSMA/CA Algorithm and the Duty Cycle

To secure the links from packet loss and to create a temporal redundancy, we propose the Hybrid TDMA-CSMA/CA Algorithm where the TDMA slots are reinforced in case of low LQI by using CSMA/CA depending on the predicted PRR class. To optimize the lifetime of a WSN node, the sensor, if it is not active, enters a sleep mode [4]. This mode obliges the sensor's physical layer to turn off if not needed. If the physical layer was not well managed, the outcome can be a rapid reduction of the lifetime of a WSN node.

Moreover, since it is necessary to transfer information to the server, the node should compromise between waking up to send data and sleeping to conserve energy, and at the same time ensure that the sensor information is sent correctly to the server.

To solve this problem, we define a periodical duty cycle (cf. Fig. 7) that is composed of three time intervals: the TDMA cycle, the CSMA/CA cycle, and the sleep cycle.

Fig. 7. WSN node duty cycle.

The *TDMA cycle* is the part where the nodes can communication synchronously without hidden terminal packet collisions and without concurrency. Each node can send its packet during its reserved time slot, and listen to all the neighbors during their transmission time slots. The TDMA weaknesses can be summarized as follows:

1. In the case of coexistence with Wi-Fi technology, the sensor radio is submitted to extensive interference, which can cause a high number of packet loss. This is because all these technologies (Wi-Fi, ZigBee, Bluetooth, etc.) share the same free frequency band without any coordination among them.
2. TDMA needs to synchronize the neighboring nodes among themselves, and at the same time, it needs to synchronize their clock rates due to the clock drift problem.
3. Mobility causes topology variation which causes nodes desynchronization.

These weaknesses are solved by using *CSMA/CA cycle*, because this protocol does not need any requirement similar to the TDMA protocol. However, CSMA/CA has its own weaknesses:

1. It consumes a lot of energy since each node needs to listen to the channel before sending packets, and during this time, all the neighboring nodes should stay awake to listen to their neighbors, without knowing when they are going to transmit.
2. In the case of a hidden terminal, two nodes can transmit at the same time causing collision and packet loss to their neighbors.

The *sleep cycle* is the time interval where a sensor turns off most of its components, keeping active only the necessary modules to collect the monitored data like temperature, pressure, speed, luminosity, etc. This is to conserve energy and to expand the life span of the node.

Finally, for ensuring that there are always some nodes awake for an emergency, our hybrid algorithm selects in rotation a random number of nodes to stay awake during all the CSMA/CA cycle. These nodes are interchanged at the end of each cycle to prevent the depletion of their batteries.

3.4 Hybrid TDMA-CSMA/CA Duty Cycle Algorithm

We map for each PRR class (as described in Sect. 3.1) a specific action at the link layer. Algorithm 1 summarizes the proposed model shown in Fig. 8.

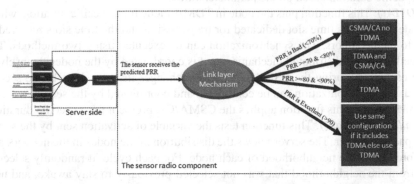

Fig. 8. For each PRR, the radio proactively adapts its configuration

Algorithm I: Hybrid TDMA-CSMA/CA Duty Cycle Algorithm
1.   radio_initalisation()
2.   **while (True)**
3.   **if** (PRR = Bad)
4.   CSMA-CA()
5.   Sleep()
6.   Sleep()
7.   **else if** (PRR = Good(-))
8.   TDMA()
9.   CSMA-CA()
10.   Sleep()
11.   **else if** (PRR = Good(+))
12.   TDMA()
13.   Sleep()
14.   Sleep()
15.   **else if** (PRR=Excellent)
16.   **if** (TDMA_not_used())
17.   TDMA()
18.   Sleep()
19.   Sleep()
20.   **End if**
21.   **End if**
22.   **if** (random_selection())
23.   **if** (CSMA-CA_Not_Used())
24.   CSMA-CA()
25.   **End if**
26.   **End if**
27.   **End while**

The corresponding functions are described as follows.

radio_initalisation(): This function initializes the radio CSMA/CA, and sets the node ID, the time of day, the mobility state for a node, etc.

Sleep(): By setting the parameter for this function, the node goes into a deep sleep for a specific duration based on the parameter value.

TDMA(): This function puts the node in TDMA mode for a specific duration, where the node receives its time slot dedicated for transmission and the time slots reserved to listen to the neighbors. The synchronization can be executed using two methods. The first method uses a distributed mechanism and is coordinated by the nodes themselves, where each node during the CSMA/CA cycle exchanges its time slots. In the second method, the synchronization can be centralized and coordinated by the server.

CSMA-CA(): This function applies the CSMA/CA protocol for a specific duration.

random_selection(): This function tests the variable of activation sent by the server in the packets header. The server knows the distribution of the nodes in the network and therefore knows the neighborhood of each node. For each cycle, it randomly selects a node from the neighborhood that was not selected previously to stay awake, and uses CSMA/CA by setting the variable of activation. The random waking up of specific nodes is to ensure that there are always some nodes awake for an emergency transmission. Moreover, the selected node activates a periodical beacon so that it can be detected.

TDMA_not_used(): to test if TDMA is used in the duty cycle.

CSMA-CA_Not_Used(): to test if CSMA/CA is used in the duty cycle.

4   Simulation Configuration and Results

To test our system and configure the simulator, we analyze the structure of different industrial and manufacturing facilities. The simplified standard topology is shown in Fig. 9.

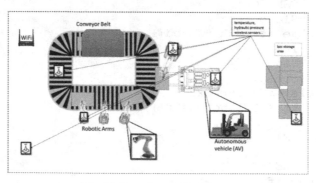

Fig. 9. Top view of the factory.

We classify three different mobility speeds for the WSN nodes that we categorize as fixed, low speed, high speed. For instance, sensors can be fixed in strategic places to monitor the room temperature in different parts of the facility. Mobile sensors with relatively low speeds are attached to the conveyor belt to monitor its pressure and temperature. Moreover, they are attached to the robotic arms (cf. Fig. 11) to monitor the hydraulics, etc. The high mobility sensor is attached to the forklift truck to monitor the speed and load of the fully automated forklift. In addition, each palette can contain an integrated sensor characterized as highly mobile to monitor the temperature. The palette is assembled in the cargo bay area for shipping. This part is monitored by fixed sensors. The facility can be divided into four zones shown in Fig. 10. The scenario considered for the simulation is as follows:

- **Zone A:** The zone where WSN node are under interference by the Wi-Fi technology. This interference exists as long as the workers, supervisors and administrators are using Wi-Fi network. In the simulation, we modeled the Wi-Fi packet arrivals following the Poisson model and the Wi-Fi transmissions as active only between 8h00 and 17h00.
- **Zone B:** The zone contains a mix between fixed nodes and low speed mobile nodes with periodic movement. This situation creates a favorable circumstance for the machine-learning algorithm, as there are a limited number of mobility states that can be studied and adapted to.
- **Zone C:** The zone where the nodes have the highest mobility speed as it can contain a number of mobile forklifts, which can affect the LQI due to distance variations, and can disconnect the nodes from the network.
- **Zone D:** The fixed nodes zone where nodes remain stationary as long as they stay in the facility. This region is not affected by interference.

The factory is fully automated and the production process is continuously on, day and night, unless there is a request for maintenance. Moreover, it is worth noting that we use the Poisson Point Process to distribute each node in each zone. At each hour, the state of the WSN nodes is collected to verify the following features: the mobility, the LQI, the PRR and the Predicted PRR. Later the data is fed to the ML platform as described earlier. Noting that the *duty cycle* duration is equal to the sum of the CSMA/CA duration, TDMA duration and sleep duration. The sleep cycle is when most of the node's components go off to preserve energy (at this point the radio module is turned off). Moreover, the duration to transmit one packet is 0.5 s which is equal to the length of one slot in TDMA, and the energy cost to send or receive one packet is considered one energy unit.

The physical layer of each node using CSMA/CA mode stays active for all the CSMA/CA defined cycle. In the simulation, the CSMA/CA duration is set to 10 s. As the radio is always on, the energy consumption is constant and equal to the average energy for the duration of the cycle.

The cycle duration in seconds for TDMA is related to the number of neighboring nodes: *TDMA Cycle = (nb_of_neighbor nodes + 1) * Time_Slot_Length.*

To calculate the energy cost for TDMA:

. $E_{TDMA} = (nb\_of\_neighbor\_nodes + 1) * energy\ cost\ per\ packet.$

In our hybrid system, a part of the energy and delay is affected by the random selection of some nodes to stay awake in CSMA/CA mode.

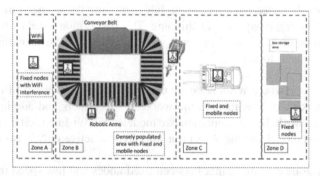

Fig. 10. Factory divided by type of mobility for the wireless sensor nodes

The energy consumption for our proposed system (cf. Fig. 12) evolves linearly but slower than the pure TDMA protocol. This is relative to the number of neighbors that affects the PRR (quality of the link) and due to the dynamic selection of the configuration. When the number of neighbors becomes higher than eight, our mechanism clearly becomes better in energy consumption then CSMA/CA and TDMA. Whereas, the average energy consumed when using CSMA/CA is constant and equal to 20 units of energy. This is because the physical layer is constantly on, listening to the channel or transmitting.

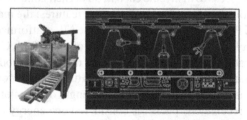

Fig. 11. On the left, a real view of the mobile robotic arms on top of a conveyor belt; on the right, a schematic view of the robotic arms.

The delay shown in Fig. 13 represents the average waiting time where a packet is queued before being transmitted. As our system has different mode of transmission, we calculated the average maximum for the worst-case scenario and the average minimum waiting duration in the best-case scenario.

For our proposed system, we conclude from Fig. 13 that the average maximum wait for the worst-case scenario (cf. Fig. 13, cross mark) is approximately 10 s (the sleep duration) added to the average waiting time in TDMA mode in respect to the time slot position. This due to the dominant combination of TDMA-CSMA/CA-Sleep duty cycle. This represents in average the half of the waiting duration for the static pure TDMA (cf. Fig. 13, diamond shape). This is equal to all the duty cycle duration (10 s sleep + 10 s sleep + duration of the TDMA cycle). Moreover, as the CSMA/CA protocol is part of the mechanism's duty cycle, a node can send its packet whenever it needs during CSMA/CA cycle unless there was a back off from transmission.

The average minimum waiting time (cf. Fig. 13, triangle shape) is estimated as being the average of the minimum between the need to transmit and the available transmission time slot (in case of TDMA), and the listening before transmission (in case of CSMA/CA). It is worth noting that, in the case of using the static CSMA/CA protocol, the node will need to sleep at least for two cycles (20 s) before entering the CSMA/CA cycle for transmitting. Then, it is necessary to take into account the back offs and the listening time. For this reason, the delay is approximately constant near 25 s as shown in Fig. 13.

Figure 14 represents the time needed for a new node (added to the WSN) to calculate its PRR based on the number of neighbors. To accurately calculate the PRR (with a confidence interval of 10%), a node needs at least 100 packet [10].

To estimate the PRR (in hours), we calculate the delay as $D = N * (100 * B)/3600$, where N is the number of neighbors, and B is the duration of one duty cycle (10 + 10 + TDMA cycle) with a time slot length of 0,5 s.

In contrast, the time needed to get the predicted PRR for initialization from the server will not exceed two sleep cycles independently from the number of neighbors.

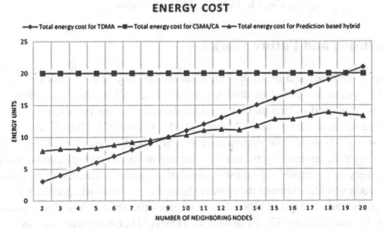

Fig. 12. The average energy consumed by a node during one duty cycle relatively to the number of neighbors

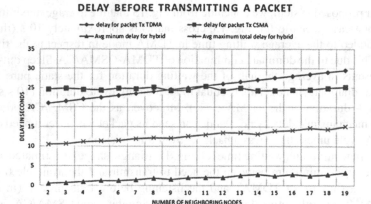

Fig. 13. The average delay needed to send one packet by a node relatively the number of neighbors

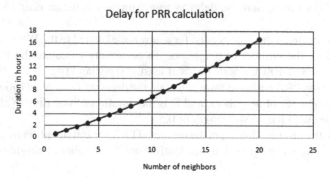

Fig. 14. Delay for PRR calculation

5   Conclusion and Future Work

In this paper, we propose a mission-critical surveillance system for industrial environments. The system assured time diversity for critical packet delivery with minimum delays. It is composed of two parts, a machine-learning server installed on centralized network management server, and a Hybrid TDMA-CSMA/CA Duty Cycle Algorithm installed on a WSN node. The system uses the PRR predictions to predict the channel quality and by that, minimizing the energy cost and delays of transmissions, and assure packet delivery to destination. Extensive simulation results validate our proposed system. The prediction algorithm of the system showed a classification accuracy exceeding 73%. Also, the radio adaption algorithm minimizes the energy cost, for a node of 20 neighbors, for one cycle by 37% relatively to TDMA. That is possible thanks to its distribution of the energy cost on multiple cycles and the avoidance of packet loss due to interference by the Wi-Fi technology. Moreover, it minimizes the energy cost compared to CSMA/CA by 35%. Furthermore, we show that calculating the average PRR using the classical method along with slow link layer adaptation, is a time consuming task, and It results in critical transmission failures.

As future work, the system will be implemented on a real platform. Moreover, the PRR prediction will be used in proactive routing algorithm to choose the most stable and critical pathways in the network. By that, we will have a complete proactive system that adapts dynamically to the predicted quality of the radio channels.

References

1. Frank, E., Hall, M.A., Witten, I.H.: The WEKA Workbench. Online Appendix for "Data Mining: Practical Machine Learning Tools and Techniques", 4th edn. Morgan Kaufmann, Burlington (2016)
2. Kazandjieva, M.A., Jain, M., Srinivasan, K., Levis, P.: PRR is not enough. Technical report SING-08-01
3. Ahmed, A.A., Fisal, N.: Experiment measurements for packet reception rate in wireless underground sensor networks. IJRTE 2(2), 71 (2009)
4. Nicolas, C., Marot, M., Becker, M.: A self-organization mechanism for a cold chain monitoring system. In: IEEE 73rd Vehicular Technology Conference (2011)
5. Qiao, M., Zhao, H., Huang, S., Zhou, L., Wang, S.: An intelligent MAC protocol selection method based on machine learning in wireless sensor networks. KSII Trans. Internet Inf. Syst. 12(11) (2018)
6. Duan, Y., Li, W., Fu, X., Luo, Y., Yang, L.: A methodology for reliability of WSN based on software defined network in adaptive industrial environment. IEEE/CAA J. Autom. Sin. 5(1), 74–82 (2018)
7. Srinivasan, K., Levis, P.: RSSI is under appreciated. In: EmNets (2006)
8. Bildea, A., Alphand, O., Rousseau, F., Duda, A.: Link quality metrics in large scale indoor wireless sensor networks. In: PIMRC (2013)
9. Nicolas, C., Marot, M.: Dynamic link adaptation based on coexistence-fingerprint detection for WSN. In: 2012 The 11th Annual Med-Hoc-Net (2012)
10. Woo, A., Culler, D.: Evaluation of efficient link reliability estimators for low-power wireless networks. Technical report UCBCSD-03-1270, University of California, Berkeley (2003)
11. Zhang, Y., Feng, C.H., Demirkol, I., Heinzelman, W.B.: Energy-efficient duty cycle assignment for receiver-based convergecast in WSN. In: GLOBECOM (2010)
12. Guidara, A., Derbel, F., Fersi, G., Bdiri, S., BenJemaa, M.: Energy-efficient on-demand indoor localization platform based on wireless sensor networks using low power wake up receiver. Ad Hoc Netw. 93 (2019)
13. Komguem, R.D., Stanica, R., Tchuente, M., Valois, F.: Ground level deployment of WSN: experiments, evaluation and engineering insight. Sensors (2019)
14. CC2420 Datasheet. From TI. http://www.ti.com/lit/ds/symlink/cc2420.pdf. Accessed 2019
15. Erpek, T., O'Shea, T.J., Sagduyu, Y.E., Shi, Y., Clancy, T.C.: Deep learning for wireless communications. In: Pedrycz, W., Chen, S.-M. (eds.) Development and Analysis of Deep Learning Architectures. SCI, vol. 867, pp. 223–266. Springer, Cham (2020). https://doi.org/10.1007/978-3-030-31764-5_9
16. Praveen Kumar, D., Amgoth, T., Annavarapu, C.S.R.: Machine learning algorithms for wireless sensor networks: a survey. Inf. Fusion 49, 1–25 (2019)
17. Sitanayah, L., Sreenan, C.J., Brown, K.N.: A hybrid MAC protocol for emergency response wireless sensor networks. Ad Hoc Netw. 20, 77–95 (2014)

Analyzing Architectures of Reservoir Computing Models Using Particle Swarm Intelligence

Sebastián Basterrech$^{(\boxtimes)}$

Faculty of Electrical Engineering and Computer Science,
VŠB-Technical University of Ostrava, Ostrava, Czech Republic
`Sebastian.Basterrech@vsb.cz`

Abstract. The Reservoir Computing (RC) area has gain relevance during the last years. An RC model is a neural network with a recurrent hidden subnetwork (named reservoir) composed by randomly initialized hidden-hidden weights over the edges, and the rest of the model parameters are trained using linear regression. In this paper, we study the effect of training a selected subset of hidden-hidden weights and the linear regression parameters. For the training, we use a popular evolutionary technique named Particle Swarm Intelligence. The proposed method is inspired in Extreme Learning machines, where only a good selection of adjustable parameters is trained. Empirical analysis was made over well-known simulated time-series benchmarks and a real-world problems.

Keywords: Reservoir Computing · Particle Swarm Intelligence · Evolutionary computation · Neural Networks

1 Introduction

Nowadays, one of the most popular techniques in the wide field of Artificial Intelligence is the family of Neural Network (NN) models. The family has grown up on the last decades, due mainly to its success for solving machine learning problems. A NN with a recurrent topology (RNN) has been successfully applied for solving machine learning problems with sequential data. It is also a powerful tool for times series analysis [21]. A RNN is a dynamical systems that satisfies the property of universal Turing machine [28]. Even though a RNN has good theoretical properties and enormous potential for solving machine learning problems, in many real-world problems is hard to adjust its parameters. In particular, it is a complex problem to adjust the model parameters when the network is big and has a large amount of recurrences [25]. Therefore, it is still an important challenge in the NN community to define an optimal architecture in large recurrent networks.

Almost 20 years ago a new computational concept for designing a RNN topology and for learning its parameters was introduced with the names of Liquid

© Springer Nature Singapore Pte Ltd. 2020
S. M. Thampi et al. (Eds.): SoMMA 2019, CCIS 1203, pp. 16–26, 2020.
https://doi.org/10.1007/978-981-15-4301-2_2

State Machine (LSM) [23] and Echo State Network (ESN) [16,17]. Since 2007 the approach was unified with the name of Reservoir Computing (RC) [29]. The architecture of an RC model is characterized by two structures. A subset of the network has recurrences and its parameters are fixed during the training (untrainable structure so-called *reservoir*). Another structure doesn't have recurrences and its parameters are adjusted according to the training data (trainable structure so-called *readout*). The functionality of an RC model can be seen as a convolution of at least two operations. In the first operation a dynamical system given by the untrainable structure is performed. The second operation is a parametric mapping between the projected data by the reservoir and the output space. The operation made by the reservoir structure has the double role of memorizing the input sequence, and to project the input data in a feature map. The linear separability of the input space may be enhanced by the reservoir projection [21]. On the other hand, the operation made by the readout has the role of fitting the target data. Typically, the weight connections of the reservoir are untrained after an initialization procedure, and only the readout weights are adjusted through classic learning methods. Despite of having some untrainable parameters, RC models are populars for achieving accurate and robust results [1]. As a consequence, the family of RC models have been extended over the past few years.

Here, we present a preliminary work where is applied an evolutionary algorithm for finding the readout weights (as usually is done in the RC area), and also the evolutionary technique adjusts a selected subset of reservoir weights. This is a difference with respect of other works. We analyze the potential of the novel approach using Particle Swarm Optimization (PSO), that is popularly used for solving optimization problems when the searching space is continuous. The presented algorithm is more efficient in terms of computational costs than our previous work in [3].

The rest of the article is organized as follows. In the next section are presented RC and PSO. Section 3 introduces the proposed approach. Next, we present and discuss the results. The article ends with a discussion about the presented work, its limitations and good possibilities.

2   State of the Art

2.1   Reservoir Computing

The canonical ESN model is probably still the most popular in the RC area. The model is composed by n input neurons that are fully connected with N_x reservoir neurons, which are also fully connected with N_y output neurons. The reservoir neurons are interconnected among them, forming a graph with circuits. The network weights are collected in three matrices. The input-reservoir weights are collected in a N_x by n matrix denoted by $\mathbf{w}^{in}$. A N_x squared matrix $\mathbf{w}^h$ contains the hidden-hidden weights of the reservoir, and the readout matrix $\mathbf{w}^{out}$ collects weights from the projected space to the output space of dimensions $N_y \times N_x$. For the sake of notation simplicity, it is usual to omit the bias term in the matrices.

The reservoir with its recurrences is a dynamical system characterized by the following state:

$$\mathbf{x}(t) = \phi_1(\mathbf{w}^{\text{in}}\mathbf{a}(t) + \mathbf{w}^{\text{r}}\mathbf{x}(t-1)), \tag{1}$$

where $\phi_1(\cdot)$ is a predefined Lipschitz function, most often the $\tanh(\cdot)$ function [16]. The prediction of the model in the case of ESN is computed by a function:

$$\hat{\mathbf{y}}(t) = \phi_2(\mathbf{w}^{\text{out}}\mathbf{x}(t)), \tag{2}$$

where $\phi_2(\cdot)$ is a predefined coordinate-wise functions. Note that, in case that $\phi_2(\cdot)$ is linear the previous expression is a linear regression. In case that $\phi_2(\cdot)$ has a defined inverse function, then the system also can be easily solved using the ridge regression technique [22].

The ESN with leaky-neurons is a popular variation of the canonical model, in which the reservoir neurons have an additional parameter (leaky rate) that controls the trajectories speed [18]. The reservoir state is computed by:

$$\mathbf{x}(t) = (1 - \alpha)\mathbf{x}'(t) + \alpha\mathbf{x}(t-1), \tag{3}$$

where the leaky rate parameter α belongs to $[0, 1)$.

An RC model has important global parameters that impact in the computational cost and accuracy of the model. According to the literature, the most relevant global parameters are related to the dimensionality of the feature space, stability of the dynamics, memorization capacity of the system, non-linear transformations of the activation functions, and type of the readout mapping [7,21,22]. The dimension of the feature space is given by the reservoir size. A large number of neurons in the reservoir may improve the linear separability of the data. However, there is a tradeoff to pay attention, because a large reservoir can also provoke overfitting. A parameter named *input scaling factor* impacts in the recurrent expression (1), and can modify the trajectories of the reservoir. The pattern of connectivity of the reservoir also has been studied [22]. In [26] was studied also particular graphs and analyzed the degree of the reservoir nodes. A topology generated with a cascade of reservoir projections also was developed in [13]. There are several analyses about the stability of the recurrent expression (1). When the activation function is a Lipschitz continuous function, then the system can be controlled by the singular value and the spectral radius of reservoir matrix. Also some analyses were done concerning the singular values of the reservoir matrix. For more details, we suggest [2,21,24,30]. Another important parameter of an RC model is the type of projection made by the reservoir, which can be partially controlled by the activation functions. Hyperbolic tangent and linear neurons were studied in [7,21], leaky neurons were presented in [18], neurons inspired from self-organization were studied in [4,20] and random spiking neurons in stationary state were developed in [5,6]. The most common readout structure defines a linear model. However, there have been developed several other operations such: Support Vector Machine (SVM), FNN, CART.

2.2   Particle Swarm Optimization

Particle swarm optimization is an optimization method popularly used for find-ing solutions represented in a continuous searching space. The technique effi-ciently explores high dimensional complex solution spaces [19]. PSO is popular for its simplicity, theoretical background, and for achieving a record of outstand-ing results in many domains [8,10]. The PSO is a population based algorithm, for instance similar to genetic algorithm, where at each iteration several feasi-ble solutions are combined in order of generating a new more accurate set of solutions. The technique was originally based on the computational simulation of a swarm of birds, and motivated by the analysis of propagation of groups of social animals [9,11,19]. The swarm represents a group of problem solutions, also mentioned as particles. At each iteration, the particles in the swarm exchange information (a kind of simulation of cognitive and social behavior), and the par-ticles learn from each other. Each particle i explores a M–dimensional space and it is characterized by its position $\mathbf{p}_i$ and a velocity $\mathbf{v}_i$. The position has associated a value according to a fitness function, which measures how well this particle solves the optimization problem. Each particle keeps its best position (in terms of the fitness function value), and the technique also keeps the best discov-ered position of the whole swarm. Let's denote by $\mathbf{b}_i$ the best position obtained by the particle i, and $\mathbf{b}^*$ the best position obtained by the whole swarm. The dynamics are given according to the following two update rule [11]:

$$\mathbf{v}_i(t+1) = \iota \mathbf{v}_i(t) + c_1 \mathbf{r}_1(t)(\mathbf{b}_i(t) - \mathbf{p}_i(t)) + c_2 \mathbf{r}_2(\mathbf{b}^*(t) - \mathbf{p}_i(t)) \qquad (4)$$

where ι is a parameter in $(0,1)$ called inertia, c_1 and c_2 are positive acceleration and $\mathbf{r}_1$ and $\mathbf{r}_2$ are vectors of random values sampled from uniform distribution. The vector $\mathbf{b}_i(t)$ represents the best position known by particle i at iteration t and vector $\mathbf{b}^*(t)$ is the best position visited by the swarm at iteration t. The position of a particle, i, is updated by [11]:

$$\mathbf{p}_i(t+1) = \mathbf{p}_i(t) + \mathbf{v}_i(t+1) \qquad (5)$$

PSO is particularly helpful when the solution can be represented as a mul-tidimensional point in a continuous space. After some iterations, the swarm is attracted downhill towards the locations in the searching space where local minima are presented. There is a number of PSO alternatives, these include: self-tuning PSO, niching PSO, and multiple-swarm PSO [9,11].

3   Proposed Methodology

It is still a challenge to define an optimal architecture of the reservoir. Due to the vanishing and exploding phenomena is hard to train the weights. Besides, there are several global parameters that require to be optimized, such as: input scaling factor, the reservoir size, the spectral radius of the reservoir matrix. In spite of the effort made by the research community in finding "good" architectures, as far as we know an algorithm for defining optimal network is still missing [21]. Evolutionary and genetic algorithms were applied for optimizing some global parameters and for designing specific aspects of the reservoir connectivity [12].

The PSO technique was already used for defining the spectral radius and other main parameters of the reservoir in [12]. An evolutionary algorithm was applied to define the reservoir size, the spectral radius and the density of the reservoir matrix [15]. However, to define the reservoir global parameters seems to be insufficient. Different reservoirs with the same size and spectral radius can produce substantial different accuracy [27]. Another disadvantage, it is that to compute the spectra of the reservoir has a high computational cost. In [3], we proposed a hybrid algorithm that applies PSO for adjusting a small subset of the reservoir weights. The method doesn't require to compute the spectrum of the reservoir matrix. The algorithm combines the PSO and linear regression algorithm for adjusting both: subset of reservoir weights and readout weights. The algorithm has achieved good results. However, at each PSO iteration is computed the inverse of a large matrix (that is necessary for solving the linear regression). Then, the computational cost of matrix inversion at each iteration is a drawback of the method.

In this short article, we present an empirical analysis of a variation of our previous work in [3]. A selected subset of reservoir weights and the readout parameters are adjusted using only PSO. Then, we avoid to compute matrix inversion. Note that to adjust the whole reservoir weights can be very expensive, therefore is selected a weight subset. We selected the $g\%$ of reservoir nodes with higher node degree (in this ongoing work, we selected $g = 10$). Therefore, there are two searching spaces one is defined by the subset of reservoir nodes, and another one corresponds to the output weights. Both, problems are analyzed by PSO. In the case of the readout weights we applied a small variation of the dynamics of the PSO given by (4) and (5). The initialization of the particles that represent the readout weights is made using solving linear regression with a ridge small parameter. Then, we update the velocity using a learning rate (it is for controlling the changes of output weights at each iteration) We apply for the output weights:

$$\mathbf{v}_i(t+1) = \eta(\iota\mathbf{v}_i(t) + c_1\mathbf{r}_1(t)(\mathbf{b}_i(t) - \mathbf{p}_i(t)) + c_2\mathbf{r}_2), \qquad (6)$$

the learning rate η belongs to $(0,1)$. The proposed algorithm is presented in Algorithm 1. We denote by $\mathbf{p}^r$ and $\mathbf{v}^r$ the position and velocity of the particles that represent the subset of reservoir weights. On the other hand, we denote by $\mathbf{p}^{out}$ and $\mathbf{v}^{out}$ the position and velocity of particles searching in the space of readout weights.

4   Empirical Results

In this ongoing work, we evaluate the proposed approach over two well-known benchmarks, which are commonly used in the RC area. The goal is to predict next time-step value, using the previous inputs.

Algorithm 1: Specification of the proposed method.

$t = t_0$;

Initialize population $(\mathbf{p}_i^r, \mathbf{v}_i^r)(t), \forall i$;

Initialize population using linear regression for $(\mathbf{p}_i^{out}$ and random values for $\mathbf{v}_i^{out})(t), \forall i$;

Evaluate fitness function for all particle;

Set $\mathbf{b}^{r*}$, $\mathbf{b}_i^r(t)$ for all i;

Set $\mathbf{b}^{out*}$, $\mathbf{b}_i^{out}(t)$ for all i;

while (termination criterion is not satisfied) **do**

    for (each particle i) **do**

        Compute $\mathbf{v}_i^r(t+1)$ using (4);

        Compute $\mathbf{p}_i^r(t+1)$ using (5);

        Compute $\mathbf{v}_i^{out}(t+1)$ using (6);

        Compute $\mathbf{p}_i^{out}(t+1)$ using (5);

        Evaluate fitness function $F(\mathbf{p}_i)(t)$;

        Control and update local best $\mathbf{p}_i(t+1)$;

    end for

    Control and update global best $\mathbf{p}^{r*}$;

    Control and update global best $\mathbf{p}^{out*}$;

    $t = t+1$;

end while

Return $\mathbf{p}^{r*}$ and $\mathbf{p}^{out*}$;

4.1 Benchmark Datasets and Results

1. **Henon map.** The Henon map is an invertible mapping of a two-dimensional plane unto itself [14]. The sequence is generated by the following dynamics:

$$x(t+1) = 1 - rx^2(t) + y(t), \quad y(t+1) = bx(t).$$

where $r = 1.4$, $b = 0.3$. The initial states are $x(0) = 1$, and $y(0) = 1$. Often the previous sequence is presented as a 2-step recurrence

$$x(t+1) = 1 - rx^2(t) + bx(t-1).$$

The learning data is composed by a training sequence with 13107 instances, and 3277 instances for testing the parameters of the model.

2. **Rossler attractor.** It is a sequence generated for the dynamics [2]:

$$\frac{\partial x}{\partial t} = -z - y, \frac{\partial y}{\partial t} = x + ry, \frac{\partial z}{\partial t} = b + z(x - c),$$

where the parameters values are $r = 0.15$, $b = 0.20$, $c = 10.0$. The learning data is a sequence of 8192 samples, the first 80% is used for the training procedure.

We present results over the ESN model with leaky neurons. As we mentioned before the ESN has some global parameters to be optimized. In Fig. 1 the impact of the reservoir size and the spectral radius in the model accuracy is illustrated. Figure 2 shows the evolution of the accuracy of the PSO iterations when the ESN with leaky neurons is used for solving the Hénon map problem. Figure 3 shows the difference between the accuracy obtained by the proposed approach (red line) and the classic ESN with leaky neurons (30 blue dots). A similar graphic for the Rossler dataset is presented in Fig. 4.

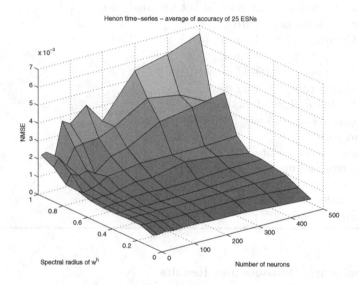

Fig. 1. Accuracy of ESN with leaky neurons for Hénon time series.

4.2 Discussion

The proposed approach has several parameters that require further investigation. Here, we present some possible future research avenues. However, the list obviously isn't complete:

- Here we only present results using PSO. However, there are other metaheuristic techniques that can be similarly applied for tackling the optimization problem.
- The PSO method has several parameters that require to be better analyzed. In this short study we used 20 particles and $\iota = 0.729$, $c_1 = 1.5$, $c_2 = 1.5$, r_1 and r_2 random values in $[-0.5, 0.5]$.
- The method can be extended in order of finding also the best ESN global parameters (reservoir size, spectral radius and density of reservoir matrix).
- We select only a subset of the reservoir weights ($g = 10\%$). This value was arbitrary selected, then it is missing an empirical analysis for finding good values of g.
- We selected the nodes with higher degree on the reservoir, an analysis about the relevance of the degree in the reservoir is missing as well.

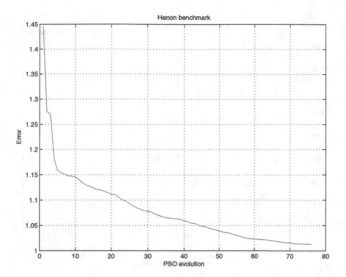

Fig. 2. Evolution of the accuracy according to the iterations of PSO, when the learning data is the Hénon map.

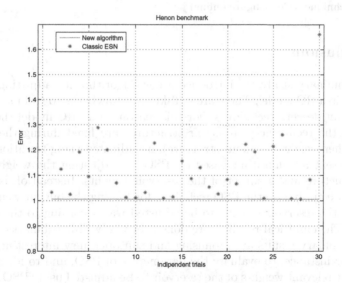

Fig. 3. Comparison between the proposed approach and the ESN with leaky neurons. Dataset corresponds to Hénon map. The graphic shows the results of 30 different independent ESNs (blue dots) and one horizontal red line marking the error of the proposed technique. (Color figure online)

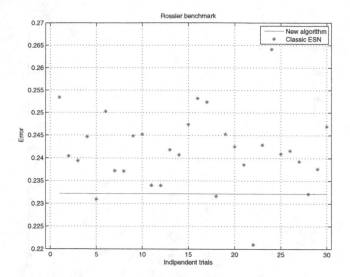

Fig. 4. Comparison between the proposed approach and the ESN with leaky neurons. Dataset corresponds to Rossler data. The graphic shows the results of 30 different independent ESNs (blue dots) and one horizontal red line marking the error of the proposed technique. (Color figure online)

5   Conclusions

In this preliminary study, we introduce a new algorithm for adjusting relevant parameters in a RC model. There are well-known drawbacks to train large RNNs using gradient descent techniques. For this reason, in an RC model the weights involved in the recurrences (reservoir structure) are fixed during the training process. Other weights (readout structure) are adjusted using traditional learning. We present an algorithm based on PSO for adjusting the weights of the readout structure and a subset of the reservoir weights. Instead of using ridge regression, we apply also the PSO technique for finding the output weights. The selection of the reservoir weights to be adjusted was according to the degree of the nodes. The empirical results were done over two well-benchmarks. The presented preliminary results are promising and can open new interesting research avenues. For instance, to evaluate the parameters of PSO, and to identify what are the most relevant weights of the reservoir to be adjusted using PSO. It would be also interesting in a future work to evaluate other metaheuristic techniques.

Acknowledgment. This work was supported by the Technology Agency of the Czech Republic in the frame of the project no. TN01000024 "National Competence Center-Cybernetics and Artificial Intelligence", and by the projects SP2019/135 and SP2019/141 of the Student Grant System, VSB-Technical University of Ostrava.

References

1. Bacciu, D., Barsocchi, P., Chessa, S., Gallicchio, C., Micheli, A.: An experimental characterization of reservoir computing in ambient assisted living applications. Neural Comput. Appl. **24**(6), 1451–1464 (2014)
2. Basterrech, S.: Empirical analysis of the necessary and sufficient conditions of the echo state property. In: 2017 International Joint Conference on Neural Networks, IJCNN 2017, Anchorage, AK, USA, 14–19 May 2017, pp. 888–896 (2017)
3. Basterrech, S., Alba, E., Snášel, V.: An experimental analysis of the echo state network initialization using the particle swarm optimization. In: 2014 Sixth World Congress on Nature and Biologically Inspired Computing (NaBIC), pp. 214–219, July 2014
4. Basterrech, S., Fyfe, C., Rubino, G.: Self-organizing maps and scale-invariant maps in echo state networks. In: 11th International Conference on Intelligent Systems Design and Applications, ISDA 2011, Córdoba, Spain, 22–24 November 2011, pp. 94–99, November 2011
5. Basterrech, S., Rubino, G.: Echo state queueing network: a new reservoir computing learning tool. In: 10th IEEE Consumer Communications and Networking Conference, CCNC 2013, Las Vegas, NV, USA, 11–14 January 2013, pp. 118–123 (2013)
6. Basterrech, S., Rubino, G.: Echo state queueing networks: a combination of reservoir computing and random neural networks. Probab. Eng. Inf. Sci. **31**, 457–476 (2017)
7. Butcher, J.B., Verstraeten, D., Schrauwen, B., Day, C.R., Haycock, P.W.: Reservoir computing and extreme learning machines for non-linear time-series data analysis. Neural Netw. **38**, 76–89 (2013)
8. Cleghorn, C.W., Engelbrecht, A.P.: A generalized theoretical deterministic particle swarm model. Swarm Intell. **8**(1), 35–59 (2014)
9. Clerc, M.: Particle Swarm Optimization. ISTE. Wiley, Hoboken (2010)
10. Clerc, M., Kennedy, J.: The particle swarm - explosion, stability, and convergence in a multidimensional complex space. IEEE Trans. Evol. Comput. **6**(1), 58–73 (2002)
11. Engelbrecht, A.: Computational Intelligence: An Introduction, 2nd edn. Wiley, New York (2007)
12. Ferreira, A.A., Ludermir, T.B.: Comparing evolutionary methods for reservoir computing pre-training. In: The 2011 International Joint Conference on Neural Networks (IJCNN), pp. 283–290, July 2011
13. Gallicchio, C., Micheli, A., Pedrelli, L.: Deep reservoir computing: a critical experimental analysis. Neurocomputing **268**(Suppl. C), 87–99 (2017). Advances in artificial neural networks, machine learning and computational intelligence
14. Hénon, M.: A two dimensional mapping with a strange attractor. Commun. Math. Phys. **50**, 69–77 (1976)
15. Ishu, K., van Der Zant, T., Becanovic, V., Ploger, P.: Identification of motion with echo state network. In: OCEANS 2004. MTTS/IEEE TECHNO-OCEAN 2004, vol. 3, pp. 1205–1210, November 2004
16. Jaeger, H.: The "echo state" approach to analysing and training recurrent neural networks. Technical report 148, German National Research Center for Information Technology (2001)
17. Jaeger, H., Haas, H.: Harnessing nonlinearity: predicting chaotic systems and saving energy in wireless communication. Science **304**(5667), 78–80 (2004)

18. Jaeger, H., Lukoševičius, M., Popovici, D., Siewert, U.: Optimization and applications of echo state networks with leaky-integrator neurons. Neural Netw. **20**(3), 335–352 (2007)
19. Kennedy, J., Eberhart, R.: Particle swarm optimization. In: 1995 Proceedings of the IEEE International Conference on Neural Networks, vol. 4, pp. 1942–1948 (1995)
20. Lukoševičius, M.: On self-organizing reservoirs and their hierarchies. Technical report 25, Jacobs University, Bremen (2010)
21. Lukoševičius, M., Jaeger, H.: Reservoir computing approaches to recurrent neural network training. Comput. Sci. Rev. **3**, 127–149 (2009)
22. Lukoševičius, M.: A practical guide to applying echo state networks. In: Montavon, G., Orr, G.B., Müller, K.-R. (eds.) Neural Networks: Tricks of the Trade. LNCS, vol. 7700, pp. 659–686. Springer, Heidelberg (2012). https://doi.org/10.1007/978-3-642-35289-8_36
23. Maass, W.: Noisy spiking neurons with temporal coding have more computational power than sigmoidal neurons. Technical report TR-1999-037, Institute for Theoretical Computer Science. Technische Universitaet Graz. Graz, Austria (1999)
24. Manjunath, G., Jaeger, H.: Echo state property linked to an input: exploring a fundamental characteristic of recurrent neural networks. Neural Comput. **25**(3), 671–696 (2013)
25. Pascanu, R., Gulcehre, C., Cho, K., Bengio, Y.: How to construct deep recurrent neural networks. In: Proceedings of the International Conference of Learning Representations (ICLR) (2014). https://128.84.21.199/abs/1312.6026v1
26. Rodan, A., Tino, P.: Simple deterministically constructed cycle reservoirs with regular jumps. Neural Comput. **24**, 1822–1852 (2012)
27. Schrauwen, B., Wardermann, M., Verstraeten, D., Steil, J.J., Stroobandt, D.: Improving reservoirs using intrinsic plasticity. Neurocomputing **71**, 1159–1171 (2007)
28. Siegelmann, H.T., Sontag, E.D.: Turing computability with neural nets. Appl. Math. Lett. **4**(6), 77–80 (1991)
29. Verstraeten, D., Schrauwen, B., D'Haene, M., Stroobandt, D.: An experimental unification of reservoir computing methods. Neural Netw. **20**(3), 287–289 (2007)
30. Yildiza, I.B., Jaeger, H., Kiebela, S.J.: Re-visiting the echo state property. Neural Netw. **35**, 1–9 (2012)

A Cost-Effective Data Node Management Scheme for Hadoop Clusters in Cloud Environment

B. S. Vidhyasagar[1]($\boxtimes$), J. Raja Paul Perinbam[2], M. Krishnamurthy[3], and J. Arunnehru[4]

[1] Information and Communication Engineering,
Anna University, Chennai, Tamilnadu, India
vidhyasagar_bs@hotmail.com
[2] Department of ECE, Kings Engineering College, Chennai, Tamilnadu, India
rperinbam@yahoo.com
[3] Department of CSE, KCG College of Technology, Chennai, Tamilnadu, India
mkrishmails@gmail.com
[4] Department of CSE, SRM Institute of Science and Technology,
Chennai, Tamilnadu, India
arunnehru.aucse@gmail.com

Abstract. MapReduce framework in Hadoop is used to analyze the large set of data in a distributed storage system. MapReduce jobs are designate to the task node to perform the map-reduce operation based upon the scheduler. Each node has slots (virtual core) to process a task using the map and reduce operation. Map tasks done separately prior to the Reduce task. The different execution order of jobs and different slot configuration in the clusters affect the CPU performance significantly. In this paper, we have stated effective DataNode assignment techniques for resource allocation in the Hadoop MapReduce job. We performed various operations on Amazon EC2 and physical machine to demonstrate that our proposed technique helps to choose optimized node selection for assignment of DataNodes in the Hadoop cluster. This significantly scales down the cost of the node and increases the job execution performance in the Hadoop cluster.

Keywords: MapReduce · Virtual core · Slot · Hadoop · Big data · Cloud

1 Introduction

In present years, the expansion of cloud computing has led the world to new technologies like, Big Data, Internet of Things (IoT) and Artificial Intelligence which provides computing and storage to be interconnected together for a technological revolution. Cloud computing is the technology which provides virtual resources such as storage, network, platform as a service and software as a service on user demand basis [1]. Hadoop is an open-source tool which processes

© Springer Nature Singapore Pte Ltd. 2020
S. M. Thampi et al. (Eds.): SoMMA 2019, CCIS 1203, pp. 27–37, 2020.
https://doi.org/10.1007/978-981-15-4301-2_3

the large set of data in a distributed storage environment released by Apache's first version Hadoop-1.X contains FIRST-IN-FIRST-OUT(FIFO) scheduler and later version of Hadoop-2.X and Hadoop-3.X which gives more sustain on flexibility, adaptability, and horizontal scalability. The Hadoop 2.X and 3.X contains Capacitive and FAIR scheduler for the allocation of slots in the Map and Reduce phase [2–4]. Hadoop Map-Reduce framework processes the large set of data by splitting into multiple chunks whereas each chunk is stored in the distributed storage called Hadoop Distributed File System (HDFS) in order to execute in a parallel and distributed environment [5]. The architecture of Hadoop is shown in Fig. 1.

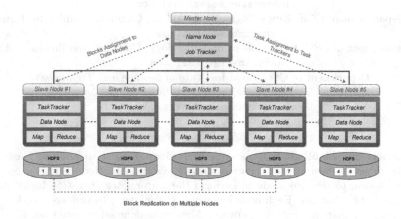

Fig. 1. Hadoop architecture.

The Hadoop cluster contains two nodes. The first one is Master node which branches into two namely Job Tracker and Name Node. Job tracker assigns the jobs to slave node whereas Name node maintains the structure of data stored in the Data nodes rather it also stores the same data is stored in multiple data nodes based on replica factor initialized in the configuration file (hdfs_site.xml) of Hadoop cluster. A Heartbeat service is implemented to check the communication between the Name node and the Data node. The second one is Slave Node which branches into two namely Task Tracker and data node. The Task Tracker assigns virtual cores to each Map and Reduce operation to run the job effectively. The Data Nodes stores the data in the HDFS layers submitted by the user. The Map operation brings the larger set of data split into multiple chunks and assigns key-value pairs to each chunk. Finally, reduce operation uses sorting, shuffling and merge functions into chunks to reduce into the smaller set of chunks [6].

Hadoop ecosystem-based component stacks [7–10] as shown in Fig. 2. MapReduce framework is used to processes a large dataset size in term of terra byte or petabyte in the distributed clusters. Hadoop map-reduce framework divides the large set of data into multiple blocks and stored into HDFS storage layer, where each block in the DataNode processed in parallel and aggregate all the results

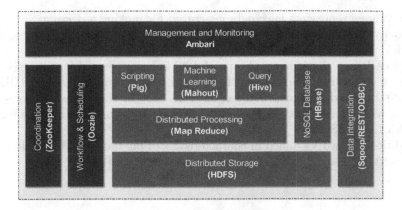

Fig. 2. Hadoop ecosystem.

which produce the reduced output using mapper and reducer function [9, 11]. Yet Another Resource Negotiator (YARN) is available in Hadoop 2.X version which manages the available resources dynamically and improves the cluster utilization for allocating various resources to the jobs without any overheads in the cluster [12, 13].

Apache Pig is an open-source tool was developed by Yahoo for analyzing the large set of data efficiently and easily. Pig handles lager sets of data with parallelization support.

- **Hive** is a NoSQL database developed by Facebook, which relies on HDFS and to offer convenient language called as HiveQL.
- The **Sqoop** component is used to pull and convert structured database to unstructured database in Hadoop environment.
- **Apache Flume** is used to collect the large amount of live streaming data from various sources like facebook, twitter, etc., which stores in HDFS.
- **HBase** is also a database which uses HDFS for storing data that offers the column-oriented database to supports random reads and stream computations using MapReduce.
- **Oozie** is another ecosystem part that offers workflow based on jobs in Hadoop. it uses workflow scheduler to execute the jobs which are expressed in Directed Acyclic Graphs. At each level, it maintains different states for managing the job in Hadoop cluster based data and time dependencies.
- **Zookeeper** is the service which maintains all the Hadoop components service which offers messaging service between the Hadoop cluster.
- **Mahout** is one of the important Hadoop components provides machine learning algorithms like frequency mining, K-means, naive Bayes and so on.
- **Ambari** is a service which provides the user interface for managing and monitoring the Hadoop clusters and its services.

Characteristics of big data based on 5V's namely Volume, Velocity, Variety, Value and Veracity shown in Fig. 3.

- The volume represents huge data generated for making a decision.
- Velocity, how much fast data is generated and get processed for big data decision.
- Variety defines the source and type of data being generated for processing. It can be structured which stores the data in rows and columns like RDBMS, semi-structured and unstructured data are not in the format of rows and columns like logs, video, images, etc. and Semi-structured data in the format of XML and JSON.
- Additionally two Vs added in characteristics of big data which is Values and Veracity represents accuracy and availability of data [14].

Fig. 3. 5V's of big data.

The Hadoop job scheduler [15] primarily classified into three types namely First-In-First-Out (FIFO) scheduler, Capacitive scheduler and the FAIR scheduler which is used for efficient resource utilization, priority and time slice. The main scope of Hadoop scheduler is to minimize the delay and maximize the throughput of allocating jobs to the cores of the processor [16,17]. Map and Reduce operations are fit to the core in order to process the job. Mapper operation takes more slots or core than reduce operation [18]. Hadoop Customized Tools are available to the end user for ease of use. Hadoop customized distribution available in a cloud as service (Eg. Amazon Elastic MapReduce (EMR), Azure-HDInsight, IBM open platform, and so on). Hadoop sandbox virtual Images are readily available for use (Eg. Cloudera, CDH Hadoop Distribution and Hortonworks Data Platform (HDP) [19–23].

2 Related Works

The algorithm [24] which minimize execution time by ordering the jobs dynamically and adjusting the cores to execute the job using the map and reduce operation. Also, it satisfies the constraints based jobs to manage the resource in the heterogeneous cluster. The term data locality plays a vital role in a distributed cluster, to minimize the latency of data in Hadoop cluster which brings the relative performance is high when executing the jobs on specialized processors [25]. In Hadoop cluster, the data nodes are always alive, in which significantly increases the power utilization. Hadoop uses to keep the same blocks in different data nodes based on replica factor for high availability of data. To mitigate power consumption decommissioning the inactive nodes and minimizing the replicas of blocks in Hadoop cluster [26]. Big data applications are generated the massive quantity of transitional data and these data is pitched after processing the MapReduce job in Hadoop which leads to increases the cost and energy. Data locality concept is introduced to avoid the overhead in the cluster. Cache manager act as data locality ensures to store transitional information after the task is submitted by the client for execution. A new cache request and reply protocols are intended to improve the finish time of Map-Reduce occupations and spare the CPU execution time [27]. In heterogeneous Hadoop cluster has different computing resources in each DataNode resulting affects the output performance due to latency. The author proposed [28] the queue based scheduler for the various computing capacity in order to avoid the latency between the nodes which is called as Storage-Tag-Aware Scheduler (STAS) for map-reduce operations.

The author [29] proposed arranging procedure for MapReduce that increases the framework throughput in job-intensive environments and finds a powerful vitality use by picking effective task nodes to allocate the jobs to the nodes. The algorithm Tolhit [30] which efficiently analyzes the time taken for numbers of maps task and reduce task and finally it assigns the node to Hadoop distributed cluster for execution. The author [31] clearly discussed various aspects of Hadoop scheduling algorithms and its performance of jobs execution in Hadoop cluster. Whereas additionally, it requires a node assignment in Hadoop cluster based on each dataset. Heterogeneous Hadoop cluster has various computing nodes to process the job in which it affects the performance significantly because of various resource available in each node of the cluster. The author [32] addresses the issues and guidelines to overcome issues of implement Hadoop cluster on cloud environment resulting in cost efficiency. Amazon cloud service provider offers Elastic MapReduce (EMR) as a service with low cost and also provide various types of instance based on cost. The author [33] used cloud services to process the Big Data applications to avoid the capitation cost as well as the operational cost of setting up Hadoop environment. The Author [34] explained about virtualization performance by allocating the yarn container to each slot in order to achieve the execution of jobs with high performance.

3   Experimental Setup

We have configured Hadoop cluster on various environments such as the Physical machine with the single node cluster, Hadoop cluster with the Single node using Amazon EC2-Ubuntu instance and Hadoop cluster with one Master node and 5 slave nodes using Amazon EC2-Ubuntu instance. The following Table 1 shows the configuration of each Hadoop cluster.

Table 1. Multiple configuration environments

Physical machine with single node	Cloud with single node	Cloud with multi node
Intel(R) Xeon(R) CPU	Intel(R) Xeon(R) CPU	Intel(R) Xeon(R) CPU
E5-2676 v3 @ 2.40 GHz,	E5-2666 v3 @ 2.90 GHz,	E5-2666 v3 @ 2.90 GHz,
Processor: 2,	Cores: 4,	Cores: 4,
Cores: 2,	Processor: 8 VCPU,	Processor: 8 VCPU,
Total Cores: 4,	Instance Type: m1.xlarge,	Instance Type: m1.xlarge,
Ram: 8 GB	Ram: 8 GB	Ram: 8 GB
HDD: 1024 GB	HDD: 1024 GB	HDD: 1024 GB

4   Experimental Results and Analysis

The Tables 2 and 3 shows various dataset and its size used for our experiment to run various jobs on Hadoop cluster to analyze the slots occupancy and its performance of Hadoop cluster. Each block needs one slot to execute the job. In dataset 1 consists of 3.375 GB of data requires 184 slots and 368 slots by choosing the block size of 128 MB and 64 MB respectively. The number of Maps slots can be calculated using Eq. 1. The Block size can be selected based on granularity, which has a large number of small blocks or a small number of the large block with available resources in the cluster. In Map phase, the Number of map slots is fixed based on block size by reducing the map slots which has always fallen less than or equal to reduce slots dynamically by Eqs. 1 and 2.

$$No\_of\_Map\_Slots = \frac{Data\_Size}{Block\_Size} \tag{1}$$

$$No\_of\_Map\_Slots \geq No.\_of\_Reduced\_Slots \tag{2}$$

The Tables 2 and 3 and Figs. 4 and 5 are obtained from the execution of various jobs in various hardware environments, from this we can conclude strongly, physical memory (slots) plays vital role in heterogeneous or homogeneous Hadoop cluster, in order to execute the jobs effectively minimize the usage of heap memory in the Hadoop cluster and maximize the provisioning of physical memory in the Hadoop cluster. Effective node assignment in the Hadoop

Table 2. Various dataset and its sizes in HDFS blocks.

Dataset	Size	HDFS blocks	
		128 MB	64 MB
Wiki_3.375 [35]	3.375 GB	27	54
Wiki_23 [36]	23 GB	184	368
Wiki_50 [37]	50 GB	400	800
Wiki_140 [38]	140 GB	2240	1120
Wiki_150 [39]	150 GB	1200	2400
Wiki_300 [40]	300 GB	2400	4800

Table 3. A set of jobs execution in various environments.

Job_ID	Job name	MAPS	Execution time in minutes		
			Env#1	Env#2	Env#3
Job_001	WordCount	184	23.15	21.05	4.3
Job_002	Grep-Search	184	9.48	6.2	1.5
Job_003	Grep-Search	184	12.51	6.22	1.03
Job_004	Inverted_index	212	35.11	31.28	6.25
Job_005	Inverted_index	212	32.4	28.55	5.71
Job_006	SequenceCount	212	31.28	31.28	6.25

cluster is mandatory with respective of cost and utilization for allocating the resource to run the jobs. The Fig. 5 is obtained from Table 3 and it showed various jobs execution in three different environments of Hadoop cluster namely Env#1, Env#2 and Env#3 to differentiate the execution time by increasing the hardware resource. Eventually by increasing the CPU resource brings down the execution time, at the certain time the execution time of the job is constant.

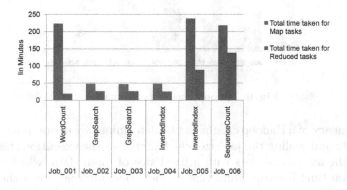

Fig. 4. Total time spent by all map and reduce tasks in single node cluster.

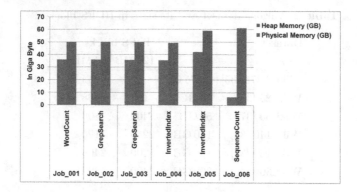

Fig. 5. Total committed Heap usage and Physical memory usage during all map and reduce tasks in single node cluster.

In this effective node allocation is mandatory in Hadoop cluster to balances the CPU cost. To Minimize the execution time of jobs is subject to maximize the cluster's DataNode assignment. The Fig. 6 horizontal axis represents various jobs namely job1, job2, job3, job4, job5 and job6 executed in three different environments namely Env1, Env2, and Env3. The vertical axis represents the execution of the job in Hadoop cluster. In this we can derive that the execution time of a job decreases linearly with increase in the number of nodes at a particular instance of time, execution time becomes constant, which is shown in the Fig. 7.

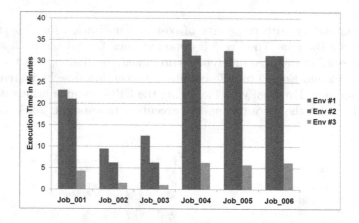

Fig. 6. Hadoop cluster performance.

The efficiency of a Hadoop cluster can be determined by maintaining the fixed number slots and scaling the job size which increases the execution time. While increasing the number of slots with a fixed size of input data, which decreases the execution time linearly. From this we can conclude that when the job size increases at different rate in order maintain the efficiency as the number of cores to be increased.

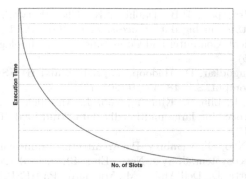

Fig. 7. Hadoop cluster performance.

5   Conclusion and Future Work

In Cloud computing, MapReduce was utilized to examine the colossal measure of information in a Hadoop system and assumes the significant job in the guide lessen activity by allocating the DataNodes and TaskNodes in the Hadoop cluster. This research paper clearly gives the in-depth knowledge and importance of choosing the exact number of DataNodes for the given dataset to process the application in the Hadoop cluster, which brings the efficiency of job execution. We have tested and executed the different jobs in the various environments with different computing resources of Hadoop cluster. In order to analyze the performance of jobs execution, additionally, the experiments are tested on single physical machine, single virtual machine and multi-node for launching the Hadoop cluster to evaluate the performance of Hadoop jobs with respect to execution time and also we used AWS EC2 for setting up Hadoop multi-node cluster and single node which is cost-effective one. Furthermore, our experimental results prove that when the number of processing elements increased when job size increased. In our Future work, we planned to analyze the jobs and dataset apriori to choose optimized scheduler in the Hadoop cluster for allocating the resource dynamically.

References

1. Al-Fuqaha, A., Guizani, M., Mohammadi, M., Aledhari, M., Ayyash, M.: Internet of Things: a survey on enabling technologies, protocols, and applications. IEEE Commun. Surv. Tutor. **17**(4), 2347–2376 (2015)
2. Apache hadoop releases. http://www.hadoop.apache.org/releases.html. Accessed 11 Feb 2018
3. Singh, N., Agrawal, S.: A review of research on mapreduce scheduling algorithms in Hadoop. In: 2015 International Conference on Computing, Communication & Automation (ICCCA), pp. 637–642. IEEE (2015)

4. Gautam, J.V., Prajapati, H.B., Dabhi, V.K., Chaudhary, S.: A survey on job scheduling algorithms in big data processing. In: 2015 IEEE International Conference on Electrical, Computer and Communication Technologies (ICECCT), pp. 1–11. IEEE (2015)
5. Ghazi, M.R., Gangodkar, D.: Hadoop, mapreduce and HDFS: a developers perspective. Proc. Comput. Sci. **48**, 45–50 (2015)
6. Bok, K., Hwang, J., Lim, J., Kim, Y., Yoo, J.: An efficient mapreduce scheduling scheme for processing large multimedia data. Multimed. Tools Appl. **76**(16), 17273–17296 (2017)
7. Demchenko, Y., Ngo, C., Membrey, P.: Architecture framework and components for the big data ecosystem. J. Syst. Netw. Eng. **49**(7), 1–31 (2013)
8. Pastorelli, M., Carra, D., Dell'Amico, M., Michiardi, P.: HFSP: bringing size-based scheduling to hadoop. IEEE Trans. Cloud Comput. **5**(1), 43–56 (2017)
9. Mavridis, I., Karatza, H.: Performance evaluation of cloud-based log file analysis with apache hadoop and apache spark. J. Syst. Softw. **125**, 133–151 (2017)
10. Apache hadoop file system. http://www.hadoop.apache.org/hdfs. Accessed 11 Feb 2018
11. Afrati, F., Dolev, S., Korach, E., Sharma, S., Ullman, J.D.: Assignment problems of different-sized inputs in mapreduce. ACM Trans. Knowl. Disc. Data (TKDD) **11**(2), 18 (2016)
12. Mathiya, B.J., Desai, V.L.: Apache hadoop yarn parameter configuration challenges and optimization. In: 2015 International Conference on Soft-Computing and Networks Security (ICSNS), pp. 1–6. IEEE (2015)
13. Cai, X., Li, F., Li, P., Lei, J., Jia, Z.: SLA-aware energy-efficient scheduling scheme for hadoop yarn. J. Supercomput. **73**(8), 3526–3546 (2017)
14. Anuradha, J., et al.: A brief introduction on big data 5Vs characteristics and hadoop technology. Proc. Comput. Sci. **48**, 319–324 (2015)
15. Suresh, S., Gopalan, N.P.: An optimal task selection scheme for hadoop scheduling. IERI Proc. **10**, 70–75 (2014)
16. Dias, L.S., Ierapetritou, M.G.: Integration of scheduling and control under uncertainties: review and challenges. Chem. Eng. Res. Design **116**, 98–113 (2016)
17. Apache hadoop yarn scheduler. https://hadoop.apache.org/docs/current/hadoop-yarn/hadoop-yarn-site/. Accessed 11 Feb 2018
18. Yoo, D., Sim, K.M.: A comparative review of job scheduling for mapreduce. In: 2011 IEEE International Conference on Cloud Computing and Intelligence Systems (CCIS), pp. 353–358. IEEE (2011)
19. Apache hadoop emr. https://docs.aws.amazon.com/emr/latest/ReleaseGuide/emr-hadoop.htm. Accessed 11 Feb 2018
20. Horton works. https://hortonworks.com. Accessed 11 Feb 2018
21. Cloudera framework. https://www.cloudera.com/. Accessed 11 Feb 2018
22. Sarkar, D.: Pro Microsoft HDInsight. Apress, Berkeley (2014)
23. MAPR framework. https://mapr.com/. Accessed 11 Feb 2018
24. Tang, S., Lee, B.-S., He, B.: Dynamic job ordering and slot configurations for mapreduce workloads. IEEE Trans. Serv. Comput. **9**(1), 4–17 (2016)
25. Polo, J., et al.: Deadline-based mapreduce workload management. IEEE Trans. Netw. Serv. Manage. **10**(2), 231–244 (2013)
26. Leverich, J., Kozyrakis, C.: On the energy (in) efficiency of hadoop clusters. ACM SIGOPS Oper. Syst. Rev. **44**(1), 61–65 (2010)
27. Zhao, Y., Jie, W., Liu, C.: Dache: a data aware caching for big-data applications using the mapreduce framework. Tsinghua Sci. Technol. **19**(1), 39–50 (2014)

28. Qureshi, N.M.F., Shin, D.R., Siddiqui, I.F., Chowdhry, B.S.: Storage-tag-aware scheduler for hadoop cluster. IEEE Access **5**, 13742–13755 (2017)
29. Wang, X., Shen, D., Yu, G., Nie, T., Kou, Y.: A throughput driven task scheduler for improving mapreduce performance in job-intensive environments. In: 2013 IEEE International Congress on Big Data (BigData Congress), pp. 211–218. IEEE (2013)
30. Brahmwar, M., Kumar, M., Sikka, G.: Tolhit-a scheduling algorithm for hadoop cluster. Proc. Comput. Sci. **89**, 203–208 (2016)
31. Usama, M., Liu, M., Chen, M.: Job schedulers for big data processing in hadoop environment: testing real-life schedulers using benchmark programs. Digit. Commun. Netw. **3**(4), 260–273 (2017)
32. Thirumala Rao, B., Sridevi, N.V., Krishna Reddy, V., Reddy, L.S.S.: Performance issues of heterogeneous hadoop clusters in cloud computing (2012). arXiv preprint arXiv:1207.0894
33. Tamrakar, K., Yazidi, A., Haugerud, H.: Cost efficient batch processing in amazon cloud with deadline awareness. In: 2017 IEEE 31st International Conference on Advanced Information Networking and Applications (AINA), pp. 963–971. IEEE (2017)
34. Jlassi, A., Martineau, P.: Experimental study on performance and energy consumption of hadoop in cloud environments. In: Helfert, M., Ferguson, D., Méndez Muñoz, V., Cardoso, J. (eds.) CLOSER 2016. CCIS, vol. 740, pp. 255–272. Springer, Cham (2017). https://doi.org/10.1007/978-3-319-62594-2_13
35. Wikipedia dataset 3.375 gb. https://dumps.wikimedia.org/enwiki/20171103/enwiki-20171103-pages-meta-history9.xml-p1947829p1952641.7z. Accessed 11 Feb 2018
36. Stanford dataset 23 gb. https://snap.stanford.edu/data/bigdata/wikipedia08/enwiki-20080103.talk.bz2. Accessed 11 Feb 2018
37. Purdue dataset 50 gb. ftp://ftp.ecn.purdue.edu/puma/wikipedia_50GB.tar.bz2. Accessed 11 Feb 2018
38. Purdue dataset 140 gb. ftp://ftp.ecn.purdue.edu/puma/wikipedia_140GB.tar.bz2. Accessed 11 Feb 2018
39. Purdue dataset 150 gb. ftp://ftp.ecn.purdue.edu/puma/wikipedia_150GB.tar.bz2. Accessed 11 Feb 2018
40. Purdue dataset 300 gb. ftp://ftp.ecn.purdue.edu/puma/wikipedia_300GB.tar.bz2

Deep Temporal Analysis of Twitter Bots

Gayathri Rajendran$^{(\boxtimes)}$, Arjun Ram, Vishnu Vijayan, and Prabaharan Poornachandran

Amrita School of Engineering, Amrita Vishwa Vidyapeetham, Amritapuri, Kollam, Kerala, India
{gayathrir,arjunram,vishnuvijayan,praba}@am.amrita.edu

Abstract. Automated accounts which are otherwise known as bots are rampant in most of the popular online social networks. Similar to email spam, these social media bots are used for spreading information with the goal of propaganda or advertisements for profit. Due to the impact they pose on influencing the user communities, understanding the bot behaviour is important. In this paper, we employ deep neural network analysis on temporal data of bot accounts and have identified the role of temporal activity in bot detection. The bidirectional LSTM network is used for studying the temporal patterns of Twitter bots and its behavioural pattern. The ability of the model to distinguish the tweeting rate and frequency of bot accounts from the genuine accounts has led to a good classification rate.

Keywords: Bot · Bot accounts · Fake accounts · Deep learning · LSTM · GRU · RNN · NLP

1 Introduction

Social media has become the biggest medium of communication/dissemination of information. The public relies on social media for vast range of usages - from daily news to sharing personal information to expressing their opinions. This aspect is exploited by many agencies for creating mass outbreak, or influencing the social political aspects, or even creating false attraction and publicity for certain products.

As the quote from Google say – "The more you see, the more you believe" is the basic human tendency taken advantage. The information whether true or false, reaches the public via manipulated accounts in social media. Such accounts could be either fake accounts or automated accounts referred as bot which takes the responsibility of getting the maximum audience for such false information and hereby, confirming the maximum reach. This information could be false information, product advertisement or that could help bring fame, thus such information is meant to go viral. Some bots have good intentions and help reduce manual intervention by automating predefined procedures but mostly they are misused and do more harm than good. Such automated accounts are seen to influence nationwide like the electoral results [1, 2]. The bots adopt various methodologies to spread news like creation of pseudo posts and spreading them in social media. For the maximum spread these accounts make sure to follow the maximum profiles having high follower count. The bots also exhibit highly activity in engagements like share, comment or like of attention seeking posts. Thus, identification of such hidden automated accounts is gaining importance and researches are ongoing

© Springer Nature Singapore Pte Ltd. 2020
S. M. Thampi et al. (Eds.): SoMMA 2019, CCIS 1203, pp. 38–48, 2020.
https://doi.org/10.1007/978-981-15-4301-2_4

to tackle the challenges involved. Bots are classified into various categories according to their actions and purposes. For example, some bots are active in engagements or increasing followers, making friends and contribute in creating a network for other bot accounts, thus increasing the reach of the bot tweets. Some other category bots are active in creating tweets or retweeting the same tweets and focusing on the spread. Also, based on the tweet content they fall under categories like social, political etc. In our study we are focusing on the social accounts having temporal patterns of a bot which marks them apart from a normal user.

This paper focuses on the identification of automated Twitter bot accounts using the temporal activity of the accounts. The temporal activities are mainly indicated by tweeting and behavioural pattern which indicates the active shell time of the account. The other activities for such accounts will be a rare phenomenon. We can see the automated bot accounts differ from normal human accounts in numerous ways. The key feature is that bot accounts are systematic and their timely activities. Their tweeting rate exhibit hourly or daily patterns and the amount of post will also be on larger scale when compared to human accounts. These unnatural features form the basis of our work to identify whether an account is a bot or not. We have used a model which understands these patterns and helps in distinguishing the bot accounts.

Natural Language processing referred to as NLP, a component of artificial intelligence, is an important domain which analyzes human language and make inferences. The text processing is an active research area under this domain and social media is a common platform used for such studies. The bot detection problem is an NLP problem as it involves the linguistics, behavioural, temporal, analytical study of user account's metadata and its posts. Various algorithms like statistical, rule based, machine learning approaches and neural network methods are employed for these various text based problems [3]. Neural Network is an evolving branch of artificial intelligence which is very advanced in self understanding of the features and hidden relationships among the data. Its basic neural units are capable of aligning based on the non linearity of the input data and arriving at various relationships which capture the irregularities among features. Recurrent neural network is an important branch of deep neural network which uses memory neural units for storing the relevant data of the previous units. This particular characteristic makes it capable to work on textual inputs. The applications of deep neural network on this domain and its various problems have proven its effectiveness in numerous ways [4]. We have used LSTM (Long Short-Term Memory) units, a special variant of recurrent neural network with advanced capability of memory for remembering long term dependencies. The LSTM cells are used for building the deep neural network model which analyses the temporal patterns of a user's tweets. These units have a capacity of remembering the previous information without getting overloaded with the help of forget layer. This behaviour is the reason we have used LSTM neural network for analyzing daily temporal patterns. We have tested the performance with various other recurrent networks and performed a comparative study as well.

The major contribution in this paper is developing a novel deep neural study on temporal data of a user's tweets for detection of bot behaviour based on historical behavioural data. This model performs best for the bot accounts displaying temporal discrepancies when compared to a human account.

The next Sect. 2 presents a literature survey followed by Sect. 3 which describes about technical aspect of recurrent neural network. Section 4 details about the methodology and includes results and comparison reports. The final Sect. 5 states the conclusions and future work.

2 Literature Survey

The number of bots is increasing day-by-day and there are attempts by Twitter and Facebook to identify bot accounts and suspend them periodically. Thus bots are considered as potential hazards and many studies are conducted based on them. There are many survey studies [9, 10, 18, 21] analyzing bot nature and its influence.

[5] is a good machine learning approach of finding the bots by extracting 7 main feature sets from the user profile information as well as his/her tweets information. Under the seven main feature sets, they have extracted around 1150 features for each user. This group has created an online portal for bot detection [11]. [17] is a review on different types of bots in social media and various analysis performed on them. This includes improvement of the tool [11] developed using supervised approach method [5] by updating the training data and the features based on recent observations on bot behaviour. A University in Mexico has done a research on bot detection based on temporal analysis. They have analyzed bots tweeting at similar times and following rhythmic patterns [6, 7, 12, 13]. They have performed clustering based on tweeting patterns and extracted the bots. [8] is an online portal created by the group for bot detection by their system. [20] is the study of bot detection with the Twitter json structure of user data and tweet data and its application on machine learning models and deep neural models. [10] is a study on the current available solutions of bot detection and its comparison along with the Twitter methodology of detection and performance evaluation. This paper also focuses on providing prospective methods which can increase the rate of bot detection. [16] is a recent textual study which includes bot detection based on selected features from text and classifies into bot using SVM classifier achieving an accuracy of 90%. [9] is a research guide on bots which analyses the topology, behaviour and impacts of bots in social media.

3 Recurrent Neural Network

The ability of neural networks in solving the mystery of feature resolution from the input given is the main reason behind its usage in various fields. There are numerous problems in NLP domain where neural network is employed. The branch of neural network which focuses on the sequential data is recurrent neural network. The architecture of these networks are such that each units are arranged based on time series and the units are interdependent and recurrent to itself which gives it a unique ability of memory cells. Recurrent neural network units were used in understanding the continuous flow of data remembering the order of occurrence (Fig. 1).

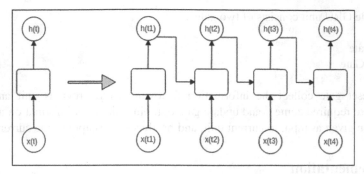

Fig. 1. Architecture of recurrent neural network.

But it was observed that given a long sequence, it failed to collect the information across the length. These networks are capable of remembering the immediate occurrences. To solve this drawback, RNN units were improved by LSTM units and GRU units. These special units were provided with gates which regulate the incoming data and outgoing data and filtering out which needs to be carried forward to the next time sequence (Fig. 2).

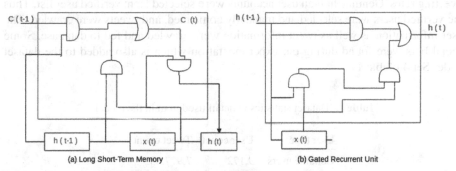

(a) Long Short-Term Memory   (b) Gated Recurrent Unit

Fig. 2. A single memory unit of (a) Long Short Term Memory Neural Network and (b) Gated Recurrent Unit Neural Network.

A single LSTM unit consists of three gates:

- Forget Gate
- Update Gate
- Output Gate

The forget gate identifies the data from the previous cell which need not be carried forward. The update gate focuses on taking in the new data coming to the current unit and converts to the current data distribution. And lastly, output gate combines the data from previous unit passing through forget gate and the vectorized new data coming through update gate, and picks the necessary data to be carried forward, combining both, to produce the output of the current unit.

A single GRU unit consists of two gates:

- Reset Gate
- Update Gate

The reset gate collect the information following from previous unit and reset according to required context and update gate combines the reset information and new information given as input to current unit, and produces the output of the current unit.

4 Implementation

The construction of bot detection system consists of different phases as mentioned below:

4.1 Data Collection

The bot users were fetched from dataset [19]. The tweets of suspended users were taken from [1] while those not suspended were crawled using Twitter API. The latter steps were taken to make sure of no data loss for the users. The accounts having high tweeting rate were chosen and rest were not selected, as we are performing a study on tweeting rates. Genuine human user accounts were selected from verified user list. Thus the verified users were selected and manually confirmed, and tweets were crawled. The user information as well as tweet information were crawled and fed to database. Some social bots were found during our experimentation which is also added to the dataset under Set 4 (Table 1).

Table 1. Dataset statistics in detail used to train the model.

User type	User count	Tweet count
Genuine users	9,172	7,977,832
Social bot set 1	831	1,210,373
Social bot set 2	3,125	3,407,624
Social bot set 3	464	1,418,626
Social bot set 4	5141	3,418,426

4.2 Data Preparation

The users having post activity of atleast one year were considered for data preparation. The timeline of the users were picked around the same duration. As the temporal feature is being experimented here, users with no major temporal activity were discarded from consideration. These tweets were aggregated based on hourly slots giving rise to 8760 slots. In case of empty slots, zeros are appended to fill in the 8760 input vector. Based on temporal information of each tweet, the hourly tweet count was recorded for each user of both types. We are using binary classification problem with 2 classes - 0 and 1.

These temporal data were tagged as 1 for bot and 0 for non-bot user. The given data were divided into training and testing set in the ratio 5:1 respectively. We have selected users which were active during the period of consideration in order to ensure the data matrix is not sparse. The training of neural network will happen accordingly.

4.3 Model Building and Results

The hourly temporal data organized from preprocessing stage is fed into deep neural network. The neural network consists of 8760 input cells to receive corresponding hourly temporal data and 2 output cells for the binary classification problem. As the historical memory of the hourly data had to be analyzed, we used RNN [14] and its variants which were best suited for analyzing the sequential data acting as memory cells. The different deep learning neural network variants used were as follows:

(1) Recurrent Neural Network (RNN) [23]
(2) Long-Short Term Memory (LSTM) [22]
(3) Gated-Recurrent Unit (GRU) [24]

The recurrent neural network and its variants are the learning models used to study the collected data due to its excellence in understanding the sequential data patterns and focusing on the hidden relationship among the data. These models are used for problems like pattern identification and pattern matching [26]. We wanted to distinguish bot accounts from normal accounts from its tweeting behaviour which will be significantly different. Multiple patterns can be followed by bots accounts like having a high tweeting rate on a daily basis when compared to a normal user and another distinguishing factor is the systematic behaviour of bot activity unlike normal users. Such data with multidimensional relationship can be fed to a recurrent neural network and used for classification.

We have experimented with different hyper-parameters [15] like hidden layer count, batch size, neuron/layer count, drop-out rate etc. to study the impact in feature extraction and classification by network layers. We have used Tensorflow to implement all the neural network models. From the result of all the three recurrent neural networks, the highest accuracy of 98.88% is attained by bidirectional LSTM network which is best suited to find the temporal activity patterns and detecting bot behaviour. The best result for bidirectional LSTM was achieved with 4 hidden layer, batch size of 32, neuron/layer of 64 and drop-out rate of 0.1. The next lower accuracy was obtained by bidirectional GRU of about 93.1% and later by RNN of about 88%. We varied the hidden layers from 2, 4 and 6 and lesser layers depicted a behaviour of under learning and more layers depicted a behaviour of over learning. Hence, we fixed the hidden layer count to an optimum value of 4. Likewise, we varied batch size from 8, 32, 64, 128 etc. where 32 seems to be the optimum value while 8 and 128 batch size yielded very less performance. The neuron unit count in layers was also experimented and selected 64 as the optimum which was observed to be margin between underfitting and overfitting scenarios. As it is a binary classification problem we have used sigmoid as activation function and Adam optimizer (Fig. 3).

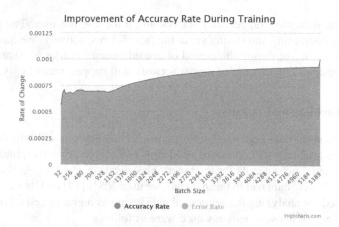

Fig. 3. The rate of improvement of accuracy rate during training phase

We have observed the training period taken by the LSTM network is highest when compared to the GRU network or the simple recurrent network. This is due to complexity in network unit. The LSTM unit has trio gates for information processing when compared to dual gate in GRU network and simple recurrent unit in RNN. The drawback of the higher training time is compensated by the superior classification accuracy provided by the LSTM network (Fig. 4).

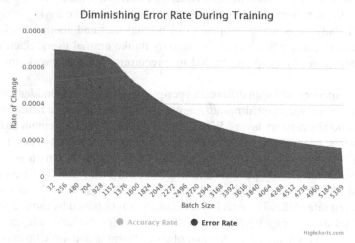

Fig. 4. The rate of decrease of error rate during training phase

For testing purposes, in case of a new user, 8760 input vector size of temporal data will be sparse as zeros will be appended in empty slots. We randomly tested the model with machine learning algorithm AdaBoost Classifier which delivered lesser accuracy when compared to deep learning models. The AdaBoost Classifier were using decision tree as baseline algorithm for the learning and were experimented with different classifier count and the best were chosen based on the classification accuracy delivered (Table 2).

Table 2. The neural network architecture and experimental results.

Experimental model	Hidden layer count	Neuron/layer	Batch size	Classification accuracy (%)
AdaBoost Classifier	–	–	–	77.54
Multi Layer Perceptron	6	128	8	71.24
GRU	4	128	32	81.07
Bidirectional GRU	4	64	32	93.1
RNN	6	128	32	88
LSTM	4	64	32	92.61
Bidirectional LSTM	4	64	32	98.88

In the Figure 6 [25], we can see that the bidirectional LSTM model have found interesting patterns as bots. The timeline of Twitter handles in a, b in the figure are following a pattern of dormant period and an active period irregularly. During the active period they are having high tweeting rate unlike normal users. The Twitter handles in c, d are job advertisement handles which tweet following a systematic patterns which are picked as bots by the model. The random patterns or decreased tweeting rate like that seen in handles e and f in the figure are marked as normal by the model. A special care has been given to avoid the active accounts like news or public figures which are highly active but due to irregular patterns and active state, they are not identified as bots by the model.

4.4 Observation Regarding the Excellence of Neural Network

The hourly based temporal aggregated data is fed to neural network and the neurons capture the pattern of the temporal data. The hidden layers seem to capture the few interesting features from the temporal patterns like continuous hourly activity, high contribution in hourly data and the rate of contribution based on time. Even if the account is occasionally very active with high tweet count patterns, the model seems to recognize them. These features captured by neural network seem very interesting and helps in segregating from the pool of human users. The neural network has the property of understanding the input and as data traverse through the hidden layers, and filters out the exact features required for classification. This very basic feature was missing in traditional learning model where the latter rely on human fed features which is always costly and has more risk involved (Fig. 5).

A challenge we faced while testing recent user was for the user who did not have one-year long data slots of temporal activity. The input given as test samples needs to be a vector of length 8760. Zero is padded in places of vacant data. Hence, we can test

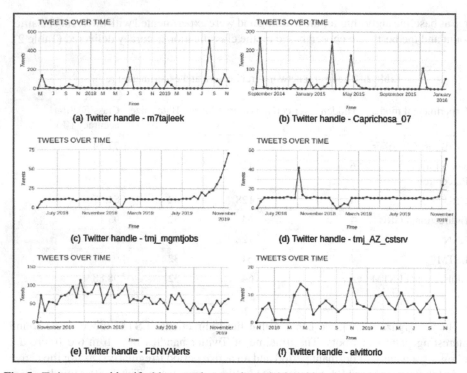

Fig. 5. Twitter users identified by neural network model in which timeline of a, b, c and d are identified as bots while e and f are identified as normal users.

a recent or an old user irrespective of the total user activity span. The LSTM network focuses more on slots where data values are present and ignores if the previous data is all empty. This feature is performed by the forget gate of LSTM units. The forget gate considers the empty slots as unwanted and remove these data and replace with new slot which contains values. But the empty slots in between the values slots indicating dormant period are considered and remembered by the LSTM units. These are taken as feature for detection.

5   Conclusion and Future Works

The temporal feature of a user account's activity is a very important feature which distinguishes a bot account from a normal one. Such timely, systematic and over rated patterns can be identified by recurrent neural network like LSTM and helps in finding bot user. As a future work, we are planning to increase the bot dataset collection and test the temporal activity to find any new timeline pattern to make sure of the full coverage of the bot users displaying temporal patterns. Also, we are looking to add post content analysis, metadata of the users etc., in order to capture generic bots as well. With such further analysis, we may find the hidden relationship among features and the correlation among them. This might help in finding different types of ever evolving, sophisticated bot accounts which are difficult to distinguish from the regular account in social media.

Acknowledgement. We thank Amrita Vishwa Vidyapeetham for providing all the support for conducting this research.

References

1. Metaxas, P.T., Mustafaraj, E.: Social media and the elections. Science **338**(6106), 472–473 (2012)
2. Bessi, A., Ferrara, E.: Social bots distort the 2016 US presidential election online discussion. First Monday **21**(11) (2016)
3. Vijayan, V.K., Bindu, K.R., Parameswaran, L.: A comprehensive study of text classification algorithms. In: 2017 International Conference on Advances in Computing, Communications and Informatics (ICACCI), pp. 1109–1113. IEEE (2017)
4. Aravinda Reddy, D., Anand Kumar, M., Soman, K.P.: LSTM based paraphrase identification using combined word embedding features. In: Wang, J., Reddy, G.R.M., Prasad, V.K., Reddy, V.S. (eds.) Soft Computing and Signal Processing. AISC, vol. 898, pp. 385–394. Springer, Singapore (2019). https://doi.org/10.1007/978-981-13-3393-4_40
5. Varol, O., Ferrara, E., Davis, C.A., Menczer, F., Flammini, A.: Online human-bot interactions: detection, estimation, and characterization. In: Eleventh International AAAI Conference on Web and Social Media (2017)
6. Chavoshi, N., Hamooni, H., Mueen, A.: Identifying correlated bots in Twitter. In: Spiro, E., Ahn, Y.-Y. (eds.) SocInfo 2016. LNCS, vol. 10047, pp. 14–21. Springer, Cham (2016). https://doi.org/10.1007/978-3-319-47874-6_2
7. Chavoshi, N., Hamooni, H., Mueen, A.: Temporal patterns in bot activities. In: Proceedings of the 26th International Conference on World Wide Web Companion, pp. 1601–1606. International World Wide Web Conferences Steering Committee (2017)
8. DeBot: Real-Time Bot Detection via Activity Correlation: Online Tool. https://www.cs.unm.edu/~chavoshi/debot/check_user.php
9. Gorwa, R., Guilbeault, D.: Unpacking the social media bot: a typology to guide research and policy. Policy Internet (2018)
10. Karataş, A., Şahin, S.: A review on social bot detection techniques and research directions. In: Proceedings of the International Security and Cryptology Conference, Turkey, pp. 156–161 (2017)
11. Botometer: Online Tool. http://botometer.com
12. Chavoshi, N., Hamooni, H., Mueen, A.: On-demand bot detection and archival system. In: Proceedings of the 26th International Conference on World Wide Web Companion, pp. 183–187. International World Wide Web Conferences Steering Committee (2017)
13. Chavoshi, N., Hamooni, H., Mueen, A.: DeBot: Twitter bot detection via warped correlation. In: ICDM, pp. 817–822 (2016)
14. Jozefowicz, R., Zaremba, W., Sutskever, I.: An empirical exploration of recurrent network architectures. In: Proceedings of the 32nd International Conference on Machine Learning (ICML 2015), pp. 2342–2350 (2015)
15. Karpathy, A., Johnson, J., Fei-Fei, L.: Visualizing and understanding recurrent networks. arXiv preprint arXiv:1506.02078. 5 June 2015
16. Bacciu, A., La Morgia, M., Mei, A., Nemmi, E.N., Neri, V., Stefa, J.: Bot and Gender Detection of Twitter Accounts Using Distortion and LSA (2019)
17. Yang, K.-C., Varol, O., Davis, C.A., Ferrara, E., Flammini, A., Menczer, F.: Arming the public with artificial intelligence to counter social bots. Hum. Behav. Emerging Technol. **1**, 48–61 (2019)

18. Hwang, T., Pearce, I., Nanis, M.: Socialbots: voices from the fronts. ACM Interact. **19**(2), 38–45 (2012)
19. Cresci, S., Di Pietro, R., Petrocchi, M., Spognardi, A., Tesconi, M.: The paradigm-shift of social spambots: evidence, theories, and tools for the arms race. In: Proceedings of the 26th International Conference on World Wide Web Companion, pp. 963–972. International World Wide Web Conferences Steering Committee (2017)
20. Kudugunta, S., Ferrara, E.: Deep neural networks for bot detection. Inf. Sci. **467**, 312–322 (2018)
21. Ferrara, E., Varol, O., Davis, C., Menczer, F., Flammini, A.: The rise of social bots. Commun. ACM (in press). Preprint arXiv:1407.5225
22. Hochreiter, S., Schmidhuber, J.: Long short-term memory. Neural Comput. **9**(8), 1735–1780 (1997)
23. Chung, J., Gulcehre, C., Cho, K., Bengio, Y.: Empirical evaluation of gated recurrent neural networks on sequence modeling. CoRR, vol. abs/1412.3555 (2014). http://arxiv.org/abs/1412.3555
24. Cho, K., et al.: Learning phrase representations using RNN encoder-decoder for statistical machine translation. arXiv preprint arXiv:1406.1078 (2014)
25. Online website. https://socialbearing.com/
26. Sutskever, I., Vinyals, O., Le, Q.V.: Sequence to sequence learning with neural networks. In: Advances in NIPS (2014)

Comparison of Metaheuristics for a Vehicle Routing Problem in a Farming Community

Aravind Mohan[2]([✉]), Anandhu Dileep[2], Sreesankar Ajayan[2], Georg Gutjahr[1,2], and Prema Nedungadi[1]

[1] Center for Research in Analytics and Technologies for Education (CREATE), Amrita Vishwa Vidyapeetham, Amritapuri, Kollam, India

[2] Department of Mathematics, Amrita Vishwa Vidyapeetham, Amritapuri, Kollam, India
mohanaravind31@gmail.com

Abstract. In a farming community, different types of commodities may need to be transported to different destinations, like the market, storage unit or a processing unit, during the harvest season. To organize efficient transportation in such a setting, the problem is formulated as a Vehicle Routing Problem with Pickups and Deliveries, by considering a virtual field and a virtual destination for delivery of each commodity. To solve this particular problem instance, four common metaheuristics - iterative hill-climbing, guided local search, tabu search, and simulated annealing - were tried and their performances based on total tour lengths for different run times were compared. Basic implementations of these metaheuristics were done using Google OR tools. Guided local search was found to produce good solutions quicker than others. In the long run, tabu search was able to find a slightly better solution. Simulated annealing was prone to get trapped in a local optimum for hours.

Keywords: Metaheuristics · Vehicle routing with pickup and delivery · Guided local search · Iterative hill climbing · Tabu search · Simulated annealing

1 Introduction

Community farming is a practice in which farmers pool their resources together, and collectively market the products. For a large community, the cost of transportation of the resources or products, forms a non- negligible part of the recurring costs, despite the benefits of having a shared economy and society. Therefore, careful planning of the logistics of transportation is important.

This paper examines a farming community in Khordha district, in the Indian state of Odisha. The community consists of a cluster of four villages, adjacent to the Chandaka forest. The farmers have ownership of their lands, and each farmer chooses the plants to be grown, based on climate, availability of resources and

© Springer Nature Singapore Pte Ltd. 2020
S. M. Thampi et al. (Eds.): SoMMA 2019, CCIS 1203, pp. 49–63, 2020.
https://doi.org/10.1007/978-981-15-4301-2_5

access to production facilities. The farmers carry out multicropping, and adopt crop rotation practices, to achieve sustainable agriculture.

In the Khordha farming community, some of the crops must be promptly transported to a market; as they are sold fresh, soon after harvest. Other crops that can be stored need to be transported to a storage silo. Some harvest like lemongrass, which needs to be processed, should be transported to a distillery, for oil extraction.

In this work, we investigate the problem of selection of optimal routes to deliver a variety of crops, in different quantities, from the fields to different destinations (the marketplace, storage unit, and the distillery). Four tractors, owned by the four villages, are available to deliver the crops. The tractors are required to return to their respective depots, at the end of their designated delivery route. In addition, no split deliveries for the quantities of a particular crop at a field are allowed, as the harvest of a crop is done completely, all at once. The farmers are informed of the pickup and delivery plans, prior to the arrival of the tractors. This leads to a type of multi-destination, multi-depot, vehicle routing problem. To solve the problem efficiently, we formulate it as a Vehicle Routing Problem with Pickups and Deliveries (VRPPD) by considering virtual fields and virtual delivery destinations, required for each crop.

In the Khordha farming community, 92 fields were considered, where up to three different crops are grown. Harvest from these fields requires a total of 185 deliveries to the different destinations. Such an instance of a VRPPD has been observed to be too difficult to solve by exact methods [33]. Hence, we try four common metaheuristics on this problem instance, namely; iterative hill-climbing, guided local search, tabu search, and simulated annealing and compare the total tour lengths of their solutions, for different run times. The study area was modelled in a geographic information system software ArcGIS [27]. The metaheuristics were implemented using an optimization software Google OR-Tools [29].

This paper is organized as follows. Section 2 introduces the optimization problem and formulates a mathematical model of the problem. Section 3 presents a short introduction to heuristic and metaheuristic algorithms in general and describes the selected four metaheuristic procedures and Sect. 4 describes their implementations briefly. Section 5 presents the results of the study. Conclusion and closing remarks are noted in Sect. 6.

2   Problem Description

2.1   Informal Description

We consider a cluster of villages in Khordha district of the Indian state of Odisha. The cluster includes Haridamada and Barapita villages of the Mendhasal Panchayat, and Guptapada and Bindiyagiri villages of the Chhatabar panchayat. The village cluster is spread around an area of $15 \, km^2$.

In 2016, a farming community was initiated in this cluster of tribal villages, as part of the Self-Reliant Villages (SeRVe) project, under the aegis of Mata

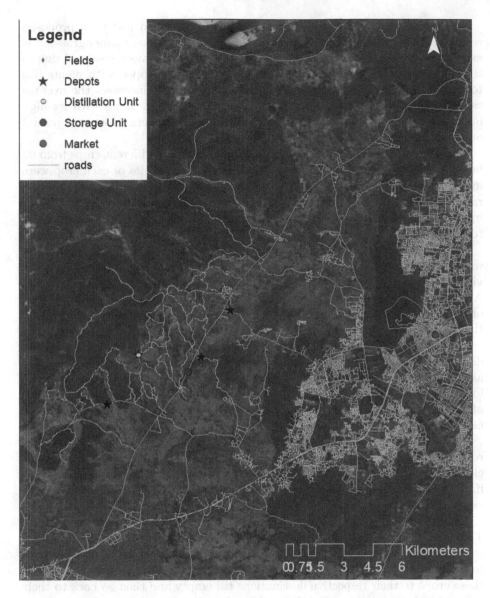

Fig. 1. Satellite image of the study area, modelled using ArcGIS.

Amritanadamayi Math [25,31]. The farmers grow vegetables such as beetroot, onions, tomatoes, eggplants, potatoes, cabbage and carrots. This study considers the winter season, where mainly tomatoes, cabbage, eggplants, potatoes and onions are harvested. Potatoes and onions are stored in a warehouse, and later sold to a wholesaler. The other vegetables are sold at a marketplace in the city of Bhubaneswar. This market, situated far into the city, is about 15 km away from the village cluster.

Additionally, a pilot project for lemongrass cultivation had been proposed recently. This required the construction of a distillery, where lemongrass oil is extracted. A common distillery for the entire community was considered due to the high cost of construction. Lemongrass, when intercropped with plants like tomatoes and eggplant, helps in pest control as well as increases the average weight and yield of eggplant fruits [6]. These incidentals, along with its high market value, make lemongrass an enticing choice for farmers. More background on the lemongrass pilot project can be found in [1,18].

This paper examines the transportation of produce of different crops from 92 fields to their respective destinations. The harvest quantities of each crop were in the range of 100–700 kg, giving total harvested quantities at each field in the range of 200–1500 kg, depending on the size of fields. Assuming deliveries of up to three destinations for each field, according to the crops grown; this leads to a total of 185 required deliveries.

The study area was modelled using ArcGIS version 10.5. The road network was obtained from Open Street Maps [26] and the more remote roads in the villages were identified in consultation with SeRVe. A satellite image from an ArcGIS map [7] of the villages, along with the roads, is shown in Fig. 1. Locations of the fields, storage unit, distillation unit, and the market are also shown on the map.

In the Khordha community, each of the four villages has a tractor at some depot, as shown in the figure. The average speed of tractor in paved roads was assumed as 25 km/h, and 15 km/h on the more remote roads (assumed to be identical for all four tractors). The cargo capacity of the tractors is about 1500 kg of harvested produce. The service time to fully load a tractor at any of the fields, can be assumed to be 30 min.

Efficient management of transportation is imperative to reduce the total recurring expenses of the community. Informally, the problem of using the vehicles in the best possible way is called the Vehicle Routing Problem (VRP) [34] if all fields must be visited and team orienteering if some fields can be skipped [13,14].

The distillery, storage unit and market act as destinations for the deliveries. The sources of pickups are the various fields. The tractors in the four villages start from their depots to go around collecting all the quantities of some crop from some of the fields in the community, until fully loaded, then deliver all these crops to their respective destinations till empty and then go back to their respective depot, at the end of the working day. Such a manoeuvre is henceforth referred to as a tour or route. Planing these tours in an optimal way leads to a of multi-depot, multi-destination vehicle routing problem [30].

This optimization problem can be solved by formulating it as a Vehicle Routing Problem with Pickups and Deliveries (VRPPD) [34]. For that, we split each field into up to three virtual sites, depending on the types of crops that are grown there. The destinations are split into multiple virtual sites so that each transportation of the produce of each commodity, from a field to its destination, can be represented as a unique pickup-and-delivery request, from a virtual field to a virtual destination. A mathematical model will be given next.

2.2   Formal Description

Model Parameters

- n, the number of pickup and delivery requests.
- $P = \{1, 2 \ldots, n\}$, the set of virtual fields.
- $D = \{n + 1, n + 2 \ldots, 2n\}$, the set of virtual destinations, where $n + i$ is the virtual destination of the ith virtual field.
- $N = P \cup D$, the set of all sites.
- $\ell_i = q_i$ and $\ell_{n+i} = 0$, if the ith request consists of transporting q_i kilogram of produce from site i to site $n + i$.
- K, the set of tours of all the tractors.
- C, capacity of the tractor in kg.
- $d(k)$, site where the kth tour starts and ends (the depot).
- $S_k = N \cup d(k)$, the set of all sites belonging to the visit of the kth tour.
- $A_k = S_k \times S_k$, the set of all edges between these sites, where an edge denotes the shortest path between two sites.
- t_{ij} and c_{ij}, the time in hours and distance in kilometers, of travel for the tractor, between the ith site and the jth site.
- s_i, the time in hours required to load the produce at i^{th} site.

Decision Variables

- $x_{ijk} = 1$, if the kth tour goes from site i to site j and 0 otherwise.
- T_{ik}, specifies the time for the kth tour to reach the ith site.
- L_{ik}, specifies the load of the kth tour after it reaches the ith site.

Objective Function. The objective function is to minimize the total tour length to satisfy all requests:

$$\min \sum_{k \in K} \sum_{(i,k) \in A_k} c_{ij} x_{ijk} \tag{1}$$

Constraints. A feasible solution has to satisfy the following constraints:

- Possible range of the decision variables:

$$x_{ijk} \in \{0, 1\}, T_{ik} \geq 0, L_{jk} \geq 0 \quad \text{for all } k \in K \text{ and } (i, j) \in A_k. \tag{2}$$

- Each request is served once, and only once:

$$\sum_{k \in K} \sum_{j \in S_k} x_{ijk} = 1 \quad \text{for all } i \in P \tag{3}$$

$$\sum_{j \in N} x_{ijk} - \sum_{j \in N} x_{j,n+i,k} = 0 \quad \text{for all } k \in K \text{ and } i \in P \tag{4}$$

- Valid multi-commodity flow structure and the requirement that the vehicles start and end tours at their respective depots:

$$\sum_{j \in P} x_{d(k),j,k} = 1 \quad \text{for all } k \in K \tag{5}$$

$$\sum_{i \in N} x_{ijk} - \sum_{j \in N} x_{ijk} = 0 \quad \text{for all } k \in K \text{ and } i,j \in N \tag{6}$$

$$\sum_{i \in D \cup d(k)} x_{i,d(k),k} = 1 \quad \text{for all } k \in K \tag{7}$$

- Pickups must happen before deliveries:

$$x_{ijk}(T_{ik} + s_i + t_{ij} - T_{jk}) \leq 0 \quad \text{for all } k \in K \text{ and } (i,j) \in A_k \tag{8}$$
$$T_{ik} + t_{i,n+i} - T_{n+i,k} \leq 0 \quad \text{for all } k \in K \text{ and } i \in P \tag{9}$$

- Maximum loading capacity of C for all tours:

$$L_{d(k),k} = 0 \quad \text{for all } k \in K \tag{10}$$
$$x_{ijk}(L_{ik} + \ell_j - L_{jk}) \leq 0 \quad \text{for all } k \in K \text{ and } (i,j) \in A_k \tag{11}$$
$$\ell_i \leq L_{ik} \leq C \quad \text{for all } k \in K \text{ and } i \in P \tag{12}$$
$$0 \leq L_{n+i,k} \leq C - \ell_i \quad \text{for all } k \in K \text{ and } n+i \in D \tag{13}$$

3   Heuristic Algorithms

3.1   Local Search Procedures

The VRPPD problem, formulated in the previous section, is NP-hard. If time windows are also added as constraints, then even finding a feasible solution becomes NP-hard [20].

Exact methods, like branch-and-cut, and branch-and-price, are only able to solve relatively small instances of VRPPD; for example, instances with up to 50 pick up and delivery requests with time-windows or capacitated VRP instances of up to 134 customers, which could be viewed as a single commodity VRP [33].

Due to the intractability of the solution space of VRPs in general, it is common to apply methods that try to create good feasible solutions, called heuristics. One way to do this is to first create feasible routes for the vehicles to get a feasible solution (also referred to as, simply "solution"), and then improve upon them by injecting minor local changes like exchanging a few vertices. These methods are collectively known as local search procedures.

Local searches form a general class of techniques, applicable to many different types of optimization problems. The usage of a local search requires firstly, a method of generating feasible solutions. This process is called a construction heuristic. Examples of construction heuristics are nearest neighbor, insertion heuristic, and savings heuristic [22].

Next, a neighborhood relationship needs to be defined, on the solution space, so that the local search algorithm can find a candidate solution from this neighborhood, according to some rules, that would be used in the next iteration. In the context of VRP, neighborhoods of solutions are defined as solutions with routes that differ by a small number of vertices. The effectiveness of a local search procedure depends on the procedure, by which a candidate solution for next iteration is chosen, and on the size and definition of the neighborhood search. An adaptive large-scale neighborhood search was found to be effective for VRPPDs [33].

Even after a large number of iterations, for local improvements, a heuristic could lead to solutions that may not be globally optimal; sometimes, they yield a poor local optimum. Calculating bounds for the difference between the heuristic and the optimal solution maybe computationally expensive; constructing algorithms for VRPs with guaranteed bounds is itself NP-hard [36].

Local searches are anytime algorithms, that is, they return a feasible solution even if interrupted before the end of the procedure [16]. This is in contrast with some exact methods, like an unmodified branch-and-cut algorithm, which returns a solution only at the end.

In summary, heuristics may be a preferred choice, when the focus is on finding decent feasible solutions, using less computational power and time. Sometimes, heuristics may lead to very bad solutions. For example, it has been proven that there are some instances of the Traveling Salesman Problem (TSP) such that the most simple heuristics for routing—the greedy algorithm and the nearest neighbor algorithm—give the worst possible feasible solution [12]. The same problem has been encountered on some TSP instances by local searches [28].

3.2 Metaheuristics

Many problem-specific heuristics have been proposed for various combinatorial optimization problems. Another approach is to develop algorithms that provide heuristic solutions for any type of combinatorial optimization problem. Such algorithms are called metaheuristics.

A simple example of a metaheuristic is to repeatedly apply a local search with different starting values. When the search is done greedily, we get the iterative hill climbing. Repeated local search can be improved by also taking the previous solutions into consideration. Methods that use this approach include tabu search [11] and guided local search [37]. Another natural way to improve the local search solution is to allow for non-improving moves to let the search escape out of local optima. This leads to metaheuristics such as simulated annealing [21] and variable neighborhood search [17]. Instead of using a single starting solution, population-based metaheuristics keep improving a set of feasible solutions, in each iteration. Examples include genetic algorithms, ant-colony optimization, and particle-swarm optimization [3].

A well-ordered bibliography of different metaheuristics applied to different vehicle-routing problems is given by Gendreau et al. [9].

There is also an interesting result that while considering the average performance on a large number of instances of different combinatorial optimization problems, the various metaheuristics essentially work with equal efficiency. This is called the no free lunch theorem [38].

Therefore, different metaheuristics may need to be tried out to know which of them will work best, on a specific problem. Here, the focus is on using the following four metaheuristics: iterative hill climbing, tabu search, guided-local search, and simulated annealing, for solving the VRPPD instance.

In general, these methods, when implemented to act on top of local search, try to escape the local search out of local optima, which is called diversification. Then, the search is continued in a new area; this is called intensification. In some cases, the restrictions of the metaheuristics are disregarded, for example, when a new solution, which would not be accepted by the metaheuristics, is the best solution hitherto; this is called an aspiration criterion. The efficiency of these algorithms also depends on how the basic version of an algorithm, used for general optimization problems, is modified to solve a specific problem, based on the knowledge of the problem.

Iterative Hill Climbing: Hill climbing, also known as Greedy descent when considering minimization problems, is a local search routine, which makes a greedy selection from the neighborhood of the current solution, for the next iteration. It tries to optimize a function, which could be the total sum of arc costs or the total number of violated constraints, like time windows in the case when it is used as a construction heuristic. This local search method is guaranteed to reach a local optimum, but not a global optimum. To avoid this problem, hill climbing can be iterated with various starting values. Even though the algorithm is quite simple, it has been found to work well on some real-world problems [10].

For vehicle routing, the important consideration for hill climbing algorithms is the definition of the neighborhood [23]. A detailed description of a hill-climbing algorithm for the Vehicle Routing Problem has been given by Braysy et al. [4].

Tabu Search: The iterative hill climbing algorithm described above, can be modified, such that solutions that have already been explored are not investigated again. There are ways by which searches that lead to a previous local optima can be avoided, by identifying certain attributes of these solutions. In tabu search, these attributes are called tabu constraints. For the performance of the algorithm, the right type of storage of the tabu constraints is important. Furthermore, the duration of the storage, called the tabu tenure, must be selected carefully to achieve the best performance [11].

Implementations of the tabu search for vehicle routing include the granular tabu search [35], the adaptive memory procedure by Rochat and Taillard [32], and the network flow-based tabu search by Xu and Kelly [39].

Guided Local Search: The local search is made to escape the local optimum by modifying the objective function that was used to decide the direction of the search, in the neighborhood of the current solution. Similar to how tabu search identifies tabu constraints, by looking at specific attributes of previously visited solutions, guided local search builds a list of features of previous solutions. The number of features that a new solution would share with previous solutions, is then used as a penalty term, in the modified objective function. The features to increase penalty are identified using a utility function, which depends on the cost of the feature and how often the feature is encountered during the search.

Guided local search was described by Voudouris and Tsang [37] for combinatorial optimization problems, such as the Travelling Salesman Problem. This work was extended for the vehicle routing problem by Kilby et al. [19]. For the Vehicle Routing Problem, the features could be the edges and the feature cost could be the edge costs.

Simulated Annealing: Simulated annealing is an iterative procedure, where, at each step, a new solution is picked at random from a large neighborhood around the current solution. If a new solution is better than the previous solution, the former is accepted as the current solution; if a new solution is worse than the current solution, the latter is accepted as the current solution, with a certain probability and rejected otherwise. This probability depends on how much worse the new solution would be and on a temperature parameter that decreases over time. Initially, if the temperature is high, the probability to accept a new solution becomes higher. As the temperature decreases, the probability to accept solutions that are worse than the current solution also decreases. In this way, simulated annealing focuses on exploring the feasible region by taking steps at random. After a large number of iterations, the algorithm will start to resemble a local search more closely, where new solutions are only accepted if they directly improve the objective function. In different implementations, parameters like the initial temperature, the decrement in temperature for a new iteration, the number of solutions checked for a given temperature, and the probability function for acceptance of new solutions, could change. These parameters are called the cooling schedule.

To apply simulated annealing to the Vehicle Routing Problem, we need a way to randomly generate new solutions from the current solution. One method for the generation of new solutions is the transfer-and-swap algorithm [15]. It is possible to combine simulated annealing with tabu search, by adding a tabu list, when generating new solutions in simulated annealing [5]. Genreau et al. gave a detailed overview of simulated annealing for vehicle routing [8].

4 Implementation

4.1 ArcGIS

As discussed previously, our problem instance is too large to be solved exactly. So, heuristic methods were tried. One simple commonly used tool for VRPs is ArcGIS, which is the geographic information system in which the maps and road network of the problem were modelled. The network analyst extension of ArcGIS can solve some variants of facility location problems, VRPs and shortest path problems [27].

ArcGIS can be used to solve small instances of VRPPD with time windows efficiently. As described previously, the fields and destinations were split into virtual fields and virtual destinations to model the problem instance as a VRPPD. The VRP solver, in ArcGIS, first creates a distance matrix of the problem, using a variation of Dijkstra's algorithm, and constructs an initial feasible solution, by inserting the vertices, one by one, to create some feasible routes for the vehicles. Then, the routes are improved by re-sequencing the vertices, or by moving the vertices between routes. A tabu metaheuristic was used to improve these operations. The algorithms are designed to return the solution within seconds and there is no way to increase the stopping time.

4.2 Google OR Tools

To obtain better solutions, four common metaheuristics were implemented using Google OR-tools and allowed them to run for a few hours. OR-tools is an open-source suite for solving optimization problems. It provides bindings to Python, C++, and Java [29].

OR-tools suite has been designed to model a variety of combinatorial optimization problems by using their predefined functions. OR-tools' local search works by changing the value of one of the decision variables in the optimization problem in a feasible way. The stopping criteria of the local search could be reaching an upper number of such operations (by default 264) or a time limit (by default 100 s).

The metaheuristic is used when the local search stops at a local optimum. The metaheuristic changes the search area and the local search acts again to reach another local optimum. The aspiration criterion is that whenever a solution better than all previous solutions is encountered, it is accepted irrespective of whether the metaheuristic allows it, or not. The iterative hill-climbing used, restarts the search, randomly and then repeatedly uses the local search for better objective value. The tabu search and simulated annealing are implemented as their most basic versions for combinatorial optimization problems in general, while an implementation of the guided local search tailored for routing problems has been used. When the default implementation is used, all these metaheuristics involve some learning while searching, to automatically alter the parameters of the algorithm. Escaping the local optimum is a byproduct of this learning.

The distance matrix, to be given as input for the metaheuristic implementations in OR-tools, was extracted by the Origin-Destination layer of ArcGIS, which solves the shortest path problems, using a modified version of Dijkstra's algorithm.

5   Results

It was found that the algorithms in ArcGIS are not capable of handling large problem instances. The solution using ArcGIS of the above formulated model was found to be 1 452 km.

A better solution for the VRP was found in ArcGIS, by splitting the problem into separate Vehicle Routing Problems, for each of the three destinations. But this approach does not guarantee the result to be near optimal [2]. The sum of the solutions for the three-single commodity VRPs, using ArcGIS, was found to be 1 320 km.

There is no control of the parameters of the heuristics and, the stopping criteria cannot be altered. The run-time of the algorithm in ArcGIS was less than a minute, the simulation below suggests that this is far too short to find a good solution. Albeit the three VRPs can be solved separately in ArcGIS, this approach will not lead to satisfactory overall solution.

Next, in OR tools, an initial feasible solution was constructed using path-cheapest arc method, where nearest neighbors among vertices were connected on a tour, if they could still form feasible tours. This was repeated until all vertices were part of some tours. In this manner. a feasible solution with an objective value of 2 954 km was obtained. This was clearly a bad solution because the solver had not yet identified the produce that went to the market, as a separate VRP due to the market being very far away.

The four metaheuristics were initialized with the feasible solution found by the path-cheapest arc algorithm mentioned above. The local search then reaches a local optimum after which the metaheuristic is applied to change the search area and then continue the local search. For each metaheuristic, the average of the total tour lengths was evaluated, when running the metaheuristic 10 times for t minutes each, where $t = 5, 10, 30, 60, 120$. The comparison was run on an Intel Xeon E3-v5 processor, with a CPU rating of 3.4 GHz. Table 1 shows the average of the 10 obtained solutions for each different time.

Tabu search and guided local search were found to be superior to simulated annealing and iterated hill climbing. Tabu search slightly outperformed guided local search for long run times, and guided local search outperforming tabu search for runtimes of 10 min and less. Both iterative hill-climbing and simulated annealing had a large chance of ending up in a local minimum solution, with a value of about 1 279 km. Run-times longer than 30 min had a low chance of improving this solution. The best solution that was found, with a run-time of 20 h of tabu search, had an objective value of 1 201 km.

To understand the usefulness of these methods for the farming community, a manual routing was used as the basis for comparison. The solution found with this approach was 1 310 km. This was better than the solution found by ArcGIS, for separation into the two or three VRPs but worse than the best solution found by a metaheuristic by over 100 km. The comparisons of manual routing with the metaheuristic solutions show that in a large farming community, optimization methods can lead to savings for the community, as transportation costs constitute a non-negligible part of the recurring costs of cultivation.

Table 1. Average of the total tour length of solutions (in km) depending on the algorithm and the algorithm's run-time, for 10 runs of each algorithm.

	Run-time				
	5 min	10 min	30 min	1 h	2 h
Hill-climbing	1 371	1 355	1 279	1 279	1 279
Guided local search	1 234	1 234	1 225	1 223	1 219
Simulated annealing	1 291	1 283	1 279	1 279	1 279
Tabu search	1 276	1 258	1 243	1 221	1 207

6 Summary and Conclusion

This paper considered the optimization of transportation of harvested crops in a farming community to their designated destinations, namely, the market, the storage and the distillery. The problem was formulated as a Vehicle Routing Problem with Pickups and Deliveries to preset destinations. This was done by splitting the destinations into virtual sites for each crop to be delivered. The large problem instance considered in this paper required heuristic approaches. Solvers designed to provide a solution in a few seconds, are not expected to work well on large VRP problem instances like the one discussed here. This was observed from the solutions, obtained using ArcGIS's VRP solver, which are only as good as a reasonably thought out manual solution.

So, to tackle the problem, four common metaheuristics; iterative hill-climbing, guided local search, tabu search, and simulated annealing, were tried and run for a few hours and the total tour length of their solutions for different run times, were compared. These metaheuristics were implemented in Google OR tools as their most basic versions. Tabu search and guided local search performed much better than simulated annealing. The implementation of guided local search was able to provide better quality solutions for shorter run times and also for longer run times, gave solutions comparable with tabu search. Simulated annealing had the tendency to be trapped in local optimal solutions for hours. This might be because a basic version of simulated annealing has been noted to be unlikely to give good results [24]. The results, thus emphasize the point that the effectiveness of a metaheuristic depends on its implementation for a specific problem type. Multiple extensions of simulated annealing for vehicle routing have been proposed in the literature and some of these may substantially improve the performance of the method on this problem. Also it might be useful to try hybrid methods which use some combination of these algorithms, to get a better performance.

In the future, we hope to perform a more extensive comparison with additional metaheuristics. Other possible extensions include stochastic modelling of the produce of the fields or the travel times, the inhomogeneous VRP, where ox-carts are used in addition to the tractors for transportation, robust optimization and the multi-objective optimization problem, where other objectives besides the sum of the total distance of the vehicles is taken into consideration.

Finally, the problem could be extended into a wider supply chain management system. Such an extension could also consider goal programming, where requirements for pickups and deliveries change dynamically.

References

1. Ajayan, S., Dileep, A., Mohan, A., Gutjahr, G., Nedungadi, P.: Vehicle routing and facility-location for sustainable lemongrass cultivation. In: 9th International Symposium on Embedded Computing and System Design (to be published)
2. Archetti, C., Campbell, A.M., Speranza, M.G.: Multicommodity vs. single-commodity routing. Transp. Sci. **50**(2), 461–472 (2014)
3. Beheshti, Z., Shamsuddin, S.M.: A review of population-based meta-heuristic algorithm. Int. J. Adv. Soft Comput. Appl. **5**, 1–35 (2013)
4. Bräysy, O., Hasle, G., Dullaert, W.: A multi-start local search algorithm for the vehicle routing problem with time windows. Eur. J. Oper. Res. **159**(3), 586–605 (2004)
5. Chiang, W.C., Russell, R.A.: Simulated annealing metaheuristics for the vehicle routing problem with time windows. Ann. Oper. Res. **63**(1), 3–27 (1996)
6. d Ebuenga, M., Gonzales, P.G.: Impact of intercropping lemon grass (cymbopogon citratus stapf.) on infestation of eggplant fruit and shoot borer (leucinodes orbonalis guenee) in eggplant (solanum melongena l.). Margaret Helen Udarbe-Alvarez, Ph.D., Editor **54**(1), 114 (2013)
7. Esri: DigitalGlobe. https://www.digitalglobe.com/
8. Gendreau, M., Laporte, G., Potvin, J.Y.: Metaheuristics for the capacitated VRP. In: The Vehicle Routing Problem, pp. 129–154. SIAM (2002)
9. Gendreau, M., Potvin, J.Y., Bräumlaysy, O., Hasle, G., Løkketangen, A.: Metaheuristics for the vehicle routing problem and its extensions: a categorized bibliography. In: Golden, B., Raghavan, S., Wasil, E. (eds.) The Vehicle Routing Problem: Latest Advances and New Challenges, vol. 43, pp. 143–169. Springer, Boston (2008). https://doi.org/10.1007/978-0-387-77778-8_7
10. Gendreau, M., Potvin, J.Y., et al.: Handbook of Metaheuristics, vol. 2. Springer, New York (2010). https://doi.org/10.1007/978-1-4419-1665-5
11. Glover, F.: Future paths for integer programming and links to artificial intelligence. Comput. Oper. Res. **13**(5), 533–549 (1986)
12. Gutin, G., Yeo, A., Zverovich, A.: Traveling salesman should not be greedy: domination analysis of greedy-type heuristics for the TSP. Discrete Appl. Math. **117**(1–3), 81–86 (2002)
13. Gutjahr, G., Kamala, K.A., Nedungadi, P.: Genetic algorithms for vaccination tour planning in tribal areas in Kerala. In: 2018 International Conference on Advances in Computing, Communications and Informatics (ICACCI), pp. 938–942. IEEE (2018)
14. Gutjahr, G., Krishna, L.C., Nedungadi, P.: Optimal tour planning for measles and rubella vaccination in Kochi, South India. In: 2018 International Conference on Advances in Computing, Communications and Informatics (ICACCI), pp. 1366–1370. IEEE (2018)
15. Han Jr, L.: Metaheuristic algorithms for the vehicle routing problem with time window and skill set constraints (2016)

16. Hansen, P., Mladenović, N.: Variable neighborhood search. In: Glover, F., Kochenberger, G.A. (eds.) Handbook of Metaheuristics, vol. 57, pp. 145–184. Springer, Boston (2003). https://doi.org/10.1007/0-306-48056-5_6

17. Hansen, P., Mladenović, N., Pérez, J.A.M.: Variable neighbourhood search: methods and applications. Ann. Oper. Res. **175**(1), 367–407 (2010)

18. Hassanzadeh, A., Mohseninezhad, L., Tirdad, A., Dadgostari, F., Zolfagharinia, H.: Location-routing problem. In: Zanjirani Farahani, R., Hekmatfar, M. (eds.) Facility Location, Contributions to Management Science, pp. 395–417. Springer, Heidelberg (2009). https://doi.org/10.1007/978-3-7908-2151-2_17

19. Kilby, P., Prosser, P., Shaw, P.: Guided local search for the vehicle routing problem with time windows. In: Voß, S., Martello, S., Osman, I.H., Roucairol, C. (eds.) Meta-Heuristics, pp. 473–486. Springer, Boston (1999). https://doi.org/10.1007/978-1-4615-5775-3_32

20. Kilby, P., Shaw, P.: Vehicle routing. In: Rossi, F., van Beek, P., Walsh, T. (eds.) Handbook of Constraint Programming, Foundations of Artificial Intelligence, Chap. 23, vol. 2, pp. 801–836. Elsevier (2006). http://www.sciencedirect.com/science/article/pii/S1574652606800271

21. Kirkpatrick, S., Gelatt, C.D., Vecchi, M.P.: Optimization by simulated annealing. Science **220**(4598), 671–680 (1983)

22. Labbé, M., Laporte, G., Tanczos, K., Toint, P.: Operations Research and Decision Aid Methodologies in Traffic and Transportation Management, vol. 166. Springer, Heidelberg (2013). https://doi.org/10.1007/978-3-662-03514-6

23. Marmion, M.E., Humeau, J., Jourdan, L., Dhaenens, C.: Comparison of neighborhoods for the HFF-AVRP. In: ACS/IEEE International Conference on Computer Systems and Applications-AICCSA 2010, pp. 1–7. IEEE (2010)

24. Michiels, W., Korst, J., Aarts, E.: Asymptotic convergence of simulated annealing. In: Michiels, W., Korst, J., Aarts, E. (eds.) Theoretical Aspects of Local Search, Monographs in Theoretical Computer Science, An EATCS Series, pp. 149–185. Springer, Heidelberg (2007). https://doi.org/10.1007/978-3-540-35854-1_8

25. Nedungadi, P.P., Menon, R., Gutjahr, G., Erickson, L., Raman, R.: Towards an inclusive digital literacy framework for digital India. Educ.+ Training **60**(6), 516–528 (2018)

26. OpenStreetMap contributors: Planet dump (2017). https://planet.osm.org, https://www.openstreetmap.org

27. Ormsby, T., Napoleon, E., Burke, R., Groessl, C., Bowden, L.: Getting to know ArcGIS desktop. Citeseer (2010)

28. Papadimitriou, C.H., Steiglitz, K.: Some examples of difficult traveling salesman problems. Oper. Res. **26**(3), 434–443 (1978)

29. Perron, L., Furnon, V.: Google's OR-Tools. https://developers.google.com/optimization/

30. Ríos-Mercado, R.Z., López-Pérez, J.F., Castrillón-Escobar, A.: A GRASP for a multi-depot multi-commodity pickup and delivery problem with time windows and heterogeneous fleet in the bottled beverage industry. In: Pacino, D., Voß, S., Jensen, R.M. (eds.) ICCL 2013. LNCS, vol. 8197, pp. 143–157. Springer, Heidelberg (2013). https://doi.org/10.1007/978-3-642-41019-2_11

31. Robert, F.C., Ramanathan, U., Durga, P., Mohan, R.: When academia meets rural India: lessons learnt from a microgrid implementation. In: 2016 IEEE Global Humanitarian Technology Conference (GHTC), pp. 156–163. IEEE (2016)

32. Rochat, Y., Taillard, É.D.: Probabilistic diversification and intensification in local search for vehicle routing. J. Heuristics **1**(1), 147–167 (1995)

33. Røpke, S.: Heuristic and exact algorithms for vehicle routing problems. Ph.D. thesis, Technical University of Denmark (2006)
34. Toth, P.: The vehicle routing problem. In: Discrete Mathematics and Applications, SIAM (2002). https://books.google.co.in/books?id=oWEEtQEACAAJ
35. Toth, P., Vigo, D.: The granular tabu search and its application to the vehicle-routing problem. Informs J. Comput. **15**(4), 333–346 (2003)
36. Trevisan, L.: Inapproximability of combinatorial optimization problems. arXiv preprint cs/0409043 (2004)
37. Voudouris, C., Tsang, E.P.: Guided local search. In: Glover, F., Kochenberger, G.A. (eds.) Handbook of Metaheuristics. International Series in Operations Research & Management Science, vol. 57, pp. 185–218. Springer, Boston (2003). https://doi.org/10.1007/0-306-48056-5_7
38. Wolpert, D.H., Macready, W.G., et al.: No free lunch theorems for optimization. IEEE Trans. Evol. Comput. **1**(1), 67–82 (1997)
39. Xu, J., Kelly, J.P.: A network flow-based tabu search heuristic for the vehicle routing problem. Transp. Sci. **30**(4), 379–393 (1996)

A Brain Computer Interface Based Visual Keyboard System Using SSVEP and Electrooculogram

D. Saravanakumar$^{(\boxtimes)}$ and Machireddy Ramasubba Reddy

Department of Applied Mechanics, Biomedical Group, Indian Institute of Technology Madras, Chennai, India
saravanabme@gmail.com, rsreddy@iitm.ac.in

Abstract. This study aims to design a steady-state visual evoked potential (SSVEP) based, on-screen keyboard/speller system along with the integration of electrooculogram (EOG). The characters/targets were designed using the pattern reversal square checkerboard flickering visual stimuli. In this study, twenty-three characters were randomly selected and their corresponding visual stimuli were designed using five frequencies (6, 6.667, 7.5, 8.57 and 10 Hz). The keyboard layout was divided into nine regions and each region was identified by using the subject's eye gaze information with the help of EOG data. The information from the EOG was used to locate the area on the visual keyboard/display, where the subject is looking. The region identification helps to use the same frequency valued visual stimuli more than once on the keyboard layout. In this proposed study, more targets were designed using less number of visual stimulus frequencies by integrating EOG with the SSVEP keyboard system. The multi-threshold algorithm and extended multivariate synchronization index (EMSI) method were used for eye gaze detection and SSVEP frequency recognition respectively. Ten healthy subjects were recruited for validating the proposed visual keyboard system.

Keywords: Steady-state visual evoked potential (SSVEP) · Electro-oculogram (EOG) · Brain computer interface (BCI) · Extended multivariate synchronization index (EMSI) · Visual keyboard

1 Introduction

Recent advancements in technology have brought about many changes in the lives of humans. Interactions between humans and computers are very common. Moreover, many types of research are being done to develop beneficial applications by using machines [1–4]. Normally people interact with their surrounding world by their physical limbs. However, there are people who are suffering from neuromuscular disorders and find it difficult for communication as normal people. In the past decades, various studies have been done to understand the complex functioning of the human brain and their neuronal activities. These studies have led to comprehend the nature of many neuromuscular diseases such as Lou Gehrig's disease, brain stroke, spinal cord injury etc. The majority of these disorders results in paralysis which is due to obstruction of neural networks that connect the

© Springer Nature Singapore Pte Ltd. 2020
S. M. Thampi et al. (Eds.): SoMMA 2019, CCIS 1203, pp. 64–74, 2020.
https://doi.org/10.1007/978-981-15-4301-2_6

central nervous system to the physical limbs. The need for rehabilitation tools has led to the development of different assistive devices that help in communication [5, 6].

Brain computer interface (BCI) has seen remarkable progress in recent years due to the developments in machine learning and neuroscience. BCI system is mainly used as an assistive device for disabled people and it uses brain signals (EEG components: steady state visual evoked potential (SSVEP), slow cortical potential, motor imagery and P300) for control or communication purpose [5, 7–9].

Most of the BCI studies use SSVEP component as a control signal because it is easy to elicit with minimal training. The signal to noise ratio (SNR) of the SSVEP signal is high as compared to other EEG components. The SSVEP based keyboard systems have a limitation on the number of targets. The harmonics of the selected frequencies cannot be used for visual stimulus design [9–12]. The visual stimulus design depends on the refresh rate of the monitor. Example, the monitor with a 60 Hz refresh rate can make only a few visual stimuli (exclude-harmonic frequencies). Therefore, the SSVEP based systems are having limitations on the number of targets. Recent studies show that the dual frequency SSVEP, frequency-shift keying, phase encoding, multiple frequencies sequential coding and sampled sinusoidal methods are used for designing or increasing the SSVEP targets [10, 12–15]. Though the above methods overcome the limitations on the SSVEP stimulus design, the target detection rate and information transfer rate (ITR) of those systems are less.

Classification accuracy and ITR are the important performance measures of a practical BCI system. Wolpaw et al. [16] explained that the ITR of the system depends on the probability of target detection rate, average time to detect the single target and the total number of targets. The main goal of this study is to increase the number of SSVEP targets using a lesser number of visual stimulus frequencies. The probability of the SSVEP target recognition rate will be high if the system uses a lesser number of visual stimulus frequencies. In this study, 60 Hz refresh rate monitor was used and the selected stimulus frequencies are 6, 6.667, 7.5, 8.57 and 10 Hz. The EOG data is used to find the region where the subject is looking on the keyboard layout. The region identification helps to reuse the same frequency valued visual stimuli into different regions of the keyboard layout. The SSVEP and eye gaze data were used for identifying the desired target character. The proposed hybrid speller system has achieved high accuracy and ITR as compared to the conventional speller systems as mentioned above.

2 Materials and Methods

2.1 Subjects and Data Acquisition

Ten healthy male subjects (average age of 25.2 ± 2.39) were volunteered for this study. Indigenously developed 8 channel data acquisition system (BioDaq v01) was used for both EEG and EOG signal acquisition. The data acquisition system is designed using the ADS1299 - 24 bit analog front end IC by Texas Instruments [17]. The data acquisition system is interfaced to a personal computer through the Arduino microcontroller. The EEG data were acquired from scalp sites O1, O2, Oz, POZ, PO3 and PO4 based on international 10–20 electrode system shown in Fig. 1(a). The EOG data were acquired using five Ag/AgCl surface electrodes and it is connected in a bipolar configuration shown in Fig. 1(b). The EEG and EOG data were acquired at 250 Hz and the data were applied to notch filter for removing power line interference (50 Hz). Further, the EOG data were down-sampled to 32 Hz for removing minor fluctuations. The signed consent was obtained from all the subjects prior to the experiment.

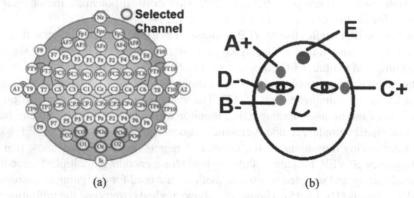

(a)   (b)

Fig. 1. Electrode configuration (a) EEG and (b) EOG

2.2 Experimental Setup

The hybrid EEG-EOG based visual keyboard system was designed for validation. The subjects were seated in front of a computer monitor in a comfortable armrest chair. The distance between the subject and monitor was kept as 50 cm (the minimum visual angle between two adjacent visual stimulus is 2°). The subject's legs were placed in a wooden rest to avoid contact with the ground. The experimental setup consists of an extended monitor (GUI-visual stimulus), computer (processor), data acquisition system (BioDaq v01), electrodes and the control unit.

2.3 Visual Stimulus Design

The Java-based Processing software platform was used for designing the SSVEP visual stimuli. For validating the proposed system, 23 characters were randomly selected (shown in Table 1) and the corresponding SSVEP visual stimuli were designed using five selected frequencies (6, 6.667, 7.5, 8.57 and 10 Hz) shown in Fig. 2. The selected frequencies are integer division of monitor refresh rate 60 Hz. The square-shaped (2.8 × 2.8 cm) checkerboard (8 × 8) pattern was adopted for SSVEP visual stimulus design. The chosen characters and their corresponding visual stimulus frequency values are listed in Table 1.

Table 1. Chosen characters and corresponding frequency

Frequency (Hz)	6	6.667	7.5	8.57	10
Characters	Q, F, T, B, K, J	A, I, Z	N, G, W	S, O, X	C, L, H, V, M, Y, E, P

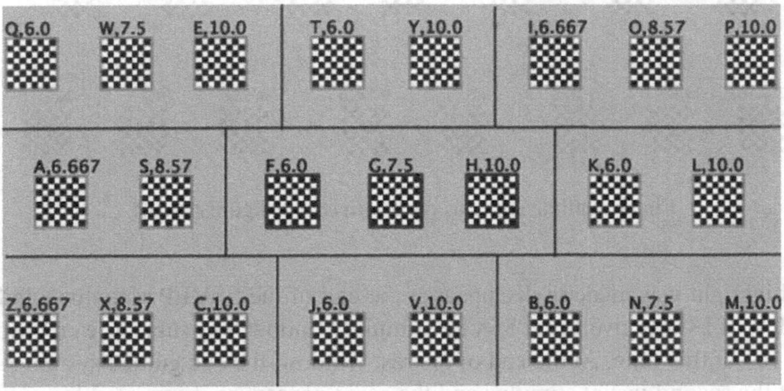

Fig. 2. Visual stimulus (speller layout) (Color figure online)

The keyboard layout was partitioned into nine segments (left top, left, left bottom, top, center, bottom, right-top, right, right bottom) for placing the visual stimulus. Two or three unique frequency valued visual stimuli were assigned to each segment. These region segregation helps to use the same frequency valued visual stimulus more than once on the keyboard layout. These segments were identified with the help of EOG data. In this study, we increased more targets using lesser stimulus frequencies with the help of EOG data. During the online process, the target segments were identified using eye gaze data and targets from the selected region will be considered for SSVEP classification.

2.4 Experimental Procedure

2.4.1 Experiment 1: SSVEP Response Time Detection

The SSVEP response to the input visual stimulus depends on the subjects. Different subjects need different SSVEP stimulus duration or time window for getting a good SSVEP response. In order to find the optimal SSVEP time window for online analysis, the cue guided offline experimental procedure was conducted on ten subjects. Five sessions of EEG data were collected for offline analysis.

An offset period of 10 s was given at the beginning of each session. The cue guided system start to highlight the visual stimulus one by one. Once the stimulus is highlighted the subjects were instructed to look or give attention to the highlighted stimulus. At the end of the offset period, the first visual stimulus is highlighted with green colour and the highlight was made to appear up to 5 s shown in Fig. 3. This highlighted time duration is called the SSVEP stimulus window.

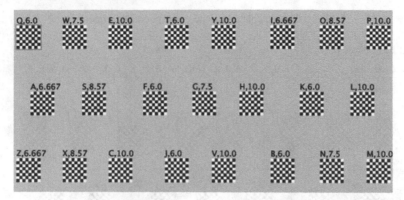

Fig. 3. Offline stimulus paradigm (Color figure online)

The highlight was made to disappear at the end of the SSVEP stimulus window. A rest window of 1 s was given after SSVEP stimulus window. The subjects were instructed to take a rest at this time. At the end of the rest window, the cue guided system starts to highlight the second visual stimulus and the same procedure is repeated for remaining targets. In each session, all the targets were highlighted once and the subjects EEG data were recorded and stored with corresponding highlighted stimulus frequency value. Figure 4 shows the timing diagram of an offline cue guided experimental paradigm.

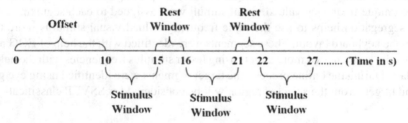

Fig. 4. The timing diagram of an offline cue based experiment

2.4.2 Experiment 2: EOG Feature Extraction and Threshold Calculation

The proposed visual keyboard adopts two-step recognition. The first step is to recognize the subject's eye gaze segment with the help of EOG data and the second step is target classification from the identified segment. Eight different types of eye movements were used for eye gaze detection. If the subject is not performing any eye movement the center segment is selected as default. In order to find the threshold values or features for various eye movement detection, five sessions of EOG data were collected. A cue guided experimental procedure was used for EOG data collection. In a single session, all the subjects were instructed to perform each eye movement twenty times. The time duration of 5 min was given in between the sessions as a rest period.

3 Results and Discussions

3.1 SSVEP Response Time Analysis (Offline)

In order to find the optimal SSVEP time window length of the online speller system, five sessions of EEG data were collected and labelled with corresponding target frequencies. The stored EEG data were analyzed at 2, 2.5, 3 and 3.5 s time window lengths. The different time window (length) data were taken from the onset of the original 5 s SSVEP data. The extended multivariate synchronization index (EMSI) method was used for identifying or classifying the target frequencies. The SSVEP classification accuracy of an EMSI algorithm is better than canonical correlation analysis (CCA) and minimum energy channel combination (MEC) [18, 19]. Therefore, EMSI algorithm is considered for SSVEP frequency recognition. The SSVEP recognition or classification accuracy was calculated using the confusion matrix.

Figure 5 illustrates the offline SSVEP classification accuracy of all the subjects at different time window lengths. The average SSVEP classification accuracy of all the subjects at different time window length's are 91.5% (2 s), 92.8% (2.5 s), 95.2% (3 s) and 96.3% (3.5 s). Information transfer rate (ITR) is one of the performance measures of a BCI system. The ITR depends on the total number of targets (N), the probability of correct classification (p) and average target detection time (T). If the target detection time is increased, the ITR of the system gets reduced. The practical BCI system should have high ITR. Therefore, from the offline SSVEP analysis 3 s (classification accuracy: 95.2%) time window was chosen for optimal SSVEP time window for all the subjects.

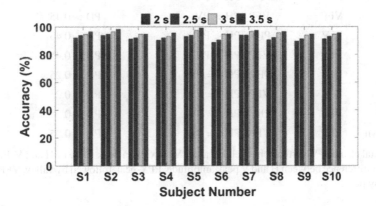

Fig. 5. Offline SSVEP classification accuracy

3.2 EOG Analysis (Threshold Calculation and Feature Extraction)

The acquired EOG data were downsampled to 32 Hz for avoiding minor fluctuations. The multi-threshold algorithm is used for eye movement classification.

Out of 5 sessions, three sessions of EOG data were used for finding features/threshold values and two session data were used for validation. The features are extracted from the first order differentiated version of EOG data shown in Fig. 6. Table 2 summarizes the threshold value and features for various eye movement classification. The average eye movement classification accuracy of 98.32% was obtained across ten subjects during validation.

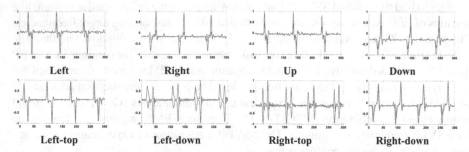

Fig. 6. First order differentiated version of different eye movement signals (samples- x axis, normalized amplitude- y axis, horizontal channel EOG- blue color and vertical channel EOG-orange color) (Color figure online)

Table 2. Threshold value and features for eye movement classification

Eye movement	Waveform pattern		Peak amplitude comparison	Difference between H and V channel peak value
	H	V		
Left	PFV	PFV	PH > PV	PD > 0.45
Right	VFP	VFP	PH > PV	PD > 0.45
Up	PFV	PFV	PH < PV	PD > 0.45
Down	VFP	VFP	PH < PV	PD > 0.45
Left-top	PFV	PFV	PH ~= PV	PD < 0.25
Left-down	PFV	VFP	PH ~= PV	PD < 0.25
Right-top	VFP	PFV	PH ~= PV	PD < 0.25
Right-down	VFP	VFP	PH ~= PV	PD < 0.25

H-Horizontal channel, V-vertical channel, PH and PV-maximum peak value of H and V, PD (peak difference)-difference between H and V peak amplitude, PFV-peak followed by valley, VFP-valley followed by peak.

3.3 Proposed SSVEP-EOG System (Online)

For validating the proposed SSVEP-EOG system, optimal SSVEP time window and threshold values for different eye movement classification were calculated from the offline analysis. Target detection in our proposed SSVEP-EOG system consists of two stages. (1) Target region selection by using eye gaze information, (2) Target identification from the selected region through SSVEP classification.

The online SSVEP-EOG paradigm consists of SSVEP stimulus window, followed by a rest window. An offset period of 10 s was given at the beginning of the experiment.

The subjects were instructed to look at the center region in the keyboard layout until the highlight comes. At the end of the offset period, all the 23 visual stimuli were highlighted with green colour. The subjects were instructed to select any character/target based on his/her interest. If the subject wants to type letter Q, he/she start moves his/her eyes from the center to the left top region. The system starts to classify the eye movement at the beginning of the SSVEP time window. If the detected eye movement is left-top, the highlighted colour of the left top region gets changed from green to blue. This colour change provides additional information to the subjects. If the subject is not moving his/her eyes, the center region is selected as default and the colour of the center region changed into blue shown in Fig. 2. The highlights were made to appear up to 3 s (SSVEP time window-evaluated from offline analysis). All the highlights were made to disappear at the end of the SSVEP stimulus window and a duration of 0.5 s was given as rest window. During this time we have instructed the subject to look center region. At the end of the SSVEP stimulus window, EMSI algorithm classifies the SSVEP target and the corresponding indexed character was displayed on the window. The same procedure is repeated.

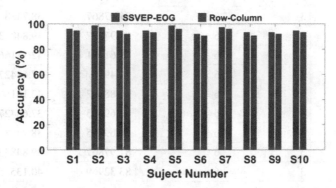

Fig. 7. Classification accuracy comparison between proposed and row-column speller system

Three sessions of online analysis were done on each subject, In each session, the subjects were instructed to type 25 characters randomly from the keyboard layout. The classification accuracy and ITR were calculated for all the subjects and it is shown in Fig. 7 and Table 3. The proposed SSVEP-EOG system is compared with traditional row-column (RC) [20] SSVEP keyboard system for proving the novelty. The RC speller system is designed with five frequencies (6, 6.667, 7.5, 8.57 and 10 Hz). The total number of targets in the RC speller system is twenty-five. The single target in the RC speller system is identified by detecting row and column coordinates. Three sessions of online experiments were performed by all the subjects. In each session, the subjects were instructed to select all the 25 targets. The classification accuracy and ITR of the RC speller system shown in Fig. 7 and Table 3. The paired T-test was conducted between the proposed and RC spelling system. There is no significant difference between the classification accuracy of both the systems. The ITR between these two systems shows a significant difference ($p < 0.001$). From that test results, we can conclude that the proposed system outperforms than traditional RC based speller system with high ITR.

Further, performance measures (accuracy and ITR) of the proposed system are compared with existing speller systems illustrated in Table 4. The classification accuracy and ITR of the proposed system are higher than the conventional speller systems (mentioned in Table 4). From the above analysis/study, we can conclude that the proposed SSVEP-EOG system has achieved more targets using a lesser number of stimulus frequencies, less target detection time, high classification accuracy and high ITR.

Table 3. ITR comparison between proposed and row-column speller system

Subject number	Proposed system (SSVEP-EOG) Time in s	Row-Column speller system Time in s	ITR of proposed system (bits/min)	ITR of Row-Column speller system (bits/min)
S1	3	6	84.36331	40.98933
S2	3	6	89.61131	43.44201
S3	3	6	81.97867	38.7488
S4	3	6	81.97867	39.84833
S5	3	6	89.61131	42.18166
S6	3	6	77.4976	37.68427
S7	3	6	86.88402	42.18166
S8	3	6	79.69665	37.68427
S9	3	6	79.69665	38.7488
S10	3	6	81.97867	39.84833
Average	3	6	83.32969	40.13575

Table 4. Comparison between proposed (SSVEP-EOG) system and conventional speller systems

Reference	Method	Average time to detect a single target (in seconds)	Classification accuracy (%)	ITR (bits/min)
[10]	Dual frequency SSVEP	4.9	87.23	33.26
[14]	SSVEP-FSK	6.32	73.5	23.24
[21]	SSVEP-P300	4.88	93.85	56.44
[22]	SSVEP-VOG	3.25	94.98	82.7
[23]	SSVEP-VOG	3.9	90.46	65.98
Proposed	SSVEP-EOG	3	95.33	83.32

4 Conclusion

The hybrid SSVEP-EOG based visual speller system was designed and validated with ten subjects. The limitations of the SSVEP based BCI system were addressed. The same frequency valued visual stimuli were used more than once on the keyboard layout in order to achieve more targets with the help of EOG data. The EOG data/eye gaze data were used to find the target region on the keyboard layout and the targets were identified from the selected region. The offline analysis was performed on all the subjects to find out optimal SSVEP stimulation time window and gaze detection threshold value for online analysis. The average online classification accuracy of 95.33% was obtained with an ITR of 83.32 bits/min. The proposed SSVEP-EOG visual keyboard system achieved more targets with lesser number of visual stimulus frequencies. The ITR of the system is high as compared to the designed RC speller system. The high ITR and classification accuracy shows that the proposed system can be easily used as a communication system for disabled individuals.

References

1. Wolpaw, J.R., et al.: Brain-computer interface technology: a review of the first international meeting. IEEE Trans. Rehabil. Eng. **8**, 164–173 (2000)
2. Fouad, M.M., Amin, K.M., El-Bendary, N., Hassanien, A.E.: Brain computer interface: a review. In: Hassanien, A.E., Azar, A.T. (eds.) Brain-Computer Interfaces. ISRL, vol. 74, pp. 3–30. Springer, Cham (2015). https://doi.org/10.1007/978-3-319-10978-7_1
3. Wu, S., Liao, L., Lu, S., Jiang, W., Chen, S., Lin, C.: Controlling a human-computer interface system with a novel classification method that uses electrooculography signals. IEEE Trans. Biomed. Eng. **60**, 2133–2141 (2013)
4. Saravanakumar, D., Vishnupriya, R., Reddy, M.R.: A novel EOG based synchronous and asynchronous visual keyboard system. In: 2019 IEEE EMBS International Conference on Biomedical & Health Informatics (BHI), pp. 1–4 (2019)
5. Wolpaw, J.R., Birbaumer, N., McFarland, D.J., Pfurtscheller, G., Vaughan, T.M.: Brain computer interfaces for communication and control. Front. Neurosci. **4**, 767–791 (2002)
6. Amiri, S., Fazel-rezai, R., Asadpour, V.: Review Article A Review of Hybrid Brain-Computer Interface Systems, vol. 2013 (2013)
7. Zhang, B., Mu, J., Wang, W., Liang, Q., Pi, Y. (eds.): The Proceedings of the Second International Conference on Communications, Signal Processing, and Systems. LNEE, vol. 246. Springer, Cham (2014). https://doi.org/10.1007/978-3-319-00536-2
8. Saravanakumar, D., Ramasubba Reddy, M.: A visual spelling system using SSVEP based hybrid brain computer interface with video-oculography. In: Abraham, A., Cherukuri, A.K., Melin, P., Gandhi, N. (eds.) ISDA 2018 2018. AISC, vol. 940, pp. 365–375. Springer, Cham (2020). https://doi.org/10.1007/978-3-030-16657-1_34
9. Saravanakumar, D., Ramasubba Reddy, M.: A high performance hybrid SSVEP based BCI speller system. Adv. Eng. Inform. **42**, 100994 (2019)
10. Hwang, H.J., Hwan Kim, D., Han, C.H., Im, C.H.: A new dual-frequency stimulation method to increase the number of visual stimuli for multi-class SSVEP-based brain-computer interface (BCI). Brain Res. **1515**, 66–77 (2013)
11. Srihari Mukesh, T.M., Jaganathan, V., Reddy, M.R.: A novel multiple frequency stimulation method for steady state VEP based brain computer interfaces. Physiol. Meas. **27**, 61–71 (2006)

12. Manyakov, N.V., Chumerin, N., Robben, A., Combaz, A., Van Vliet, M., Van Hulle, M.M.: Sampled sinusoidal stimulation profile and multichannel fuzzy logic classification for monitor-based phase-coded SSVEP brain-computer interfacing. J. Neural Eng. **10**(3), 036011 (2013)
13. Zhao, X., Zhao, D., Wang, X., Hou, X.: A SSVEP stimuli encoding method using trinary frequency-shift keying encoded SSVEP (TFSK-SSVEP). Front. Hum. Neurosci. **11**, 1–9 (2017)
14. Kimura, Y., Tanaka, T., Higashi, H.: SSVEP-based brain – computer interfaces using FSK-modulated visual stimuli. IEEE Trans. Biomed. Eng. **60**, 2831–2838 (2013)
15. Jia, C., Gao, X., Hong, B., Gao, S.: Frequency and phase mixed coding in SSVEP-based brain-computer interface. IEEE Trans. Biomed. Eng. **58**, 200–206 (2011)
16. Wolpaw, J.R., Ramoser, H., McFarland, D.J., Pfurtscheller, G.: EEG-based communication: improved accuracy by response verification. IEEE Trans. Rehabil. Eng. **6**, 326–333 (1998)
17. Texas Instruments Incorporated: ADS129x Low-Power, 8-Channel, 24-Bit Analog Front-End for Biopotential Measurements (2015)
18. Zhang, Y., Guo, D., Yao, D., Xu, P.: The extension of multivariate synchronization index method for SSVEP-based BCI. Neurocomputing **269**, 226–231 (2017)
19. Zhang, Y., Xu, P., Cheng, K., Yao, D.: Multivariate synchronization index for frequency recognition of SSVEP-based brain-computer interface. J. Neurosci. Methods **221**, 32–40 (2014)
20. Yin, E., Zhou, Z., Jiang, J., Yu, Y., Hu, D.: A dynamically optimized SSVEP brain–computer interface (BCI) speller. IEEE Trans. Biomed. Eng. **62**(6), 1447–1456 (2014)
21. Yin, E., Zhou, Z., Jiang, J., Chen, F., Liu, Y., Hu, D.: A novel hybrid BCI speller based on the incorporation of SSVEP into the P300 paradigm. J. Neural Eng. **10**(2), 026012 (2013)
22. Saravanakumar, D., Ramasubba Reddy, R.: A visual keyboard system using hybrid dual frequency SSVEP based brain computer interface with VOG integration. In: 2018 International Conference on Cyberworlds (CW), vol. 1, pp. 258–263 (2018)
23. Saravanakumar, D., Ramasubba Reddy, M.: A novel visual keyboard system for disabled people/individuals using hybrid SSVEP based brain computer interface. In: 2018 International Conference on Cyberworlds (CW), pp. 264–269 (2018)

Stock Market Prediction Using a Hybrid Model

Zuhaib Akhtar[1(✉)] and Mohammad Omar Khursheed[2(✉)]

[1] Department of Computer Engineering, Aligarh Muslim University, Aligarh, India
akhtarzuhaib@gmail.com
[2] Department of Computer Science, University of Massachusetts Amherst, Amherst, USA
mkhursheed@umass.edu

Abstract. Stock market prediction is important topic in economics and finance which has garnered the interest of researchers. This paper attempts to explore the usage of hybrid model to predict stock market movements. The data under consideration was sourced from Quandl, a repository that provides data related to the stock market for a wide variety of companies, and in order to forecast the prices of said stocks in the future, ensemble machine learning methods together with ARIMA for feature prediction have been employed. Hybrid approach for prediction stock price is proposed. Comparisons among ensemble learning algorithms are discussed, and interesting results has been obtained and future possibilities are touched upon in this paper. Intensive testing was done by gathering various stock market data from various sectors to explore robustness of the proposed model.

Keywords: Stock market prediction · ARIMA · Ensemble learning · Bagging · Boosting

1 Introduction

The typical Wall Street trading firm has been immortalized in popular culture as a large space full of desk upon desk, and men in loose ties and expensive shirts screaming into phones in order to make the right trade for their clients. But in 2019, the reality is often quite different. The typical trading firm has a bunch of computer scientists sitting at sophisticated workstations applying machine learning algorithms and trading electronically. Machine learning, or simply the process of teaching a computer how to think about a certain problem, has swiftly become one of the core components of trading today. This is especially true in the area of high frequency trading, or HFT, where hundreds of thousands are carried out in the time that it would take to execute a trade manually. Previously, work has been conducted in this area, using various machine learning algorithms, but before the advent of machine learning in the field, statistical models such as ARIMA (auto-regressive integrated moving models) were used to model the trends in data. These models were of limited use, and required various preprocessing techniques to be applied to the data before they could be used.

The use of machine learning techniques when applied to stock market data, the availability of which has increased dramatically in recent years, is an excellent example of how the field can transform an industry. In fact, some of the best hedge funds, such as

© Springer Nature Singapore Pte Ltd. 2020
S. M. Thampi et al. (Eds.): SoMMA 2019, CCIS 1203, pp. 75–89, 2020.
https://doi.org/10.1007/978-981-15-4301-2_7

Renaissance Technologies and Two Sigma, have almost completely scaled back manual investing methods, instead relying on machine learning techniques and modelling in order to post record-breaking returns on the investments made. Among various methods, ANN are most popular as they can learn complex patterns from the data if enough hidden layers are provided [1]. With neural networks having exploded into widespread usage in the past few years, especially in areas such as Deep Learning.

The proposed methodology consists of a two-step approach, first step is to predict the features and then predicting the final stock price by using these generated features. The data that we used was sourced from Quandl. Literature Review, proposed methodology, results and discussions are presented in subsequent sections.

2   Literature Review

Refenes, Zapranis and Francis examined the use of neural networks as an alternative to classical statistical techniques for forecasting within the framework of the APT (arbitrage pricing theory) model for stock ranking [2]. They showed that neural networks outperform these statistical techniques in forecasting accuracy terms, and give better model fitness in-sample by one order of magnitude. Althelaya, El-Alfy and Mohammed considered both stacked and bidirectional LSTM and benchmarked them against simple LSTM and neural networks based networks for stock market closing price [3]. Oncharoen and Vateekul used both CNN and LSTM based networks and then performed experiments on three datasets. It utilised both textual and numerical information as input to the neural network [4]. Calzon et al. performed visualization on the data collected together with No Free Lunch theoretical framework and got results which shows that inefficient strategies and priori less accurate algorithms can give good results in some subsets of data [5]. Fekri presented portfolio based the Markowitz Mean-Variance-Skewness with weight constraints model which can be used for short-term investment opportunities in Iran's stock market. Eight different portfolio with low, medium and high risks were designed using genetic algorithm [6]. Kusuma et al. used various types of neural networks and converted stock prices to candlestick charts. These charts were fed to neural networks to analyse the patterns to finally predict the future movements of stock price. Taiwan and Indonesian stock market dataset was used in this research [7]. Lee et al. propose to design both undirected and directed volatility networks of global stock market based on simple pair-wise correlation and system-wide connectedness of national stock indices using a vector auto-regressive model [8]. Vangara et al. predicted mutual fund NAV by using various factors such as macroeconomics. Cascaded SVM was further used to optimize the results. The experiments in this research were performed for the Indian market [9]. Basak et al. developed framework for classifying whether stock prices will increase or decrease with respect to 'n' previous days. They selected some technical indicators as features to predict medium to long term prediction of stock price. Random forests, and gradient boosted decision trees were used in this research [10]. Nadh and Prasad explored various tools such as artificial neural networks, genetic algorithms and support vector machine for stock market forecasting [11]. Umadevi et al. analyzed various parameters related to stock price followed by visualization of various stock prices in the form of plots. Finally, ARIMA was used for predicting the final scores [12].

In this paper, we propose a hybrid approach for predicting the values of stock market closing prices of various companies. We explored ensemble machine learning algorithm, bagging and boosting, for predicting stock prices as they show better behavior than standalone machine learning algorithms such as, linear regression, support vector-based regression, and multi-layer perceptron. As these machine learning algorithms require features to generate the output, we predicted them by using ARIMA model. This model generate features of time varied data by learning the pattern from past (features of training data). In this research, we attempted to predict values of the closing stock price in the future, rather than predicting upward or downward movement over a period of time.

3 Methodology

The implementation methodology has been divided into four major steps (Fig. 1):

- Collection and preprocessing of data
- Feature selection and extraction
- Predicting features of future using ARIMA
- Running robust machine learning algorithms for final prediction.

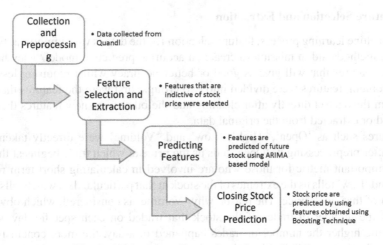

Fig. 1. Methodology for stock market prediction

3.1 Collection of Data and Preprocessing

Many different repositories were looked upon that offer financial data, including Google and Yahoo finance, but finally ended up using Quandl, a relatively new option dedicated to providing clean, high-quality data. An example of a Quandl dataset is shown below in Fig. 2.

WIKI-ABC

Date	Open	High	Low	Close	Volume	Ex-Dividend	Split Ratio	Adj. Open	Adj. High	Adj. Low	Adj. Close	Adj. Volume
1995-04-04	23.5	23.75	22.5	23.62	5048400	0	1	2.4471972036812	2.4732312164863	2.3430611524607	2.459693529276	40387200
1995-04-05	23.25	23.75	22.75	22.75	1529600	0	1	2.421163190876	2.4732312164863	2.3690951652658	2.3690951652658	12236800
1995-04-06	22.75	23.5	22.75	23.13	472000	0	1	2.3690951652658	2.4471972036812	2.3690951652658	2.4086668647296	3776000
1995-04-07	23.25	23.25	22.75	22.75	240100	0	1	2.421163190876	2.421163190876	2.3690951652658	2.3690951652658	1920800
1995-04-10	22.75	23.25	22.75	23	255900	0	1	2.3690951652658	2.421163190876	2.3690951652658	2.3951291780709	2047200
1995-04-11	22.75	23.25	22.75	22.88	512100	0	1	2.3690951652658	2.421163190876	2.3690951652658	2.3826328510245	4096800
1995-04-12	22.5	23	22.75	22.88	307200	0	1	2.3690951652658	2.3951291780709	2.3690951652658	2.3826328510245	2457600
1995-04-13	22.75	23	22.75	23	287200	0	1	2.3690951652658	2.3951291780709	2.3690951652658	2.3951291780709	2297600
1995-04-17	22.75	23.62	22.75	23.62	279200	0	1	2.3690951652658	2.4596935298276	2.3690951652658	2.459693529276	2233600
1995-04-18	23.13	23.62	23	23.5	306200	0	1	2.4086668647296	2.4596935298276	2.3951291780709	2.4471972036812	2441600
1995-04-19	23	23.25	22.5	22.75	177800	0	1	2.3951291780709	2.421163190876	2.3430611524607	2.3690951652658	1422400
1995-04-20	22.5	22.5	21.75	21.87	127900	0	1	2.3430611524607	2.3430611524607	2.2649591140453	2.2774554401916	1023200
1995-04-21	21.75	22.5	21.75	22.38	350400	0	1	2.2649591140453	2.3430611524607	2.2649591140453	2.3305648263142	2803200
1995-04-24	22	22.5	22	22	80600	0	1	2.2909931268504	2.3430611524607	2.2909931268504	2.2909931268504	644800
1995-04-25	22	22.5	22	22.5	60600	0	1	2.2909931268504	2.3430611524607	2.2909931268504	2.3430611524607	484800
1995-04-26	22	22.5	22	22	18900	0	1	2.2909931268504	2.3430611524607	2.2909931268504	2.2909931268504	151200
1995-04-27	22	22.5	22	22.25	444000	0	1	2.2909931268504	2.3430611524607	2.2909931268504	2.3170271396556	3552000
1995-04-28	22.25	22.5	22.12	22.12	134500	0	1	2.3170271396556	2.3430611524607	2.3034894529969	2.3034894529969	1076000
1995-05-01	22.5	22.5	22.12	22.12	285900	0	1	2.3430611524607	2.3430611524607	2.3034894529969	2.3034894529969	2287200
1995-05-02	22.12	23.13	22.12	22.75	151500	0	1	2.3034894529969	2.4086668647296	2.3034894529969	2.3690951652658	1212000
1995-05-03	22.5	23.13	22.25	22.88	98900	0	1	2.3430611524607	2.4086668647296	2.3170271396556	2.3826328510245	791200
1995-05-04	22.75	23.13	22.5	22.5	126400	0	1	2.3690951652658	2.4086668647296	2.3430611524607	2.3430611524607	1011200
1995-05-05	22.5	23	22.5	22.5	20500	0	1	2.3430611524607	2.3951291780709	2.3430611524607	2.3430611524607	164000
1995-05-08	22.5	23.13	22.5	22.5	7400	0	1	2.3430611524607	2.4086668647296	2.3430611524607	2.3430611524607	59200
1995-05-09	22.5	22.75	21.87	22	74100	0	1	2.3430611524607	2.3690951652658	2.2774554401918	2.2909931268504	592800
1995-05-10	22.5	22.5	21.87	22	102200	0	1	2.3430611524607	2.3430611524607	2.2774554401918	2.2909931268504	817600
1995-05-11	22	22.5	21.87	22	76900	0	1	2.2909931268504	2.3430611524607	2.2774554401918	2.2909931268504	615200
1995-05-12	22.5	22.5	21.87	22	126700	0	1	2.3430611524607	2.3430611524607	2.2774554401918	2.2909931268504	1013600
1995-05-15	22.38	22.38	21.63	21.63	461200	0	1	2.3305648263142	2.3305648263142	2.252462787898	2.252462787898	3689600
1995-05-16	21.63	21.87	21.63	21.75	310200	0	1	2.252462787898	2.2774554401918	2.252462787898	2.2649591140453	2481600

Fig. 2. Quandl dataset of ABC. Each row represents stock market value among other statistics of each day.

3.2 Feature Selection and Extraction

In any machine learning process, feature selection for the data is very important. Feature selection methods aid in mission to create an accurate predictive model. They help by choosing features that will give as good or better accuracy whilst requiring less data. In the problem, features were divided into two groups; first were the features that were used from the dataset directly after cleaning and the other were new features that were generated or extracted from the original data.

Features such as 'Open', 'High', 'Low' and 'Volume' were directly taken from dataset after preprocessing it. 'Open' tells us the price at which trade begins at the day. It is an important metric for those who are involved in calculating short term results. 'High' and 'Low' tells us the extremes of the stock at that particular day, which tells us the variation of that stock price. The reason why 'Volume' is considered, which obviously indicates the number of trades of the stock that traded on each specific day, simply because the higher the number of trades happened in a day, the more conclusive our data point for that day. Higher the volume simply means that more money is moving the stock up and hence, more the demand of that stock is. Similarly, if stock is appreciating on low volume means that small amount of money is moving the price of that stock, and hence, the lesser is the demand.

Other features were High-Low Percentage Change (HL_PCT) and Open-Close Percentage Change (OC_PCT) which were extracted from the dataset. The rationale behind these two choices of features was that they indicate volatility of a stock, and can therefore be expected to be indicative of future stock price. These were calculated as follows:

$$HL\_PCT = \frac{High - Low}{Low} \times (100)$$

$$OC\_PCT = \frac{Close - Open}{Open} \times (100)$$

3.3 Model for Stock Market Prediction

Subsequent sub-sections discuss the complete hybrid model for stock price prediction.

3.3.1 Feature Predictive Model

Autoregressive Integrated Moving Average (ARIMA) model is generally used when data varies with time. It is based on the assumption that current value are correlated with own past values [13]. It is a combination of Auto-Regressive (AR) and Moving-Average (MA) which results in the equation expressed as follows:

$$X_t = \mu + \emptyset_1 X_{t-1} + \emptyset_2 X_{t-2} + \cdots + \emptyset_p X_{t-p} - \theta_1 \varepsilon_{t-1} - \theta_2 \varepsilon_{t-2} - \cdots - \theta_q \varepsilon_{t-q}$$
$$(1)$$

where, X_t is the true value and ε_t is random error at 't', $\emptyset_i$ and θ_i are coefficients, 'q' and 'p' are integral values which are known as auto-regressive and moving-average respectively. Three terminologies are used in ARIMA which are integers, namely, 'p' which is the order of auto-regressive terms, 'q' is the order of moving-average and 'd' is the differencing required on the time series data to make it stationary.

This research focused on applying the model on various companies of different sectors, each one was having its own trend in data, therefore careful examination of various stock price was done to choose the values of 'p', 'd' and 'q' for our model. This is because the stock price of various companies varies according to supply and demand among other market forces (competition, innovation, investor valuation, etc.). These forces are different for each companies which guides their stock market value. Various criteria were examined and analyzed such as plots of differenced series (stationarized), auto-correlation and partial autocorrelation to choose the values of 'p', 'd' and 'q'.

For these models to work, time series data should be stationary. What that mean is its variance, mean, autocorrelation, etc. should not vary with time i.e., it should be constant over time. It has been found that almost all of the data were non-stationary. Such non-stationary behavior in the time series data can be removed by differencing the data. First difference generally did remove the non-stationary behavior. Second difference too made the time series data stationary but that auto-correlation plot of the time series data went into far negative zone. Therefore, value of 'd' was chosen as 1.

The number of auto-regressive terms i.e., 'p' values were found by examining partial auto-correlation plot of time series data. Auto-regressive terms allows to incorporate the affect of previous values in our model. Therefore, it tells us the correlation between the time series and its lag. It does not include the affect of intermediate lags. From partial auto-correlation plot of time series when plotted, it was found that value of 'p' as lag 1 was quite large and was above significant region, which was not a suitable value of 'p'. But, 'p' as lag 2 was under the significant region in most of the cases. Therefore, p was fixed as 2. These plots which includes significant region is shown in succeeding section.

Similarly, the order of moving average i.e., 'q' values were found by examining auto-correlation plot of the time-series data. It decides the number of moving-average terms needed in the time series data to make it free from any autocorrelation. It allows the model to incorporate error values noticed at the past. Plots of various time series data was analyzed and reached to the conclusion that 1 was most suitable value of 'q', as, for most of the plots, its value was under the significant region.

After determining all the parameterized value of ARIMA, then proposed model was identified as ARIMA (p = 2, d = 1, q = 1). Substituting these values in Eq. 1, Eq. 2 has been obtained:

$$X_t - X_{t-1} = \emptyset_1(X_{t-1} - X_{t-2}) + \emptyset_2(X_{t-2} - X_{t-3}) - \theta_1\varepsilon_{t-1} \tag{2}$$

On rearranging the terms of Eq. 2, the final equation of ARIMA model becomes:

$$X_t = X_{t-1} + \emptyset_1(X_{t-1} - X_{t-2}) + \emptyset_2(X_{t-2} - X_{t-3}) - \theta_1\varepsilon_{t-1} \tag{3}$$

Model represented by Eq. 3 is used to predict the features of time series data. These predicted features were then send to next model which predict the closing stock price of the day.

3.3.2 Closing Stock Price Predictive Model

For predicting the actual stock price of the companies, machine learning models were chosen. Out of various models available, search of the model was narrowed to bagging and boosting. These models were selected as they show better accuracy than standalone model as they are ensemble of these standalone models. This is because single model is prone to many factors like variance, bias and noise in the data. Ensemble of classifiers reduces these factors and prevents over-fitting. Such models combine the results of individual models either by voting on the results or taking the average of the results to get the final predicted value.

Bagging

In bagging or bootstrap aggregation, the base model was chosen as decision tree and number of models in the bagged model was 50. Each get its new training data which is produced from original dataset by random sampling with replacement. Each element has the same probability to occur in the dataset. After formation of dataset, each of the model train independently and in parallel fashion i.e., models are trained sequentially [14]. During testing phase, individual output of the model is averaged to generate the new output. Figure 3 shows the bagging model composed of 'k' decision trees, which in this case of proposed model, 'k' is equals to 50.

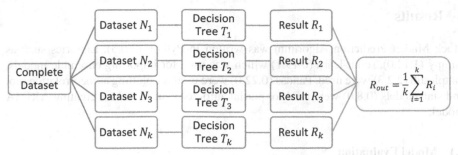

Fig. 3. Bagging model composed of 'k' decision trees and each one having its independent dataset sampled from original dataset. Output of the model, R_{out} is average of all the models

Boosting

In Boosting, the decision tree as the base model was selected and total number of models were chosen as 50. The observations in the dataset have weights associated with them. Therefore, observation with higher weight will appear more often. Rather than parallel training in bagging, boosting creates sequential model where each model learns from the mistakes of previous classifier [14]. After each and every training step, weights of the data changes. Weights of misclassified data points increases in weight so that subsequent models focus on these misclassified data points in order to increase these difficult cases. After training, each model gets weight assigned to it. A model that results in less error on the training dataset is assigned more weight than one which produces more error. Due to this, subsequent models need to keep track of previous models. Final output is given by taking the weighted mean of the results of all the individual models. Figure 4 shows the boosting model composed of 'k' decision trees, which in the case of proposed model, 'k' is equals to 50.

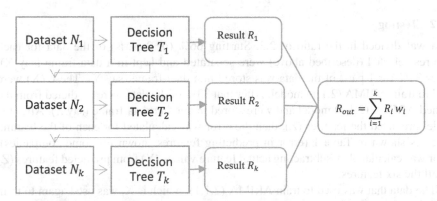

Fig. 4. Boosting model composed of 'k' decision trees and each one adjusts the weight of data-samples in attempt to rectify error of preceding model. Output of the model, R_{out} is weighted average of all the models

4 Results

Stock Market Prediction Algorithm was written in Python (3.6.5). Libraries such as numpy (1.14.0), scikit-learn (0.19.1) which was used for importing ensemble models, matplotlib (2.2.3) were used. Pandas (0.22.0) were used for plotting autocorrelation plot and statsmodels (0.8.0) were used for partial auto-correlation and for creating ARIMA model.

4.1 Model Evaluation

Subsequent sections discusses about the dataset and testing performed on the final model.

4.1.1 Dataset

All data were in csv format downloaded from Quandl. To have a rigorous testing of the proposed model, data from companies of different sectors were taken which had totally different level (value above and below which time varied data is oscillating), trend (growth or decline i.e., slope of the values) and seasonality (pattern of time varied data repeating after a time interval). Data from 21 different companies were selected and ran the hybrid prediction model.

Among various companies, autocorrelation and partial autocorrelation plots of features are shown of company named Alcoa as our accuracy was ranging between around 55%–95% and accuracy of Alcoa was in between this range. So, the average case rather than showing extreme cases are shown. But overall accuracy and plot between actual and predicted stock price is shown for all the 21 different companies selected for testing is shown. Percentage error in predicting features are shown for some companies in subsequent section.

4.1.2 Testing

Data was divided in the ratio of 2:3. Starting 66% (or 2 parts) of the data for each features selected (described above) were separated and kept in a data-frame (say X). Other 33% (or 1 part) of the data was stored in a data-frame (say Y). These (X) were used to train ARIMA (2,1,1) model. After that 33% of the data were predicted from the trained ARIMA (2,1,1) model and were stored in another data-frame (say Z). After the model predicted the features (Z), then the error was calculated for each of the feature, which is shown in Table 1 (error in predicting features shown for some companies). Error was calculated by subtracting actual feature values (Y) from predicted features (Z) for all the six features.

The data that was used to train ARIMA (2,1,1), which is X, was used again to train ensemble models. But this time target values (closing price of the stock) were also given as ensemble models are machine learning models that need target value at the time of training. After training was completed, features that were predicted using ARIMA model (which are Z) were given as input in ensemble model to predict the closing stock price (Y'). Error was then calculated between predicted stock price (Y') and actual stock price (Y). Plots of Autocorrelation and Partial Auto Correlation of features of Alcoa (AA) are plotted in Figs. 5 and 6 which were predicted by ARIMA (2,1,1). The method was performed for all the 21 different companies' stock market dataset. Final accuracy of all the stocks with actual and predicted plots are shown in Table 2. Plots of bagging approach was shown as it was giving better accuracy than boosting. Results clearly shows that the proposed hybrid approach is better for both short and long term stock price prediction.

Table 1. Percentage error in features predicted by ARIMA (2,1,1) of some companies

Feature name	Percentage Error (%) while predicting feature using ARIMA (2,1,1)					
	Alcoa	Asbury automotive group	Acadia pharmaceuticals	Apple	Cisco systems	General electric
Open	0.80	0.09	0.60	−1.81	−0.21	0.27
High	−0.32	0.07	2.20	−1.59	−0.39	0.12
Low	−3.07	0.16	0.18	−0.47	−0.45	1.91
Volume	−39.94	−19.99	−8.32	−59.24	9.96	−14.37
HL_PCT	15.88	28.06	−32.70	29.24	−30.77	33.91
OC_PCT	29.93	−8.30	−22.65	−35.55	−20.79	−15.62

5 Discussions

Bagging model was showing greater accuracy than boosting in 21 different company data that were tested. Although, boosting works by reducing error of previous individual models which is a better approach than bagging, but it seems like overfitting is the issue. This is because regular weight update of data points overfits the subsequent individual models. This is not the case with bagging and hence, it performs better in most of the cases than boosting.

In most of our test cases, accuracy was hovering around 80% to 90%. In some cases, it jumped above 90% but in some cases it was observed that it drops to 60% to 70%. By examining the results of cases where the accuracy was slightly low, it was found that the hybrid model predicts well for most of the days but deviates slightly far ahead in future. This is seen for companies such as Ascent Capital Group, Apple, Boeing, etc. In case of Apple, it was found that we were able to predict well for 400 odd days and then the hybrid model deviates from the actual stock price. Same is the case with Ascent Capital Group were the model works till 120 days in the future. Accuracy greater than 50% means hybrid model is still making profit.

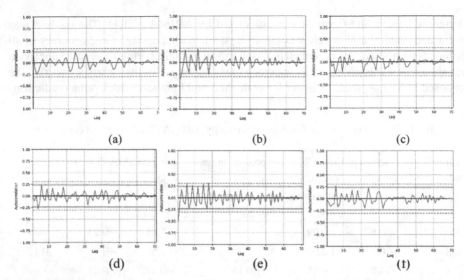

Fig. 5. Autocorrelation plots features of Alcoa (AA) predicted by ARIMA (2,1,1), (a) High, (b) HL_PCT, (c) Low, (d) Open, (e) OC_PCT (f) Volume

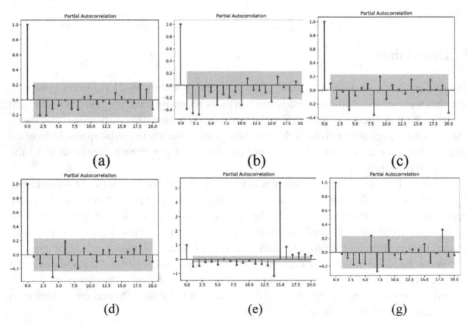

Fig. 6. Partial Autocorrelation plots features of Alcoa (AA) predicted by ARIMA (2,1,1), (a) High, (b) HL_PCT, (c) Low, (d) Open, (e) OC_PCT (f) Volume

Table 2. Accuracy of predicted stock price using Bagging and Boosting approach, and including plot of both actual and predicted price

Company	Bagging (% accuracy)	Boosting (% accuracy)	Plot of actual vs predicted stock price using Bagging approach
Asbury Automotive Group	95.05	**95.36**	
Acadia Pharmaceuticals	**92.14**	92.03	
ArQule	**94.08**	94.04	
Ascent Captial Group	**73.13**	73.12	
Alcoa	**81.65**	79.89	
AmerisourceBergen	**92.41**	92.36	
Apple	**55.22**	55.09	

(continued)

Table 2. (*continued*)

Abbott Laboratories	62.14	**62.46**	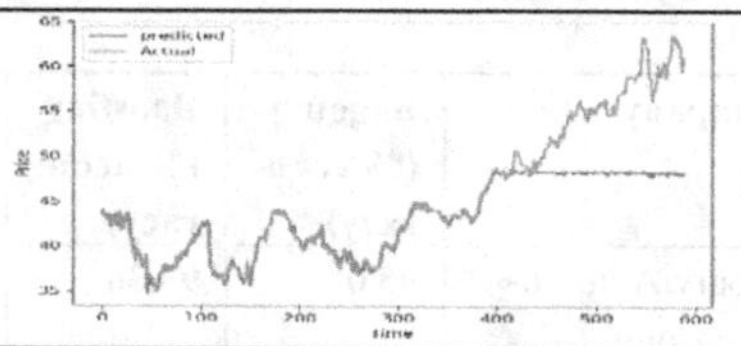
Boeing	**67.90**	65.71	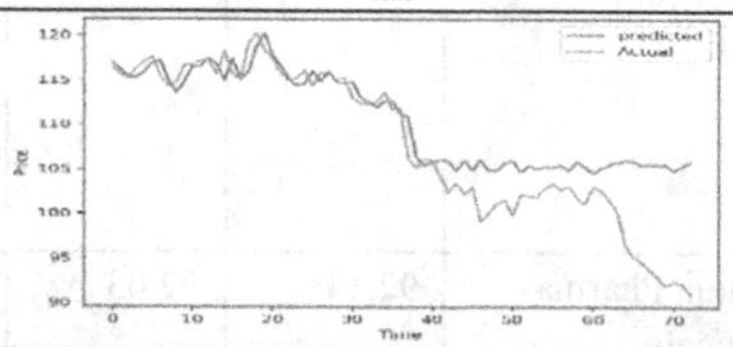
Cisco Systems	87.30	**87.65**	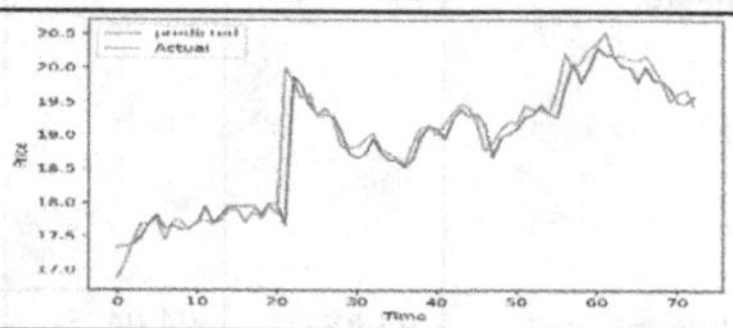
General Electric	**80.67**	79.23	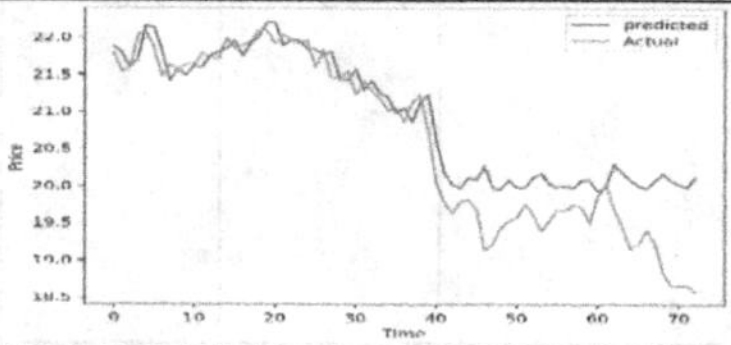
Goldman Sachs	**88.52**	85.31	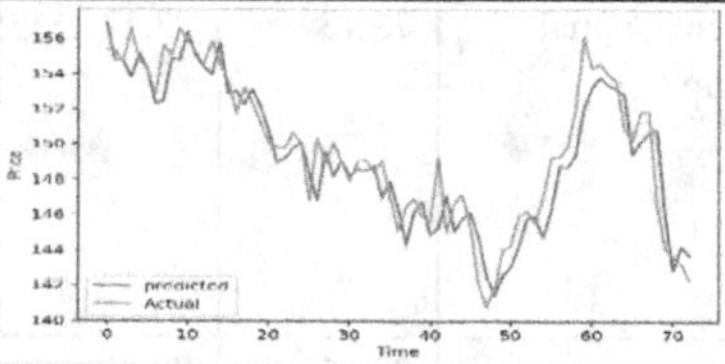
IBM	**86.27**	83.74	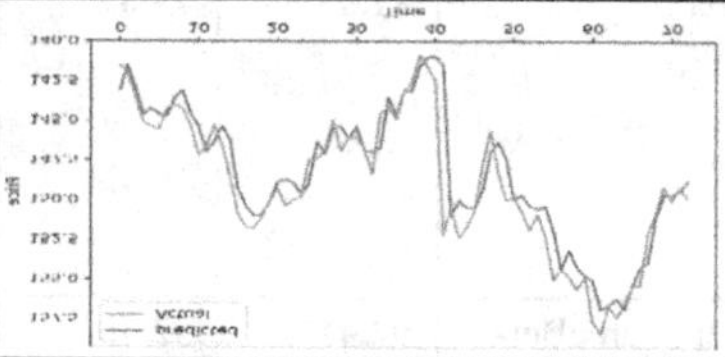
The Coco-Cola Company	**93.17**	91.22	

(*continued*)

Table 2. (*continued*)

McDonald's	82.43	81.02	
Murphy Oil	75.46	**76.82**	
Mylan	**94.77**	93.26	
Nabros Industries	**94.34**	94.15	
Nike	**76.95**	75.47	
Verizon Communications	**91.03**	90.16	
ExxonMobil	**62.62**	58.58	

6 Conclusion and Future Work

This study shows a novel method for predicting stock prices of companies of various sectors. The hybrid model was formulated by analyzing various data of stock prices. Feature prediction was done using ARIMA model which was then fed to the machine learning model. Ensemble machine learning based model were explored for predicting final stock price. Testing was done on companies from various sectors to evaluate the robustness of the model. Results show our composite model gives high accuracy in most of the cases. This can guide investors to make profitable investment decisions. This model was able to predict the plot of stock prices for short and long term and hence, opens door for further analysis of hybrid based models in stock market prediction. Feature-based learning, which we have used, is an interesting avenue, but building models using deep learning may also work. The use of satellite imagery to pinpoint oil fields to predict oil prices and similar creative methods should be employed to produce feature-based learning methods.

References

1. Shafi, I., Ahmad, J., Shah, S.I., Kashif, F.M.: Impact of varying neurons and hidden layers in neural network architecture for a time frequency application. In: 2006 IEEE International Multitopic Conference, Islamabad, pp. 188–193 (2006). https://doi.org/10.1109/INMIC.2006.35816
2. Refenes, A.N., Zapranis, A., Francis, G.: Stock performance modeling using neural networks: a comparative study with regression models. Neural Netw. 7(2), 375–388 (1994). ISSN 0893-6080
3. Althelaya, K.A., El-Alfy, E.M., Mohammed, S.: Evaluation of bidirectional LSTM for short- and long-term stock market prediction. In: 2018 9th International Conference on Information and Communication Systems (ICICS), Irbid, pp. 151–156 (2018). https://doi.org/10.1109/IACS.2018.8355458
4. Oncharoen, P., Vateekul, P.: Deep learning for stock market prediction using event embedding and technical indicators. In: 2018 5th International Conference on Advanced Informatics: Concept Theory and Applications (ICAICTA), Krabi, pp. 19–24 (2018). https://doi.org/10.1109/ICAICTA.2018.8541310
5. Bousoño-Calzón, C., Bustarviejo-Muñoz, J., Aceituno-Aceituno, P., Escudero-Garzás, J.J.: On the economic significance of stock market prediction and the no free lunch theorem. IEEE Access 7, 75177–75188 (2019)
6. Fekri, M.: Designing an optimal portfolio for Iran's stock market with genetic algorithm using neural network prediction of risk and return stocks (2019). arXiv:1903.06632
7. Kusuma, R.M.I., Ho, T.-T., Kao, W.-C., Ou, Y.-Y.: Using deep learning neural networks and candlestick chart representation to predict stock market (2019). arXiv:1903.12258
8. Lee, T.K., Cho, J.H., Kwon, D.S., Sohn, S.Y.: Global stock market investment strategies based on financial network indicators using machine learning techniques. Expert Syst. Appl. 117, 228–242 (2019). https://doi.org/10.1016/j.eswa.2018.09.005. ISSN 0957-4174
9. Vangara, A., Thouseef, S., Bhat, S.S., Rao, V.V.: Mutual fund NAV prediction using cascaded SVM models. In: 2018 3rd International Conference for Convergence in Technology (I2CT), Pune, pp. 1–6 (2018). https://doi.org/10.1109/I2CT.2018.8529733
10. Basak, S., Kar, S., Saha, S., Khaidem, L., Dey, S.R.: Predicting the direction of stock market prices using tree-based classifiers. N. Am. J. Econ. Finance 47, 552–567 (2019). ISSN 1062-9408
11. Lalithendra Nadh, V., Syam Prasad, G.: Stock market prediction based on machine learning approaches. In: Satyanarayana, Ch., Rao, K.N., Bush, R.G. (eds.) Computational Intelligence and Big Data Analytics. SpringerBriefs in Applied Sciences and Technology. Springer, Singapore (2019). https://doi.org/10.1007/978-981-13-0544-3_7
12. Umadevi, K.S., Gaonka, A., Kulkarni, R., Kannan, R.J.: Analysis of stock market using streaming data framework. In: 2018 International Conference on Advances in Computing, Communications and Informatics (ICACCI), Bangalore, pp. 1388–1390 (2018). https://doi.org/10.1109/ICACCI.2018.8554561

13. Ariyo, A.A., Adewumi, A.O., Ayo, C.K.: Stock price prediction using the ARIMA model. In: 2014 UKSim-AMSS 16th International Conference on Computer Modelling and Simulation, Cambridge, pp. 106–112 (2014). https://doi.org/10.1109/UKsim.2014.67
14. Singhal, Y., Jain, A., Batra, S., Varshney, Y., Rathi, M.: Review of bagging and boosting classification performance on unbalanced binary classification. In: 2018 IEEE 8th International Advance Computing Conference (IACC), Greater Noida, India, pp. 338–343 (2018). https://doi.org/10.1109/IADCC.2018.8692138

An Internet of Things Framework to Forecast Indoor Air Quality Using Machine Learning

Krati Rastogi and Divya Lohani$^{(\boxtimes)}$

Department of Computer Science and Engineering, Shiv Nadar University,
Gautam Buddha Nagar, Greater Noida, Uttar Pradesh, India
{kr777,divya.lohani}@snu.edu.in

Abstract. Good air quality is critical to healthy and productive life in the indoor environment. Quality of air inside buildings depends on several factors. Till now, it was not possible to measure and monitor indoor air quality (IAQ) through mobile phones and wireless sensors in real time, as standardized miniature sensors were not commercially available. With the introduction of wireless air quality sensors that can pair with most contemporary smartphones, it is now possible to monitor indoor environment pervasively in real time, take precautionary measures, and maintain a healthy life. In this work, we have created an IoT sensing system to monitor and analyse the time variation of carbon dioxide in a university classroom. Using the sensed data, forecast models have been developed to predict the build-up of carbon dioxide, an indicator of IAQ.

Keywords: Indoor Air Quality · Carbon dioxide · IoT · Forecasting · Regression · Support vector · ARIMA

1 Introduction

People spend around 90 percent of the time in an indoor environment [1], which these days are mostly heating, ventilation and air conditioning (HVAC) controlled. An indoor environment is a combination of thermal, mechanical/non mechanical, electronics, atmospheric, psychological and various other types of factors. Controlling all these components of the environment is critical for human beings to work and live indoors. One of the most important components of an indoor environment is fresh and clean air. Indoor air can be polluted due to several factors: (a) Quality of outdoor air that flows inside the building, and its filtration and ventilation systems, (b) Indoor activities like cooking, various sources of smoke, scientific experiments, use of electronic items, cleaning activities involving use of aerosols, liquids, sprays, etc., (c) building materials, electronic and mechanical systems, and (d) human breathing, as it releases CO_2. CO_2 is often used as an indicator to Indoor Air Quality (IAQ) [2].

The volume of CO_2 exhaled by a human depends upon his/her body surface area and physical activity. Indoor CO_2 levels are sometimes used an indicator to IAQ levels. Relationships have been explored and established [3, 4] between (a) CO_2 concentration and its health effects, (b) CO_2 and indoor ventilation rates, (c) Combined effects of

© Springer Nature Singapore Pte Ltd. 2020
S. M. Thampi et al. (Eds.): SoMMA 2019, CCIS 1203, pp. 90–104, 2020.
https://doi.org/10.1007/978-981-15-4301-2_8

CO_2 and other indoor contaminants, etc. With the availability of new mobile sensors and smartphones, and modelling techniques, many of these relationships can now be explored in real time and in greater detail, and CO_2 levels can be used to directly assess the quality of indoor air.

Humans exhale about 40000 ppm of CO_2 every day. That is not a concern outdoors, and a concentration of 380–400 ppm is considered normal for outdoor environment. Depending upon the environment, the CO_2 levels can increase significantly indoors. Several factors like quality of HVAC system, building design, indoor population, type of operations performed indoors, and human's daily habits can affect the level of CO_2 indoors. Humans typically spend 21–22 h in indoor environments like home, car, and office. Elevated levels of CO_2 indoors affect IAQ. Poor IAQ can cause several types short term illness like breathing problems, irritation in eyes, nose and throat, reduced activity levels, nausea, dry skin or itching. Long term presence of poor IAQ can cause several chronic illnesses. It has been researched and reported that high levels of CO_2 impacts decision making abilities [5]. This can be dangerous, especially when a person is driving. Hence, if CO_2 concentration can be measured in indoor environment pervasively and in real time, immediate remedial measure can be taken to avoid such illness, which will eventually prevent accidents and lead to better health and improved productivity. One of the ways of collecting real time data is mobile participatory sensing. Mobile participatory sensing allows use of smart devices and Bluetooth sensors to collect and report data in real time with good accuracy.

Contribution of the Work: This work presents a smartphone based IoT system that is capable of sensing, visualizing and forecasting build-up of CO_2 concentrations in university classrooms. Typical university classrooms can accommodate more than hundred persons at a time which makes the task of maintaining good IAQ a challenge. Linear, non-linear as well as hybrid forecast models have been investigated to predict the build-up of CO_2. MAPE, RMSE and R^2 have been explored as performance metrics to determine the most accurate forecast model. The models are able to accurately forecast as to when the CO_2 concentration will cross 2500 ppm mark (threshold at which human cognition begins to get affected) and IAQ will become bad. Ventilation rates can be adjusted accordingly so as to maintain IAQ at a satisfactory level.

2 Related Work

Participatory sensing is a well-researched method in which people collect data using available sensors in smart devices or otherwise and upload it to a server for further processing. Persily et al. [6] introduced and explored this architecture as an effective way of data collection, reporting and analysis. Various works [1, 7, 8] have reported collection and analysis of gases inside buildings. In [7], CO_2 levels and Ventilation rates were monitored and analysed. Tracer gas decay technique has been proposed as an easier and inexpensive technique that is alternative to traditional methods like pilot tube traverses. While [1, 9] used a standard wireless sensor network based technique to compute IAQ. In [10], author discussed the relationship between the CO_2 level and ventilation and developed a model to predict the concentration of CO_2 in building envelopes when the rate of occupancy is high. Modelling of ventilation rates is often useful to find the concentration of CO_2. In [11], such work is carried out using parameters like building characteristics and occupant behaviour. Air change rates were evaluated through several linear regression models and the effect of independent variables on the total air change rates were identified.

Effect of IAQ on health is a well discussed topic. In [1], authors discussed the effects of CO_2 when the people are exposed to it for different durations of time. The effects of CO_2 range from physiologic to toxic, anaesthetic and lethal depending upon the exposures. The study found out that people who had been exposed to high CO_2 for the longest time also underwent a marked personality change and suffered from loss of eye movement. Although long-term low-level CO_2 exposure is not immediately life threatening, it causes several health conditions like elevated systemic and pulmonary blood pressure, and increased cerebral blood flow. A recent and detailed study [11] explored effects of CO_2 on human decision making performance. The subjects of the study were twenty-two participants who were exposed to CO_2 at 600, 1000 and 2500 ppm. This is one of the detailed works that established clear relationship between concentration of CO_2 and its effects on health.

2.1 The Science of Air Quality

In quantifying the body's CO_2 production, a molar ratio of the volume of CO_2 exhaled to the volume of O_2 consumed is considered, and it is called the respiratory quotient (RQ). A healthy individual maintains a RQ value of 0.83 for light and sedentary activities. This value is appropriate for our experiments as it involved similar activities. A person's metabolic rate (MET) is related to oxygen consumption and CO_2 production and RQ as follows [12]:

$$MET = 1200 * (0.23\,RQ + 0.77) * \frac{VO_2}{Ad}(Btu/hrsqft) \qquad (1)$$

Where, RQ = Respiratory quotient
VO_2 = Volumetric rate of oxygen consumed
Ad = DuBois area, the average surface area of an adult (1.83 m^2)

Table 1. MET rates for activities

Activity	MET rate
Sleeping	0.7
Seated, quiet	1.0
Standing, relaxed	1.2
Slow walk	2.0
Office writing and typing	1.1–1.2
Office lifting and packing	2.1

Some standard MET values are given in Table 1 [12]. For our activity which primarily involves sitting and typing indoors, the MET rate will be 1.2, which will lead to an average CO_2 generation rate of 0.30 L/min per person.

The CO_2 concentration in a chamber depends on number of people present, their level of physical activity, and the ventilation rate of the chamber. The ventilation rate needed to maintain a steady state concentration of CO_2 is given by:

$$V_o = N/(C_s - C_o) \qquad (2)$$

Where, V_o = ventilation rate per person (Litres/min)
N = CO_2 generation rate per person (Litres/min)
C_s = CO_2 concentration in the chamber (%)
C_o = CO_2 concentration outdoors (%)

For volumetric units of CFM and CO_2 concentration in ppm, the equation becomes:

$$V_o = 10600/(C_s - C_o) \qquad (3)$$

If activity level is more than the standard (MET = 1.2) we have considered, increased ventilation of the chamber would be required to maintain the same CO_2 levels. As ventilation is maintained these days using HVAC systems in controlled environments, this will lead to increased energy usage. If ventilation rate is not demand controlled, this will lead to more production and higher concentration levels of CO_2.

3   IoT System Architecture and Test Bed

An IoT sensing setup has been developed by using an Arduino Uno and a Smartphone. The CO_2 concentration is measured with the help of MQ135. It is a gas sensor which detects CO_2 levels inside the classroom. The sensor data is collected by an Arduino Uno and transferred using HC-05 Bluetooth module to the smartphone. Additionally, in order to standardize the CO_2 values, we have used an off-the-shelf senor Sensordrone, which can directly transmit data to an Android Application over Bluetooth [13]. It has

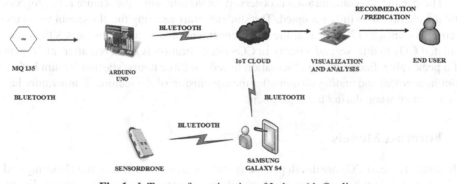

Fig. 1. IoT setup for estimation of Indoor Air Quality

11 on-board sensors, important ones being ambient temperature, relative humidity, CO_2, CO with an option to use various add-on sensor modules as attachment.

The study has been conducted in the classrooms of the Engineering building of the University. The rooms have centralized heating, ventilating and air conditioning (HVAC) system. The classroom windows are fully covered and the doors are sealed during the experiment. The sensing setup was kept in a classroom of the department of computer science and engineering. Setup is placed in such a manner that no direct contact to human breathing and 6 feet away from door/windows and at-least 2 feet above the floor from the time the class began till the time the class ended. Data was collected at a sampling rate of 1 sample per minute for an average of 2.5 h.

3.1 Details of Data Collection

The time variation of CO_2 concentration in the classroom during a lecture session is shown in Fig. 2. The plot shows the variation in CO_2 concentration starting 30 min before the commencement and finishing 60 min after the conclusion of the lecture. As shown in the graph in Fig. 2, the classroom is fully occupied 40 min after the sensing begins and build-up in CO_2 concentration is observed.

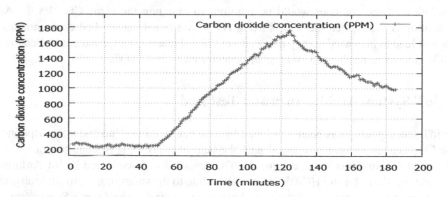

Fig. 2. Time variation of CO_2 in a university classroom

The rise in CO_2 concentration is observed for 90 min while the lecture is in progress and the classroom is fully occupied. The students start vacating the classroom when the lecture is finished (120 min after the commencement of sensing). This causes the accumulated CO_2 to diffuse, and a decay in CO_2 concentration is observed after attainment of a peak value. Each sensing observation lasted for three hours, starting 30 min before commencement and ending 60 min after the conclusion of the lecture. Temperature has been kept constant during the experiment.

4   Forecast Models

Models to forecast CO_2 are developed using statistical, stochastic, machine learning and hybrid models in this work. Statistical models involve the use of linear, multiple linear, quantile, ridge, lasso and other regression techniques. Stochastic modeling techniques may include auto-regressive moving average (ARMA), auto-regressive integrated moving average (ARIMA), exponential smoothing, etc. Some examples of machine learning models are fuzzy logic, support vector regression, random forests and artificial neural networks (ANN). Two or more of these models may be combined to improve prediction accuracy in hybrid methods. In this section, we have presented our statistical and stochastic models for forecasting air quality. Linear as well as non-linear forecast models are developed to predict the change in CO_2 concentration with time. The forecast models that assume a linear relationship between independent variables are described first, followed by non-linear models. The forecast models use approximately 80% of observation data for training and the rest 20% for testing.

4.1 Linear Regression

Linear regression is a linear approach to model the relationship between a dependent variable and one or more independent variables. The mathematical model of a multiple linear regression model with multiple independent variables (X) and single dependent variable (Y) is given as:

$$Y = a_1X_1 + a_2X_2 + .. + a_nX_n + c \qquad (4)$$

Where,

$Y = dependent\ variable\ (CO_2\ concentration),$
$X_1, X_2, .., X_n = independent\ variables,$
$a_1, a_2, .., a_n = coefficients\ of\ independent\ variables,\ and$
$c = intercept.$

There is a single dependent variable Y that uses CO_2 as input in our case, reducing the equation to (Fig. 3):

$$Y = -138.2 + 13.89X \qquad (5)$$

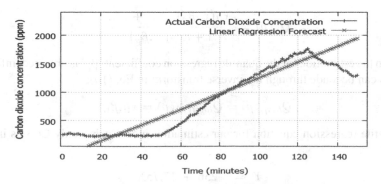

Fig. 3. Actual and forecasted CO_2 concentrations using LR

4.2 Quantile Regression

The linear regression technique is highly sensitive to outliers. An outlier is an observation that significantly differs from other observations of the time-series. Spikes and dips in the observed time-series of occupant count is best handled using quantile regression. Quantile regression is an extension to the linear regression technique, and serves to nullify or offset the effect of outliers on the trend line or regression line. To define quantile regression model, we consider 'n' observations of CO_2 concentration (X_i). The Y_i is bound within a known interval y_{min} and y_{max}:

$$Y_i = X_{1i}.\beta_{1i} + \epsilon_i \tag{6}$$

Where, Y_i is the CO_2 concentration to be predicted, X_1 is the CO_2 concentration and β_i represents the unknown regression parameters. The 'p' quantile of the conditional distribution of the estimated CO_2 concentration y_i, given CO_2 concentration x_{1i} is described as [14, 15]:

$$Q_y(p) = x_{1i}.\beta_{1p} \tag{7}$$

Where, $(0 < p < 1)$ indicates the proportion of the population having scores below the quantile at p. In this way, we are able to eliminate the outliers, and get better trend-line. For $p = 1/2$, the value $Q_y(1/2)$ splits the conditional distribution of the estimated CO_2 concentration y_i into 2 parts with equal probability, known as conditional median. For any quantile p, there exists a fixed set of parameters p and the non-decreasing function 'h' from the interval (y_{min}, y_{max}) to the real line such that:

$$h\{Q_y(p)\} = x_{1i}.\beta_{1i} \tag{8}$$

The logistic transformation function or logit function 'h' is defined as:

$$h(y_i) = \log\left(\frac{y_i - y_{min}}{y_{max} - y_i}\right) = \text{logit}(y_i) \tag{9}$$

Where, y_{max} and y_{min} are the maximum and minimum values attained by the estimated CO_2 concentration respectively. Combining Eqs. (8) and (9) and taking the inverse exponential function, we get:

$$Q_y(p) = \frac{exp(x_i.\beta_p).y_{max} + y_{min}}{1 + exp(x_i.\beta_p)} \tag{10}$$

When the estimation for the quantile regression coefficient 'β_p' is obtained, inference on $Q_y(p)$ can be made through the inverse transform in Eq. (10):

$$Q_{h(y_i)}(p) = Q_{logit(y_i)}(p) = x_{1i}.\beta_{1i} \tag{11}$$

Quantile regression equation for our estimation model using only CO_2 as input is (Fig. 4):

$$Y = -256 + 17.75X \tag{12}$$

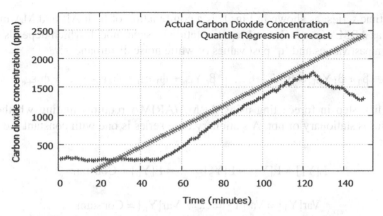

Fig. 4. Actual and forecasted CO_2 concentrations using QR

4.3 ARMA/ARIMA

As our time series is not stationary, it cannot be assumed that the statistical properties of the time series, i.e. correlations with each other, are constant over time. Such a time series is better analysed by using Auto Regressive Moving Average (ARMA) model or the Box-Jenkins model. The ARMA model is a combination of AR and MA models. Our AR model is one in which Y_t (present CO_2 conc.) depends on its own past values. Thus:

$$Y_t = f(Y_{t-1}, \ Y_{t-2}, \ Y_{t-3}, \ Y_{t-4}, \ldots, \ Y_{t-n}, \varepsilon_t) \tag{13}$$

Where, Y_t is the CO_2 conc. value to be predicted,

$Y_{t-1}, Y_{t-2}, Y_{t-3}, Y_{t-4}, \ldots, Y_{t-n}$ are the 'n' previous observations of CO_2 conc.

And ε_t is the error term. Our AR model, when Y_t depends on 'p' past values, is represented with the help of the equation:

$$Y_t = \beta_0 + \beta_1 Y_{t-1} + \beta_2 Y_{t-2} + \beta_3 Y_{t-3} + \ldots + \beta_p Y_{t-p} + \varepsilon_t \tag{14}$$

(here $\beta_0, \beta_1, \beta_2, \beta_3, \ldots, \beta_p$ and ε_t are the unknown coefficients to be determined).

Our Moving Averages (MA) model uses the random error terms, which follow a white noise process, to predict Y_t:

$$Y_t = f(\varepsilon_{t-1}, \varepsilon_{t-2}, \varepsilon_{t-3}, \varepsilon_{t-4}, \ldots, \varepsilon_{t-n}) \tag{15}$$

Where, Y_t is the CO_2 conc. value to be predicted,

$\varepsilon_{t-1}, \varepsilon_{t-2}, \varepsilon_{t-3}, \varepsilon_{t-4}, \ldots, \varepsilon_{t-n}$ are the 'n' previous random error terms of CO_2 conc. Our AM model depends on 'q' past values of error terms (MA(q) model):

$$Y_t = \phi_0 + \phi_1 \varepsilon_{t-1} + \phi_2 \varepsilon_{t-2} + \phi_3 \varepsilon_{t-3} + \ldots + \phi_q \varepsilon_{t-q} \tag{16}$$

(where, $\phi_0, \phi_1, \phi_2, \phi_3, \ldots, \phi_q$ are the unknown coefficients to be determined).

Our time series, as shown in Fig. 1, is a combination of both AR and MA models, referred as ARMA (p, q). General representation of such model, which depends on 'p' of its own past values and 'q' past values of white noise disturbances:

$$Y_t = \beta_0 + \beta_1 Y_{t-1} + \beta_2 Y_{t-2} + \ldots + \beta_p Y_{t-p} + \phi_1 \varepsilon_{t-1} + \phi_2 \varepsilon_{t-2} + \ldots + \phi_q \varepsilon_{t-q} \qquad (17)$$

The first step in forecasting using ARMA/ARIMA requires finding whether our time series is stationary or not. A stationary time series is one with constant mean and variance:

$$E[Y_1] = E[Y_2] = E[Y_3] = \ldots = E[Y_n] = \text{Constant} \qquad (18)$$

$$\text{Var}[Y_1] = \text{Var}[Y_2] = \ldots = \text{Var}[Y_n] = \text{Constant} \qquad (19)$$

Where 'n' is the number of observations of CO_2 conc. We performed the *stationarity test* on our CO_2 conc. time series and found that it was not stationary. So, we differenced the time series to obtain a stationary time series, with constant mean and variance. Our time series became stationary after differencing it once, so it is known as Integrated of Order 1 and is denoted by I(1). A series which is stationary after differencing it 'd' times is known as Integrated of Order 'd' and is denoted by I(d).

The next step is to find the auto-correlation function (ACF) and the partial auto-correlation function (PACF). The ACF refers to the way the observations of CO_2 conc. Are related to each other, and is measured by a simple correlation between current CO_2 conc. Observation (Y_t) and the observation 'p' periods from the current one (Y_{t-p}).

$$\rho = Corr\left(Y_t, Y_{t-p}\right) = \frac{Cov\left(Y_t, Y_{t-p}\right)}{\sqrt{var\left(Y_t,\right)} . \sqrt{var\left(Y_{t-p}\right)}} \qquad (20)$$

It is used to find out how much the current value of CO_2 concentration is related to the previous values, and how many lags or previous values must be considered for finding the current or future value. A comparison of *correlograms* (plot of sample ACFs versus lags, as shown in Fig. 5) of the time series data with the theoretical ACFs leads to the selection of the appropriate ARIMA (p, q) model.

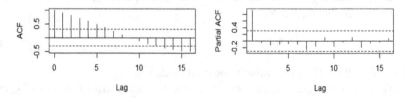

Fig. 5. ACF and PACF of CO_2 concentrations

As shown in Fig. 5 the peaks are obtained at lag values of 0, 2 and 3 for ACF and 1 for PACF. On fitting the appropriate ARIMA model, the goodness of fit is estimated by plotting the ACF of residuals of the fitted model. As most of the sample autocorrelation coefficients of the residuals of our selected model lie within the limits, $-1.96/\sqrt{N}$ and $+1.96/\sqrt{N}$, where N is the number of observations, the residuals being white noise. It indicates that the model fit is appropriate. The actual and forecasted CO_2 concentration using ARIMA model is shown in Fig. 6.

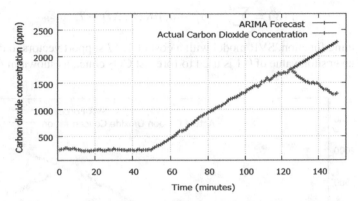

Fig. 6. Actual and forecasted CO_2 concentrations using ARIMA

4.4 Support Vector Regression

Support vector regression is a machine learning technique based on statistical learning. It realizes non-linear mapping of three dimensional space by kernel function. The basic idea is to map the input variables into high dimensional feature space via nonlinear mapping function. After that, the risk minimization principle is used to create the optimal decision function in the feature space. This optimal function approximates the relationships between the input and output. The optimal approximation of future CO_2 concentration using historic CO_2 concentration X is given as

$$f(X, \alpha) = w.\Phi(X) + T \tag{21}$$

Where Φ is the mapping function from the original data space of indoor CO_2 concentration X to a high-dimensional feature space, w is the parameter of the learning machine and **T** is the threshold. The kernel function is represented as:

$$K(X, Y) = \Phi(X).\Phi(Y) \tag{22}$$

The SVR problem is solved by maximizing:

$$W(\alpha^*, \alpha) = -\frac{1}{2} \sum_{i,j=1}^{l} (\alpha_i^* - \alpha_i)\left(\alpha_j^* - \alpha_j\right) K(X_i, X_j) - \varepsilon \sum_{i=1}^{l} (\alpha_i^* + \alpha_i)$$
$$+ \sum_{i=1}^{l} y_i(\alpha_i^* - \alpha_i) \tag{23}$$

Subject to the condition:

$$\sum_{i=1}^{l} (\alpha_i^* - \alpha_i) = 0 \tag{24}$$

$$0 \leq \alpha_i^*, \alpha_i \leq C \tag{25}$$

Where l is the number of CO_2 concentration observations. Solving the above equations, Eq. (25) is simplified as:

$$f(X) = \sum_{i=1}^{l} (\alpha_i^* - \alpha_i) \, K(X, X_i) + T \tag{26}$$

Using tuning function, SVR model with a cost of 1, 17 support vectors, radial basis kernel, and an epsilon value of 0.1 is used to forecast CO_2 conc., as shown in Fig. 7.

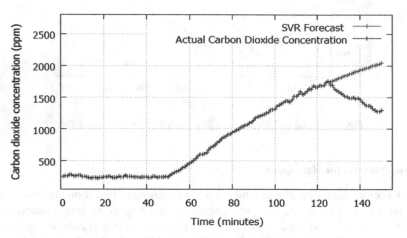

Fig. 7. Actual and forecasted CO_2 concentrations using SVR

4.5 Hybrid Model (SVR + ARIMA)

To further improve the forecast results, we developed a hybrid model that uses a combination of SVR and ARIMA models. Time series analysis is performed by stochastic models to identify the time series pattern and the future value is forecasted based on the obtained pattern. The ARIMA or Box-Jenkins model works under the assumption that the time series under observation is linear and stationary. On the other hand, non-linear models such as genetic algorithm (GA), artificial neural networks (ANNs) and supported vector machines (SVM) aim to capture the non-linear pattern among the independent and dependent variables.

In order to capture both linear and non-linear characteristics of the time-series under study, a hybrid model is proposed in this work. A hybrid model is represented by the equation:

$$y_t = L_t + N_t \tag{27}$$

Where, L_t is the linear and N_t is the non-linear part of the model. The actual and forecasted CO_2 concentration using the proposed hybrid model is shown in Fig. 8.

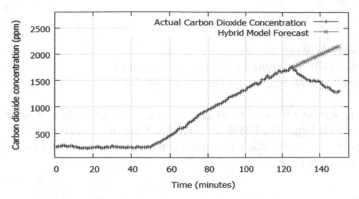

Fig. 8. Actual and forecasted CO_2 concentrations using hybrid (SVR + ARIMA) model

The final plot which gives a comparative performance of all the forecast models along with the actual CO_2 concentration in parts per million (ppm) is shown in Fig. 9.

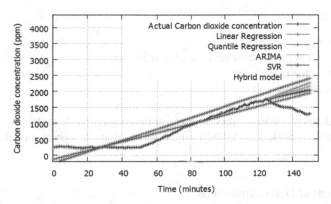

Fig. 9. Actual and forecasted CO_2 concentrations using forecast models

5 Performance Evaluation

Next, we compare the prediction performance or accuracy of the prediction techniques using Root Mean Square Error (RMSE), mean absolute percentage error (MAPE) and Coefficient of determination (R^2).

5.1 RMSE

$$RMSE = \sqrt{\frac{1}{N}\sum_{i=1}^{N}(y_i - f(x_i))} \tag{28}$$

Where,

N is the number of observations,
y_i is the actual CO_2 concentration value at time instant i,
x_i is the input vector (time), and f is the forecast model.

RMSE is sensitive to outliers, as errors are squared and effect of large errors is disproportionately large. The RMSE for ARIMA, SVR and hybrid models is 1.18, 1.73 and 1.05 ppm respectively, which indicates that the hybrid and ARIMA models perform fewer or lesser large errors.

5.2 MAPE

$$MAPE = \frac{1}{N} \sum_{i=0}^{N} |\frac{y_i - f(x_i)}{y_i}| * 100 \tag{29}$$

Where,

N is the number of observations,
y_i is the actual CO_2 concentration value at time instant i,
x_i is the input vector (time), and
f is the forecast model.

MAPE defines the size of forecast error in percent terms. It is the least for hybrid model, followed by SVR and ARIMA which shows that the hybrid model is the most accurate.

5.3 Coefficient of Determination (R^2)

Another metric to be used in this work to compute accuracy is the *coefficient of determination* (R^2). It is defined as

$$R^2 = 1 - \frac{u}{v} \tag{30}$$

Where 'u' is the residual sum of squares and 'v' is the total sum of squares. The best possible value is 1. The coefficient of determination (R^2) is also highest for the hybrid model.

As hybrid model is the most accurate, it is used to compute the time taken for IAQ to become poor with full occupancy in classroom, i.e. the CO_2 concentration to reach 2500 ppm. It is found that it takes 46 min for the IAQ in a university classroom with full occupancy to become poor (Table 2).

Table 2. MAPE, RMSE and R^2 for forecast models

Forecast model	MAPE (%)	RMSE (ppm)	R^2
LR	5.61	7.31	0.84
QR	4.25	5.34	0.87
ARIMA	2.18	1.18	0.91
SVR	1.25	1.73	0.94
Hybrid	0.52	1.05	0.97

6 Conclusion

In this work, CO_2 concentrations have been used as an indicator of classroom IAQ. Sharp rise in CO_2 concentration is observed in fully occupied classrooms during lecture sessions. This work aims to forecast the CO_2 build-up so that the requirement of ventilation is estimated. For this purpose, linear and non-linear forecast models have been developed. A hybrid forecast approach which combines ARIMA and SVR models is investigated. The forecast performance is measured using MAPE, RMSE and R^2. It is found out that hybrid model performs the best, as it is able to capture both linear and non-linear characteristics of the CO_2 concentration time series and records lowest values among all performance parameters.

References

1. Kim, J.Y., Chu, C.H., Shin, S.M.: ISSAQ: an integrated sensing systems for realtime indoor air quality monitoring. IEEE Sens. J. **14**(12), 4230–4244 (2014)
2. Cui, S., Cohen, M., Stabat, P., Marchio, D.: CO_2 tracer gas concentration decay method for measuring air change rate. Build. Environ. **84**, 162–169 (2015)
3. Rice, S.A.: Human health risk assessment of CO_2: survivors of acute high-level exposure and populations sensitive to prolonged low-level exposure. Environments **3**(5), 7–15 (2014)
4. Burke, J., et al.: Participatory sensing. In: World Sensor Web Workshop, ACM Sensys 2006, Boulder, Colorado, 31 October 2006
5. Nabinger, S.J., Persily, A.K., Dols, W.: A study of ventilation and carbon dioxide in an office building. ASHRAE Trans. **100**, 1264–1274 (1994)
6. Persily, A.K.: Evaluating building IAQ and ventilation with indoor carbon dioxide. ASHRAE Trans. **103**, 193–204 (1997)
7. Chen, X., et al.: Indoor air quality monitoring system for smart buildings. In: Proceedings of the ACM International Joint Conference on Pervasive and Ubiquitous Computing, pp. 471–475 (2014)
8. Bhattacharya, S., Sridevi, S., Pitchiah, R.: Indoor air quality monitoring using wireless sensor network. In: 6th IEEE International Conference on Sensing Technology (ICST), pp. 422–427 (2012)
9. Aglan, H.A.: Predictive model for CO_2 generation and decay in building envelopes. J. Appl. Phys. **93**(2), 1287–1290 (2003)

10. Beko, G., Toftum, J., Clausen, G.: Modeling ventilation rates in bedrooms based on building characteristics and occupant behavior. Build. Environ. **46**(11), 2230–2237 (2011)
11. Satish, U., et al.: Is CO_2 an indoor pollutant? Direct effects of low to moderate CO_2 concentrations on human decision making performance. Environ. Health Perspect. **120**(12), 1671–1677 (2014)
12. Carbon Dioxide and Ventilation Rates. www.dtic.mil
13. Sensordrone: The 6th Sense of Your Smartphone. https://www.kickstarter.com/projects/453951341/sensordrone-the-6th-sense-of-your-smartphoneand-be. Accessed 30 Sept 2019
14. Koenker, R., Xiao, Z.: Inference on the quantile regression process. Econometrica **70**, 1583–1612 (2002). https://doi.org/10.1111/1468-0262.00342
15. Cade, B.S., Noon, B.R.: A gentle introduction to quantile regression for ecologists. Front. Ecol. Environ. **1**, 412–420 (2003)

Strategy Inference via Real-Time Homeomorphic and Isomorphic Tree Matching of Probabilistic Graphical Models

D. Michael Franklin[✉]

Kennesaw State University, Marietta, GA, USA
mfranklin@kennesaw.edu

Abstract. In many common gaming and real-world scenarios agents are trying to predict the behavior of the other agents. This assumes that there is some underlying strategy that these players are following, that such strategies can be inferred, and that a reasonable player can counter such strategies in real-time. These strategies can be modeled as various graph structures such as trees, finite state machines (FSMs), or probabilistic graphical models (PGMs). With these models created, one approach to best determine which strategy an agent is following is to match prospective trees, built from observed behaviors or policies, with known trees, representing previously learned strategies and policies. While matching two trees can be done in super-linear time in the small scale, the matching problem quickly becomes NP for the more complicated cases. This leads to a well-known NP-Complete problem (e.g., (Kumar et al. 2011)) when one considers homeomorphic trees (one is a subgraph of the other) and isomorphic trees (the bijection is true (i.e., homeomorphic in both directions)) and their matching. Isomorphic graph matching is much more complex (Vazirani 1989). At scale, most solutions for graph matching utilize highly-parallel processes running on high-performance computing clusters. This is intractable for real-time low-power computer systems. This paper presents an approximation algorithm for tree matching in order to accomplish strategy inference in real-time multi-agent systems.

1 Introduction

It has been shown that strategies offer significant performance enhancement to artificially intelligent agents, that strategies can be recognized in real-time when complexity is limited, and that AI agents utilizing strategy inference will outperform their originally superior opponents (Franklin 2015). To do strategy inference in more complex environments necessitates discovering better approximation algorithms for this kind of tree matching.

Classical machine learning requires repetitive trials and numerous iterations to begin to form a hypothesis as to the intended actions of a given agent. There

© Springer Nature Singapore Pte Ltd. 2020
S. M. Thampi et al. (Eds.): SoMMA 2019, CCIS 1203, pp. 105–125, 2020.
https://doi.org/10.1007/978-981-15-4301-2_9

are numerous methodologies employed in an attempt to reduce the number of examples needed to form a meaningful hypothesis. The challenge arises from the difficulty created by the diversity of possible scenarios in which the machine learning algorithm is placed. Given enough time and stability a machine learning algorithm can learn reasonably well in a fixed environment, but this does not replicate the real world very accurately. As a result, we utilize strategies, defined and explained in the Methodology section. Strategies offer an opportunity to encapsulate much of this policy-space in a compact representation. They have to be learned as well, but they are transmutable to another instance of a similar problem. Additionally, they can be pre-built and then modified to suit the exact situation. If these strategies are represented as graphs then they can be classified, categorized, identified, and matched. In particular, they can be represented as a variety of highly expressive graphs such as PGMs, FSMs with probabilistic progression, or other tree structures composed of complex elements. The strategy inference engine created in (Franklin 2015) uses PGMs to build a belief network of candidate strategies from which it selects the most likely strategy an opposing agent is using. This matching is workable in fixed-size implementations and low-complexity environments. It is also restricted to known strategies so it does not learn new strategies currently nor does it approximate solutions. The belief networks utilized are successful in estimating solutions, but they require more experience than may be available in a real-world scenario. To learn strategies and form hypotheses in real-time we utilize approximation algorithms. This paper introduces an approximate solution to the real-time, complex tree matching. First, we explain and propose algorithms for an exact solution. Next, an approximation algorithm is introduced to create approximate solutions in real-time. After this, the approximate solution is improved upon to produce the final approximation algorithm. Finally, there is an analysis of the solutions and relative performance of each algorithm in a variety of applications.

2   Related Works

The work of Vazirani (1989) describes the complexity classes of finding complete matchings in variations of complete graphs. It documents how to decompose the problem of $K_{3,3}$ into subsets of examination using K_5 discrete elements. This decomposition brings the problem from the complexities of intractability into the tractable realm. Namely, considering the decomposition as a set of parallel sub-optimizations that can be discretely considered provides a lower-NP bound, though it requires parallel processing. Further, the paper introduces the exponential increase in complexity when considering homeomorphic graphs. The insight of graph decomposition is utilized herein to inform the process of culling the list of viable candidate trees and confirms the intractability of isomorphic graphs.

In (Das et al. 2013), the authors investigate paths and matchings within k-trees. They analyze the complexity classes of such matching and searches in these trees. Their experiments substantiate the claims of the complexity of matching trees and offer motivation for approximate solutions to this class of problems.

Their insight into tree-decomposition is also helpful in organizing solutions to large-scale problems in the realm of tree-matching. Their work stops short of larger scale graphs and does not consider approximate solutions to the more intractable issues of homeomorphism and isomorphism.

Datta et al. study the effects of moving the graph matching problem into the area of bipartite graphs. In (Datta et al. 2010) they established an algorithm to find matches within and between graphs and analyzed the relevant complexities, assigning simplex matching to NC. This lays the groundwork herein where the limits of this complexity were pushed into higher bounds by matching homeomorphic and isomorphic graphs. Their work also helped to inform the baseline algorithm used herein for comparison to the approximate solution (along with several other works and the author's own research).

An approach to distributed graphical representations and clarifications of the complexities of comparing these graphs is offered in (Lotker et al. 2015). This work is instrumental in constructing a portion of the complexity analysis for these graphs and their search functions. Further, the work of (Wang et al. 2015) explores the combinatorial growth and complexity of both these structures and the search functions/comparator functions of this work.

The work of Fukuda, et al., further explores the complexity of matchings within bipartite graphs and aims to make improvements to the process. Their work (Fukuda and Matsui 1994) elucidates the difficulties and complexities of such matchings. In particular, they move from $O((c+I)n^2)$ to $O(c(n+m)+n^{2.5})$. While they do not deal directly with homeomorphic and isomorphic matchings, they do further describe the relationship with complexity and memory management. The algorithm they propose does, in fact, lower the computational complexity, but at the cost of increased memory utilization. Additionally, they recognize that computing such difficult matchings pushes the limits of computability. As a result, herein, the entire problem of doing these matchings in real-time is further clarified as intractable and in need of the approximate solution proposed in this research.

3   Methodology

Graph matching is complex enough on its own as can be seen in the literature (e.g., (Kumar et al. 2011; Vazirani 1989)). Adding the subgraph generalization of homeomorphism makes this substantially more difficult and more complex in both time and memory. Further, the bijection of isomorphic matching adds even more complexity and an increased memory requirement. Because of this complexity there needs to be a method of approximating solutions to such matchings. This may include both approximate culling, where the target set of graphs or trees may be reduced through simple algorithmic considerations, and approximate matching, where the partial candidate graph is best-matched with target graphs that remain after culling.

In multi-agent strategic interactions, the complexity of strategic inference quickly leaves the computable range and becomes intractable. Learning in such an environment is even more difficult (Franklin 2015). When the strategies, and their associated policies, can be derived (or provided) probabilistically then they can be represented as either FSMs or PGMs. These models can then be encapsulated in two ways: first, as diverse sets of graphs for each such policy where the relevant walks in the graph represent action chains (representing policies); second, as multiple isomorphic graphs where the weighting of the edges encodes the decision process. Both are described in the following sections after the background information is presented. This means that multiple agents interacting within the same environment can use strategies (with their related set of policies) to execute their actions and, thus, act intelligently. In this scenario, then, it is possible to reverse engineer this strategic interaction based on observations of the actions taken by a particular agent. By comparing the observed actions with the probable actions of each strategic possibility a belief network (BN) can be formed that leads the particular agent to infer the strategy of another agent within the system. This requires the ability to match these candidate graphs (e.g., PGMs) with the currently forming belief network image (another graph) in real time.

To accomplish this task this paper seeks to first implement a complete matching (exact tree match with all vertices and edges identical) solution, as informed by the various reference papers and this research. This complete matching is then optimized to perform complete matching across graphs and to consider homeomorphs and isomorphs. Next, an approximation algorithm is presented to both cull the target set and to provide approximate matching in real-time, thus realizing the goal of recognizing strategies in real time. After these algorithms are fully implemented, several experiments are conducted to validate the hypothesis proposed herein. To be considered a success, these algorithms must find matchings and must do so in less time, less memory, or both. The methods are analyzed and compared according to accuracy, complexity and time.

3.1   Strategy

It is necessary to define strategy as it is a term often abused in literature. Many researchers use the terms policy and strategy interchangeably. In this paper, as elucidated in (Franklin 2015), policies are defined as they are in classical machine learning problems. Strategies are the amalgamation of policies into a larger super-policy that can select from among these various member policies to see which one should be in place in a given circumstance. They also have various factors that influence strategic choices. Each policy has defined states and actions. A state, s, is a discrete or measurable value or set of values at a specific time t. All s are in S, the set of all states. An action, a, is any transition from state s to a subsequent state s', or anything that changes a state. All a are in A, the set of all possible actions. A policy, π, is a mapping from $S \rightarrow A$, or that chooses a', the next action, from A for all $s \in S$ (1, generically). There are several ways this can be derived and several considerations for the method used. First, there is the generic formulation shown in (1). To evaluate the results of taking each of the actions from a given state, and thus determine the optimal action, a valuation function is needed. This function (e.g., 2) generally determines a value of taking a certain action from a certain state by capturing the reward of that action. It may additionally consider the current action plus the previous action or actions. While the valuation function, $V^\star$, is left generalized here, it is defined specifically during implementation. This function is critical to the success of the policy and essential for it to have decidability from among the various available actions.

Additionally, when looking backwards multiple steps of reward for this valuation, it is possible (and likely) that the reward is diminished by a certain factor that grows over time. In this manner the cumulative value of the valuation is weighted in proportion to how long ago that action was taken (e.g., epsilon decay). In a fully-explored deterministic environment choosing a' is distinct and simple. Each state s would have an optimal action a that maps to the highest valued option, thus the optimal action. In non-deterministic environments these evaluations must use the underlying probabilities or experimental values derived thus far (3). When time constraints or complexity create bounds then a heuristic must be used. These heuristics may range from scores or values to expected values and rewards. In this environment a' is determined by choosing the maximum value of the available choices (4). Here $E(a, s)$ is the expected value based on experience thus far of taking action a from state s.

$$a' \leftarrow \pi : \operatorname*{argmax}_{a} V^a(s), \forall s \in S \tag{1}$$

$$where : V^\star(s_t) = \max_a V^a(s_t) \tag{2}$$

$$\hat{a}' \leftarrow \pi : \operatorname*{argmax}_{a \in A} P(s|a) V^a(s_t), \forall s \in S \tag{3}$$

$$\hat{a}' \leftarrow \pi : \operatorname*{argmax}_{a \in A} E(s, a), \forall s \in S \tag{4}$$

These values can be determined through machine learning, experience, or domain knowledge. When the agent has no prior knowledge they must make their choices stochastically to explore each option and track their rewards for taking each action. Once enough states have been visited and actions taken, the exploration (i.e., favoring stochastic selection to maximize testing each option) transitions to exploitation (i.e., taking the best actions seen thus far to maximize reward). Once these most-favorable choices ($w.r.t.$ reward or utility) have been learned, they can be saved and re-used. This forms a policy that the agent can now start from and not have to relearn an environment. This is assuming that either the states stay the same or are only marginally different from the states in the learning environment. Additionally, it is not necessary to assume a fully exploitation-oriented approach. The agent can, $w.l.o.g$, take the favorable actions from its experience 90% of the time and make stochastic choices the other 10% of the time to make sure there is not a better choice. Once this policy π has been learned, it can be added to the set of policies Π to form a collection of policies. The agent or set of agents can then share this collection of policies as prior experience for each of them. Selecting the best policy to utilize from among these available policies is the domain of strategy.

A strategy, σ, selects the optimal (or desired) policy, π, from the set of policies, Π, to accomplish a goal, g, or meta-set of goals, G (5). All σ are in Σ, the set of all strategies. As seen generically in (5), this selection is simply putting in force the best policy given the current set of states and actions. The method for such selection, however, is not so easily contrived. There is a similar notion of expectation that will be used. This expectation function will examine the actions $a \in A$ taken by the current policy π in force and by those of each other known policy $\pi \in \Pi$. The *argmax* of these values is then taken, and this may indicate that either the current policy π is the best policy to have in place or there is a shift in policy that needs to occur. Further, there is a threshold ϵ that is considered before a policy change occurs in order to provide some momentum to the current policy and avoid unnecessary vacillations in policy change (6). If the δ between the current π and π' is less than ϵ, the current policy, π, stays in place; otherwise, a change is initiated. This mechanism and relevant valuations are considered within the experiments.

$$\pi' \leftarrow \sigma : \operatorname*{argmax}_{\pi} V^{\pi}(\pi_0), \forall \pi \in \Pi \tag{5}$$

$$\pi' \leftarrow \sigma : \operatorname*{argmax}_{\pi} E^{\pi}(s, a) - \epsilon, \forall \pi \in \sigma \tag{6}$$

These strategies can be represented as graphs (or trees), as stated previously. However, these graphs may not be exact matches and so the matching of candidate strategies to target strategies can be computationally complex. To reduce this problem we wish to consider finding homeomorphs and isomorphs within these graphs, as introduced below.

3.2   Homeomorphism and Isomorphism

Two graphs which contain the same graph vertices connected in the same way, perhaps with additional vertices, are said to be homeomorphic. Formally, two graphs G and H with graph vertices $V_n = (1, 2, ..., n)$ are said to be homeomorphic if there is a permutation p of V_n such that the resultant graph is a subgraph of the former. Figure 1 provides an example from (Sepp 2015).

Fig. 1. Homeomorphic graphs

Two graphs which contain the same number of graph vertices connected in the same way are said to be isomorphic. Formally, two graphs G and H with graph vertices $V_n = (1, 2, ..., n)$ are said to be isomorphic if there is a permutation p of V_n such that (u, v) is in the set of graph edges $E(G) \iff (p(u), p(v))$ is in the set of graph edges $E(H)$. Figure 2 provides an example from (Windsor 2015).

Fig. 2. Isomorphic graphs

The cost of calculating isomorphism is much higher than the cost of calculating homeomorphism so the approximation algorithm should consider these in this order. There may be graphs that are homeomorphic and not isomorphic, but there are no reasonable graphs that are isomorphic but not homeomorphic. This intuition will be used later in the intelligent pruning section of the approximation algorithm to cull the target list.

A complete matching would be one where all vertices and edges appear in both graphs (ensuring that the two graphs are identical because their lists of vertices and edges are identical). Figure 3 shows the complete match between the candidate tree on the right-hand side of the bar and its ideal target from the target trees on the left-hand side of the bar. While this is ideal, the cost to calculate it is too high. Instead, we wish to approximate the performance of complete matching with the approximate matching algorithm proposed herein.

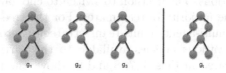

Fig. 3. Complete matching

3.3 Strategy Representation

Unlike in (Franklin 2015), strategies can instead be represented as a PGM. For example, consider the simple game of Rock-Paper-Scissors (Roshambo). In Fig. 4 the game is represented as both a PGM and the corresponding tree reproduction.

In this assembly the graph is isomorphic for all players, but the weights of the edges vary (i.e., the policy is encapsulated in the transitional probabilities of each edge). While there are many such sample trees that could be considered,

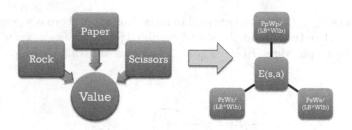

Fig. 4. RPS PGM example

there is no need to consider these variations for the purpose of this research as the focus is on the shape of the tree and not on the meaning behind them. A list of target trees is created to represent each possible known strategy. Each of these trees will be unique, though they may share subtrees. The target trees are not isomorphic with respect to one another. There will also be a candidate tree. This candidate tree will start with only a root node at the beginning of any episode.

In a further example, we wish to consider a simulation of 5-vs-5 Speedball Paintball. This fast-paced version of paintball pits two teams against each other with a vast array of objects between them (half of a field is shown in Fig. 5, the other half is a mirror of this one). All players must start in their home base and then progress from obstacle to obstacle while both avoiding enemy fire and attempting to eliminate the opponents. While there are flags for each team to capture and return to base, thus ending the match, the majority of the matches end via team elimination. There are several distinct phases of each round of the game but they can be reduced to offense, defense, and end game. Most of the teams will start out on offense and then shift to defense based on progress and eliminations. The decision to switch to end game is necessitated by the elimination of the majority of teammates. For the tree-matching algorithm we decompose the multi-agent, multi-team strategies into a graph composed of the union of the various policies available to the particular strategy. This procedure, demonstrated in Figs. 6, 7, 8 and 9, shows the progression from the field layout (with the position mappings) to the resultant graph. Each of the subfigures shows a policy (drawn from a particular strategy) being added to the diagram. This shows how the strategy graph is built. This complex graph is a directed graph but not implicitly acyclic. Each edge is weighted based on the probability of selecting this edge as a path for the agent to travel. This leads to the probabilistic graphical model representation of the strategy model. In this PGM, each policy is amalgamated into a multi-branch pathway that is a partial representation of the strategy (and, as such, could be derived from any number of cases where there is a probabilistic progression of players through a space, mappings for data, a constellation of sensor inputs, or any other scenario that can be realized as a PGM). Recall that each strategy has several variables that define it along with a set of policies to which it has access. This set of policies is a subset of all available policies available to all strategies being followed by all teams in the simulation.

The simulation of the multi-agent, multi-team 5-vs-5 Speedball Paintball is written about elsewhere (Franklin 2016a), but some of the results are shown to prove that this graph matching approximation algorithm is both valid and useful in larger, more complicated environments. The results of these experiments will be reported separately in the Results section, but the approximation algorithm performed exactly as desired.

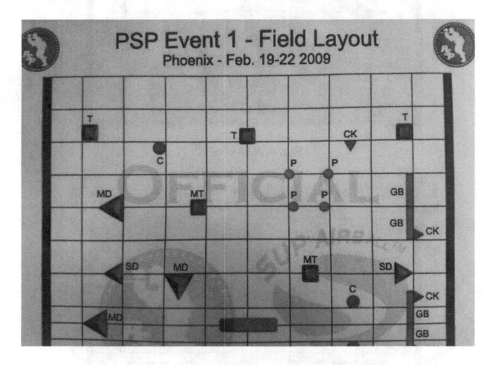

Fig. 5. Official PSP field

3.4   Tree Matching

During each episode the agent watching the other players will observe the states and actions of the players. To model this the agent builds a probabilistic tree tracking not only states and actions but the likelihood of any and all transitions (movements from one location to another, translated as traveling from one vertex to another along an edge). Each time the player makes a move (i.e., takes an action from the observed current state) the candidate tree is either expanded or updated. If the action has been observed before from this current state then the existing node is updated to reflect this event. This will help to build the

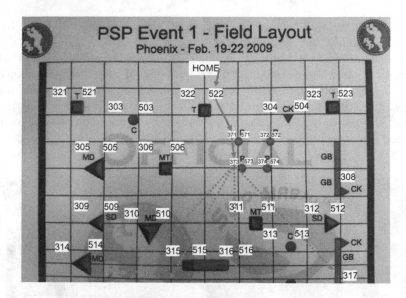

Fig. 6. Policy π_0

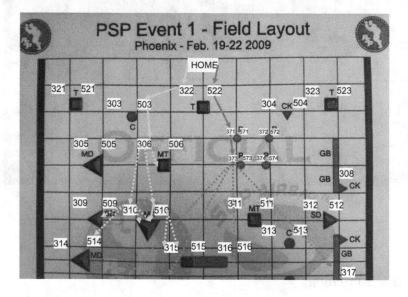

Fig. 7. Policy π_1

probability model for transitions from this state. If the state-action pair is new then a new node is created. The following series of diagrams (Fig. 10) show this progression. The left-hand side of the bar shows the three sample targets (the trees to which we are hoping to find a match). The right-hand side of the bar shows the candidate tree. As this candidate tree is being built it is constantly

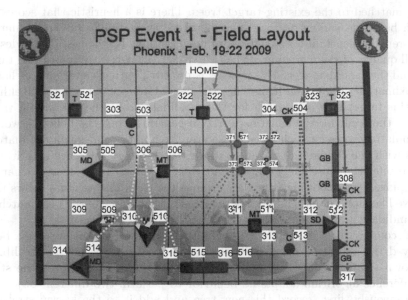

Fig. 8. Policy π_2

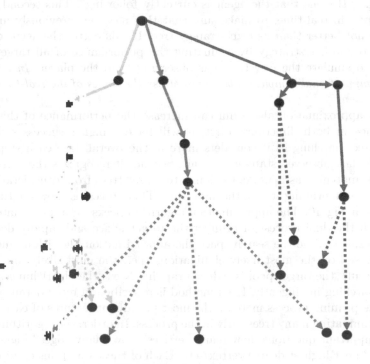

Fig. 9. Strategy σ_0

being matched to the existing target trees. There is a heuristic that scores the match based on various factors. This heuristic is adaptable to each situation, but it remains constant for any given implementation. The heuristic provides the overall quality of the matching of the two trees—the currently considered target tree and the candidate tree. This process is repeated until each target tree has an approximation of how well it matches the candidate tree. This is the likelihood that this target tree is a match for the candidate tree. These heuristic values become the seeds for the belief network. In general terms, the belief network is accumulating votes for each target based on the number and quality of matches it has with the candidate tree. As a result, the strategy inference algorithm is able to infer the most likely match, and thus the most likely strategy that the other players are following (the glow around the trees in the figure shows their relative likelihood of matching, thus their belief that they are the best match for the candidate graph).

Of course, there is another possibility, namely that the strategy being observed (i.e., the tree being built through observation) is not in the library of known strategies (i.e., not one of the target trees). In this case the strategy inference algorithm adapts its behavior to perform two different objectives simultaneously: first, record this new tree and add it to the known strategies (i.e., it becomes a target tree in the next episode); second, begin to evaluate the scoring outcome of the player's candidate tree and the currently selected target tree (i.e., the one that the agent is currently following). This second objective attempts, in real-time, to make sure that this new and previously unobserved tree is not better than its own strategy tree. If it is better the agent can either swap to another strategy by evaluating the performance of all target trees or begin to emulate the new tree it is observing from the player. *In either case, the computational complexity begins to stress the limits of the real-time analysis requirement.*

An approximation algorithm can increase the performance of this strategy inference in both directions. First, it will have a higher success rate of real-time tree matching as it considers more of the overall tree each step and not just the last observed state-action pair. Second, it recognizes the correct target tree for matching as it works to eliminate target trees from consideration in the approximate pruning step of the algorithm. This process is shown in the series of figures in Fig. 10. The approximation algorithm seeks an approximate solution through the dual process of pruning the target space and rapidly determining matches. To prune the search space the approximation algorithm ignores some trees based on the most likely eliminations (i.e., the most likely 'no' answers). As a result, the target pool is reduced rapidly. Next, the algorithm searches the tree matching intelligently. Each method is described in more detail below.

The pruning process matches the most prominent features of each tree first, thus eliminating many trees early in the process. In order, the algorithm asks several important questions: how many vertices? how many edges? highest degree vertex? next highest degree vertex? etc. Each of these questions eliminates both non-matching exact match target trees and isomorphic variants of the candidate

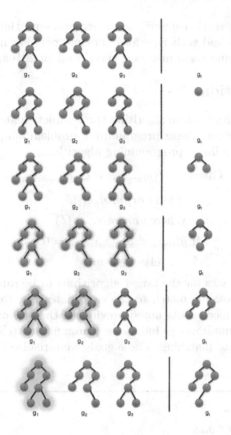

Fig. 10. Approximate matching

trees as none of the questions deal with root node orientation or other metrics that would require identical trees. This pruning is even more useful as the complexity of the trees increases. As tree complexity increases the likelihood that these quick determinants would match is even lower. As a result, the expectation is that the relative performance of the approximation algorithm will increase as the complexity increases.

The intelligent tree matching also seeks to rapidly determine 'no' answers. It must, in the worst case, perform the same edge-by-edge matching that the complete matching algorithm performs, but there are two factors that affect this. First, the order in which edges are considered is vital. The approximation algorithm orders these edges by the highest degree vertex. As a result, the approximation algorithm first considers the most difficult vertices and their corresponding edges. This is also homeomorphic and isomorphic tolerant. Second, the algorithm exits on the first non-match and need not consider any additional vertices or edges after a non-match. Many complete matching algorithms run through the entire tree either way. These two considerations work together to ensure optimal performance.

The Experiments section describes the experiments that were designed to test these hypotheses and gather performance metrics. For more elaboration on Strategy Inference using these methods, see (Franklin 2016a,b).

4   Implementation

To formulate the approximation algorithm the complete matching algorithm was transposed into an integer linear programming problem and, via a relaxation of the constraints, into a linear programming algorithm.

$$\text{Given}: Set(g_{targets}) \in G, g_{candidate}$$

$$\text{Find}: argmin_{g \in G}(\delta)$$

$$\text{Where}: argmin_{g \in G}(\delta)$$

$$\text{if } g_{target} = g_{candidate}, \delta = 0$$

$$\text{else } \delta \to min$$

This formulation asks for the target algorithms to be ranked by minimum δ so that the closest possible match to the candidate (i.e., the minimal δ differential) is the target selected. As noted previously, the approximation algorithm actually serves two simultaneous functions: prune non-matching candidates and accelerate approximate matching. These goals were realized in the experiments that follow.

Algorithm 1
Perfect Matching

Given: $g_{target} \in G, g_{candidate}$:
$\delta_g = -max; g_{prime} = null;$
For each $g \in g_{target}$
    Calculate $\delta_g(g_{candidate}, g_{target_g})$
  If $(\delta_g < \delta_{opt})$
      $g_{prime} = g_{target_g}$
      $\delta_{opt} = \delta_g$
Return g_{prime}

    Function δ_g(candidate graph, target graph):
      viewCounter, foundCounter = 0
      For each v in candidate graph
        viewCounter + +
        For each v in target graph
          If $(v_{candidate} = v_{target})$
            foundCounter + +
            break
      For each e in candidate graph
        viewCounter + +
        For each e in target graph
          If $(e_{candidate} = e)$
            foundCounter + +
            break
      Return $(1 - \dfrac{viewCounter}{foundCounter})$

Fig. 11. Algorithm 1: complete matching

4.1   Algorithms

There are three algorithms that have been implemented in this work. The first is the complete matching algorithm that matches every vertex, edge, and connection, shown in Fig. 11.

The second algorithm is the initial approximation algorithm that only focuses on matching but with the elimination of invalid candidates (quick 'no' evaluation), shown in Fig. 12.

The third algorithm is the improved approximation algorithm, shown in Fig. 13. This takes the initial approximation algorithm and improves it by quickly eliminating invalid candidates and performs in-line pruning to reduce the search space.

5   Experiments

This paper proposes a system that matches strategy trees realized as PGMs. In order to throughly test the robustness of the algorithm it was first tested against procedurally generated randomized trees. This creation process produces a large population of diverse trees that follow stochastic branching, much larger and more complex trees than may be found in standard scenarios. This process varies the depth, branching, and diversity of the trees (according to the variables described below). This sample population had no guarantees of containing any matchings. There are several variables to the tree generation algorithm:

Algorithm 2
Approximal Matching

Given: $g_{target} \in G, g_{candidate}$:
$\delta_g = -max; g_{prime} = null;$
For each $g \in g_{target}$
    Calculate $\delta_g(g_{candidate}, g_{target_g}, level\ l, goal\ goal_a)$
    If $(\delta_g < \delta_{opt})$
        $g_{prime} = g_{target_g}$
        $\delta_{opt} = \delta_g$
Return g_{prime}

    Function δ_g (candidate graph, target graph, current l, matching goal):
    For candidate graph and target graph
      While (currentMatching < goal)
        $l++$
        Generate conflict graph to length l:
          For each v in candidate graph
            neighbors = neighbors of v
            For each v_{not} in candidate graph $\neq v$
              send neighbors to v_{not}
        currentMatching = $neighbors_{sent} \cup neighbors_{received}$

      Return $(currentMatching_{candidate} / currentMatching_{target})$

Fig. 12. Algorithm 2: approximate matching

Table 1. Full and approximate tree matching (n = 1000) *(numbers are time, measured in seconds)*

Alg	Category	Trial 1	Trial 2	Trial 3	Avg
Full	H-morphs	278	289	327	**298.00**
Full	I-morphs	78	87	92	**85.66**
Full	Time (sec)	1777	1674	1689	**1713.33**
Aprx	H-morphs	278	289	327	**298.00**
Aprx	I-morphs	78	87	92	**85.66**
Aprx	Time (sec)	173	168	169	**170**

numgraphs, how many graphs to generate; *gen*, how many generations in each graph (depth of the graph); *offspring*, the number of children to have at each level; *family*, the size of the set from which the vertex labels are drawn. Each of these variables was randomized below this limit at tree generation. Once the trees were generated the algorithms analyzed the set and calculated the homeomorphic matches, the isomorphic matches, and the total time (in seconds) to execute each algorithm. The results were then recorded and analyzed. This procedure will work with any connected graph structure, not just trees, and so is widely applicable. This experiment proves that this matching of strategy trees can be done in real-time with a large population of complex trees, even these highly-complex and purposely diverse trees (Table 1).

In the second experiment the algorithm was put to the test in the Roshambo example mentioned above. While this game is simple (that is the reason it was used), it is sufficiently expressive to test the solution. The results show the time to recognize the strategy is greatly reduced by using the approximation algorithm. Additionally, the number of target strategies can be reduced because of the number of strategies that are isomorphic or homeomorphic to another strategy. The results, shown in Table 2 of Franklin (2015), reduced the number of recognition steps required to positively identify the strategy in play from hundreds of steps to less than 20 (about 13 steps, on average). This shows the algorithm working in a real environment, but not a complex one. For the complexity proof we implemented this in a more difficult real-world example, following.

The third experiment increased both the complexity and the difficulty of the matching. To increase the complexity we implemented this graph matching approximation algorithm in a multi-agent, multi-team simulation. In this simulation, 5 vs 5 Speedball Paintball, there are 5 agents on each team, each following their own policy drawn from their team strategy. They are attempting to infer the strategy of the opposing team in real time so they can switch policies or strategies to better their position. The results show that such inference can be done within the real-time limit constraint, shown in Table 3, with a significant increase in strategy recognition.

Algorithm 3
Improved Approximal

$Given:$ $g_{target} \in G, g_{candidate}$:
$\delta_g = -max;$ $g_{prime} = null;$
$For\ each\ g \in g_{target}$
$\quad Calculate\ \delta_g (g_{candidate}, g_{target_g}, goal\ goal_a)$
$\quad\quad If\ (\delta_g < \delta_{opt})$
$\quad\quad\quad g_{prime} = g_{target_g}$
$\quad\quad\quad \delta_{opt} = \delta_g$
$Return\ g_{prime}$

$\quad\quad\quad Function\ \delta_g (candidate\ graph, target\ graph, matching\ goal):$
$\quad\quad\quad\quad While\ (currentMatching < goal)$
$\quad\quad\quad\quad\quad Generate\ degreeMap\ for\ both\ graphs$
$\quad\quad\quad\quad\quad If\ (|v_{candidate}| \neq |v_{target}|)$
$\quad\quad\quad\quad\quad\quad return\ max$
$\quad\quad\quad\quad\quad If\ (|e_{candidate}| \neq |e_{target}|)$
$\quad\quad\quad\quad\quad\quad return\ max$
$\quad\quad\quad\quad\quad For\ each\ v\ in\ candidate\ graph, target\ graph$
$\quad\quad\quad\quad\quad\quad degree = degree\ of\ v$
$\quad\quad\quad\quad\quad\quad If\ (maxDegree_c \neq maxDegree_t)$
$\quad\quad\quad\quad\quad\quad\quad return\ max$
$\quad\quad\quad\quad\quad else$
$\quad\quad\quad\quad\quad\quad\quad goodCount + +$
$\quad\quad\quad\quad\quad\quad\quad maxDegree -= 1$

$\quad\quad\quad\quad currentMatching = 1 - (\frac{goodCount}{|v|+|e|})$

$\quad\quad\quad Return\ (currentMatching)$

Fig. 13. Algorithm 1: improved approximate matching

It may seem counter-intuitive that the complete matching, where every single vertex and edge are matched, would produce lower accuracy than the approximation method, but this is another side-effect of the complexity of the system. The complete matching takes so long to calculate that the 'world' has changed (i.e., this is a dynamic environment). As a result, the graphs that are being compared are becoming antiquated during the matching procedure. This was the inspiration for the goal of real-time graph matching. Further, not only did we achieve the matching, with even higher accuracy, but it was with a negligible time penalty. As you can see from Table 3, the simulation runs have an average run-time of 5.4 s, but adding in the graph matching only raises the average to 5.6. This sub-second result qualifies as real-time, especially since the variance is so high in run-times. It should be noted that the simulation was run in serial to slow it down for analysis; in parallel the difference in timing is not easily measurable.

There is another aspect of this third experiment that amplifies the results from the second experiment (the Roshambo experiment). In real-time considerations it is imperative that the algorithm utilize its belief network to constantly provide the most likely match evaluated so far. This means that another key

Table 2. Growth of algorithmic methods by complexity

Tree complexity	n	n^2	n^3
Homeomorphs	21	278	380
Isomorphs	1	78	10
Full match (time in sec)	427	1777	24310
Approx match (time in sec)	9	173	111

Table 3. Strategy recognition in 5v5 speedball

Method	Correct	Total	Accuracy	Time (sec)
Complete	60	81	74.07%	1778
Complete	63	81	77.78%	2035
Complete	66	81	81.48%	1694
Normal	38	81	46.91%	5.3
Normal	35	81	43.31%	5.1
Normal	40	81	49.38%	5.8
Approx	**72**	**81**	**88.89%**	**5.9**
Approx	**77**	**81**	**95.06%**	**5.2**
Approx	**74**	**81**	**91.35%**	**5.7**

element in evaluating the effectiveness of the algorithm is in how fast it can recognize the correct strategy. As it was with the Roshambo experiment, the Speedball experiment showed that the inference engine could recognize the correct strategy in an average of about 25 moves. A move is either a literal movement, a shot fired, or a player taking cover. Considering the complicating factor that all players start in home base (by rule of the game and the simulation), this shows that the recognition occurs very early in the encounter. Further, the fact that some players could be eliminated in fewer than 25 moves also makes the recognition (the tree matching) even more difficult. Table 4 shows the results of the experiments showing how many steps it took to recognize the correct strategy. Each time the inference engine selects another strategy as the most likely this counter is reset to the current step number. This means that even if the correct strategy is recognized early on but is discounted later on, even if the engine comes back to select this same strategy, the last time it is selected is the number of steps recorded.

Table 4. Moves to recognize correct strategy

Trial number	Recognition steps
1	22
2	27
3	24
4	26
5	25

Table 5. Complexity of algorithms

Algorithm	Complexity
Graph matching (pair)	$O(VE)$
Graph matching (weights)	$O(VEW)$
Graph matching (set of g)	$O(g^2 VEW)$
Approximate matching	$O((g-m)^2 VEW)$
Improved approximate	$O((g-m)VEW)$

6   Conclusions

The experiments showed that the growth rate for the complete matching algorithm is exponential while the growth rate for the approximate solution is linear. The complexity of tree growth has a significant effect on runtime. Complete matching is, as the related works showed and the experiments confirmed, a taxing process on a computing platform; with homeomorphic and isomorphic variants the compute time exceeds reasonable computation time even in highly parallel environments. In multi-agent interactions, where real-time decision making is critical, we have shown that the use of PGM-based Belief Networks, where this kind of approximate tree matching is required, is tractable. The algorithm also returns the most likely match observed thus far, allowing real-time decisions in multi-agent scenarios without having to wait for episodic completion or complete matching. The experiments demonstrate that this PGM-matching, even approximately, is both real-time and accurate enough for decision making even in multi-agent, multi-team environments.

Another surprising but welcome conclusion is that the pruning portion of the approximation algorithm is so effective that it keeps the growth rate constant within the linear boundary. This result is manifesting itself because as the trees increase in complexity the unique features expand; thus, there are more graphs eliminated in the culling step. This means that the size of the target set is staying consistent and manageable. Again, the greater complexity works in the improved approximation algorithms favor as there are more 'no' flags that are triggered because of the higher probability of unique vertices, edges, and degrees.

The complexity analysis is shown in Table 5, where g is the set of graphs in the set to inspect and m the number of eliminations in the set of g:

This research has pushed the boundaries of tree matching to make it tractable in real-time via an approximation algorithm. The results also show that there is no loss of precision with the approximation, though this was not a claim of the initial hypothesis. This additional benefit means that the algorithm achieves greater speed and lower complexity without compromising the integrity of the system. These results, in total, conclude that the improved approximation algorithm is a success and the hypothesis is confirmed.

7   Future Work

While this algorithm has met and exceeded the desired goals, it would be worthwhile research to consider creating and testing an optimized parallel version of this algorithm just to see how fast it can run, especially as it is tested in increasingly complex environments. This would lead to continued research into the complexity boundaries that limit the real-time claim of this hypothesis and should allow pushing those boundaries higher. It could also be expanded to include various special graph types or more complicated or intricate structures. Expanding the complexity of the systems studied will strengthen the algorithm and broaden its areas of application.

References

Das, B., Datta, S., Nimbhorkar, P.: Log-space algorithms for paths and matchings in k-trees. Theory Comput. Syst. **53**(4), 669–689 (2013). https://doi.org/10.1007/s00224-013-9469-9

Datta, S., Kulkarni, R., Roy, S.: Deterministically isolating a perfect matching in bipartite planar graphs. Theory Comput. Syst. **47**(3), 737–757 (2010). https://doi.org/10.1007/s00224-009-9204-8

Franklin, D.M.: Strategy inference in stochastic games using belief networks comprised of probabilistic graphical models. In: Proceedings of Florida Artificial Intelligence Research Society (2015)

Franklin, D.M.: Strategy inference in multi-agent multi-team scenarios. In: Proceedings of the International Conference on Tools with Artificial Intelligence (2016a)

Franklin, D.M.: Strategy inference via real-time homeomorphic and isomorphic tree matching of probabilistic graphical models. In: Proceedings of Florida Artificial Intelligence Research Society (2016b)

Fukuda, K., Matsui, T.: Finding all the perfect matchings in bipartite graphs. Appl. Math. Lett. **7**(1), 15–18 (1994)

Kumar, R., Talton, J.O., Ahmad, S., Roughgarden, T., Klemmer, S.R.: Flexible tree matching. In: Proceedings of the Twenty-Second International Joint Conference on Artificial Intelligence, IJCAI 2011, vol. 3, pp. 2674–2679. AAAI Press (2011)

Lotker, Z., Patt-Shamir, B., Pettie, S.: Improved distributed approximate matching. J. ACM **62**(5), 38:1–38:17 (2015)

Sepp, S.: Homeomorphic graph images (2015)

Vazirani, V.V.: NC algorithms for computing the number of perfect matchings in $K_{3,3}$-free graphs and related problems. Inf. Comput. **80**(2), 152–164 (1989)

Wang, T., Yang, H., Lang, C., Feng, S.: An error-tolerant approximate matching algorithm for labeled combinatorial maps. Neurocomputing **156**, 211 (2015)

Windsor, A.: Boost library: planar graphs (2015)

CNN and Stacked LSTM Model for Indian Sign Language Recognition

C. Aparna$^{(\boxtimes)}$ and M. Geetha$^{(\boxtimes)}$

Computer Science and Engineering, Amrita Vishwa Vidyapeetham,
Amritapuri, Kollam 690525, India
aparna1994c@gmail.com, geetham@am.amrita.edu

Abstract. In this paper, we propose a deep learning for sign language recognition using convolutional neural network (CNN) and long short term memory (LSTM). The architecture used CNN as a pretrained model for feature extraction and is passed to the LSTM for capturing spatio-temporal information. One more LSTM is stacked for increasing the accuracy. Deep learning model which captures temporal information is less. There is only less papers which deals with sign language recognition by using the deep learning architectures such as CNN and LSTM. The algorithm was tested in Indian sign language (ISL) dataset. We have presented the performance evaluation after testing with ISL dataset. Literature shows that deep learning models capturing temporal information is still an open research problem.

Keywords: Indian sign language recognition · Convolutional Neural Networks (CNN) · Long Short Term Memory (LSTM) · Deep learning

1 Introduction

Sign language is the most effective way of communication of the deaf with the hearing majority. Sign language is expressed by various hand shapes, body movements, and facial expressions. There are different signs associated with each movement. The deaf people use sign language as a communication medium with the hearing majority. Sign language includes dynamic sign, static sign and continuous sign. Static sign is for alphabets, dynamic sign is for isolated words and continuous sign is used for sentence. Sign language recognition is a research area which involves pattern recognition, computer vision, NLP (Natural language processing).

There are few existing deep learning models which did sign language recognition [2,3,9–12]. We propose a deep learning solution for Indian sign language recognition. Since Indian sign language dictionary is standardized very recently, not much work has happened in the area of Indian sign language recognition. We propose a deep learning architecture which use CNN based LSTM for Indian sign language recognition. When a deaf person is trying to communicate with normal person who does not know sign language, a framework which translates sign language to speech will be helpful.

© Springer Nature Singapore Pte Ltd. 2020
S. M. Thampi et al. (Eds.): SoMMA 2019, CCIS 1203, pp. 126–134, 2020.
https://doi.org/10.1007/978-981-15-4301-2_10

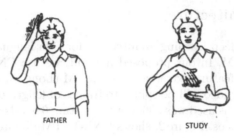

FATHER

STUDY

Fig. 1. Examples of isolated words

2 Related Work

In the work by Oscar Koller et al., they did a CNN-HMM model, which combines the strong discriminative abilities of CNNs with the sequence modelling capabilities of HMMs by taking the outputs of CNN in a bayesian fashion. The contributions associated with this paper are, they are the first one to implement the hybrid CNN-HMM model in the context of sign language and gesture recognition. With their three challenging benchmark datasets got an improvement of over 15% with the state of the arts [1]. In the work by Runpeng et al. [2] they developed a real world continuous sign language recognition by using the deep neural networks. They used CNN with temporal convolution and pooling for spatio-temporal representation from the video and RNN with LSTM (Long Short Term Memory) for the feature sequence. In the work by Geetha et al. they proposed a method which can approximate the gesture image boundary into a polygon. It also recognizes the open and closed gestures of the finger very efficiently [3]. In the work by Brandon Garcia et al. they developed a fingerspelling translator based on CNN for ASL. Their model correctly classifies a-e and a-k letters correctly [4]. In the work by Eleni et al. [5], Gesture recognition involves segmentation and feature extraction. They used frame level classification. Both training and testing is done for CNN and CNN-LSTM combination for training. In the work by Ce Li et al. they proposed hand gesture recognition for mobile by using discriminant learning. The solution is they consolidate Fisher model into the BiLSTM and BiGRU networks termed as F-BiLSTM and F-BiGRU to improve the traditional softmax loss work for improving the mobile gesture recognition performance. They proposed a gesture recognition strategy to distinguish arm movement employing a particular wearable device. Their major contribution includes broad tests that appear prevalent execution of the proposed strategy compared to the state-of- the-art BiLSTM and BiGRU on three motion recognition databases and construct a large hand gesture database for portable hand signal recognition [6]. In the work by Juan C.Núñez et al., they used supervised learning; CNN-LSTM combination for training. By using their method they solved the problem of overfitting [7]. It is different from our method, that we are using CNN for feature extraction and LSTM is used for recognition.

3   System Architecture

We proposed a new deep learning architecture for sign language recognition by using CNN and LSTM. In our proposed method, we use CNN (Convolutional Neural Network) for feature extraction and LSTM (Long Short Term Memory) for prediction. Input video will be split into frames of length 60. Batch size used was 8; number of epochs used was 300. For the testing 6 words were given, each of which contains 10 videos. Figure 2, shows CNN-LSTM architecture of proposed method.

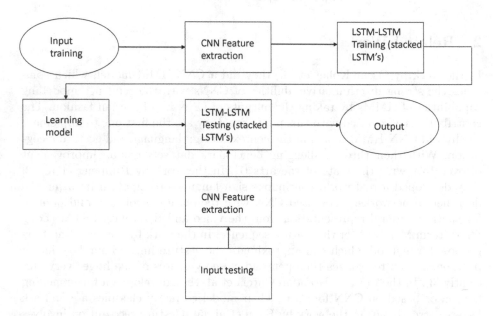

Fig. 2. CNN-LSTM architecture of proposed method

3.1   Feature Extraction

Convolutional Neural Network or ConvNet is a multilayer neural network, which consists of layers which recognize features such as edges and then these layers recombine these features. The neural network neurons are having weights and bias. Each neuron will receive some inputs and they will perform dot product and follows it with non-linearity. In ConvNet we use only images that allow us to encode certain properties. The main difference is that the hidden layer neuron is only connected to a subset of neurons in the previous layer [5]. Because of this connectivity it is capable of learning features directly. It is having convolution layer, pooling layer, fully connected layer and loss layer. Convolution layer is the one which performs computations. In the pooling layer it will perform the functions for reducing spatial size. In the fully connected layer, the neurons are connected fully to the neurons in the previous layer. Last layer is the loss layer, this layer computes the error. Here CNN is used for feature extraction, we haven't used fully connected layer. The CNN used is pretrained CNN that is the Inception net. Inception V3 Net is a pretrained CNN model which was developed by Google for the image recognition. Inception net was used to classify the images. During the feature extraction for each video, the models make use of sequence length 60 and class limit 6. Batch size used is 8 and number of epochs are 300. First, every frame from the video is taken and executed through the inception net and the output is taken from the final pool layer. We took 2048 feature vectors and passed on to the LSTM. Then these extracted features are converted to sequences. We used 60 frames sequence. These 60 frames were taken together and output is saved and the LSTM models are trained. For the LSTM layer we used 4096 wide 1024 dense layer and some drop out in between. After training it is given to the testing and the output obtained is correctly classified isolated words.

3.2 Classification

LSTM make use of Natural language processing, it is based on the concept of memory cells. Memory cells are able to retain its value for a long time or short time as a function of its inputs, which allows the cell to remember what is important. Since the RNNs have vanishing gradient problem and long term dependencies. We used LSTM instead of RNN for classification. LSTMs deal with the problem allowing for higher accuracy on longer sequences of data. For that we used single LSTM layer which is 4096 wide 1024 dense layer and some drop out in between; the dropout used is 0.5. Dropout is used where the randomly selected neurons are ignored during the training. The model used is the sequential model. The activation functions used are Softmax and ReLU. Softmax function is used for frequent classifications whereas ReLU is used for improving the neural networks by improving training by speeding up. One more LSTM is stacked with the first LSTM to get more accuracy. After the feature extraction, during classification these images are given to the LSTM for the training and the output obtained as a result of training and the validation is given for the testing, where the words are classified. Figure 3, shows the architecture diagram of stacked LSTM. Here we used LSTM for the temporal feature extraction. LSTM is having three gates, they are, input gate, forget gate and the output gate. Input gate decides what information flow should be there, forgotten gate decides what should be kept in the memory and what should be forgotten, output gate controls the flow of output. It is having four activation functions, they are tan h, and four sigmoid functions. The Sigmoid Function curve looks as if a S-shape. Sigmoid functions are used because the values are between 0 and 1. The other activation functions is the tanh or hyperbolic tangent Activation Function. tanh is likewise like logistic sigmoid but higher. tanh is having its range from -1 to 1.

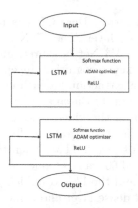

Fig. 3. Architecture diagram of stacked LSTM

4   Results and Discussion

4.1   Dataset Used

We have tested our algorithm in Indian sign language dataset. The videos were recorded on Nikon camera with 25fps. ISL dataset with 6 words, each having 20 videos for training and separate 6 words containing 10 videos for testing. Six words used are app, bull, early morning(EM), energy, crocodile and kitchen. Different variations of these videos are used. Inorder to avoid issues with complex background. Dataset containing 6 words of 20 videos each was given as the training input. It was randomly split to 70% and 30%, train and test. It uses ADAM optimizer. Keras framework was used since it is the fastest growing in deep learning framework. The open source library framework written in python is capable of running on top of Tensorflow. During training it took two days on Nvidia GeForce 940MX GPU. After the training, the accuracy obtained was 94% on the training set. The challenges faced by our model was to eliminate issues of hand segmentation in complex background. Figure 4, shows the word *"app"* from the dataset. In the experiments, the dataset was taken by wearing dark clothes with long sleeves and stand before a dark curtain under normal lighting. Total videos of around 156 were taken. Then videos are given to the preprocessing step, from there the video will be divided into frames(sequences). Then it is passed on

Fig. 4. Dataset which shows the word *"app"*

to the CNN where the feature extraction is done and a 2048 dimension vector is obtained. Then it is given to LSTM for the training and testing. Stacked LSTM is used that is two LSTMs are stacked so that the accuracy obtained is high. The training result obtained was 94%. In general existing system doesn't deal with temporal feature extraction from video in case of isolated sign language word by using the CNN based LSTM. The challenging factor about sign language is that sign language is involved with manual parameters such as hand shape, movements orientation, differentiation of the skin from background color, large vocabulary, temporal feature extraction from video.

4.2   Performance Evaluation

Comparison of words with other words Fig. 4, Showing prediction probability of app videos with other words such as bull, kitchen, energy, early morning and crocodile.

Table 1. Prediction probability of *"app"* with others

	Kitchen	Bull	Energy	Early morning	Crocodile	APP
App 1	0.01	0.016	6.63×10^{-3}	4.21×10^{-3}	6.94×10^{-4}	0.99997
App 2	7.2×10^{-3}	7.11×10^{-3}	3.59×10^{-3}	7.77×10^{-3}	6.54×10^{-4}	0.999
App 3	8.55×10^{-3}	0.024	5.77×10^{-3}	0.02	7.61×10^{-4}	0.999
App 4	0.015	5.55×10^{-3}	8.09×10^{-3}	5.17×10^{-3}	4.86×10^{-4}	0.999
App 5	0.011	4.04×10^{-3}	3.47×10^{-3}	0.02	3.85×10^{-4}	0.99
App 6	0.011	5.94×10^{-3}	8.95×10^{-3}	3.59×10^{-3}	5.56×10^{-4}	0.99
App 7	9.23×10^{-3}	5.05×10^{-3}	4.43×10^{-3}	0.01	7.11×10^{-4}	0.99
App 8	9.5×10^{-3}	4.63×10^{-3}	7.76×10^{-3}	6.4×10^{-3}	4.15×10^{-4}	0.99
App 9	0.011	0.011	8.53×10^{-3}	2.75×10^{-3}	6.5×10^{-4}	0.99
App 10	0.011	3.61×10^{-3}	6.19×10^{-3}	5.09×10^{-3}	3.45×10^{-4}	0.99998

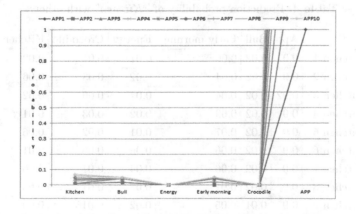

Fig. 5. Prediction probability of *"app"* with others

Table 2. Prediction probability of *"Bull"* with others

	App	Kitchen	Early morning	Energy	Crocodile	Bull
Bull 1	0.01	0.02	0.02	0.01	0.038	0.69
Bull 2	0.9	0.02	0.0003	0.04	0.012	0.89
Bull 3	0.02	0.0032	0.01	0.011	0.014	0.66
Bull 4	0.99	0.011	0.08	0.014	0.016	0.02
Bull 5	0.9	0.01	0.03	0.06	0.02	0.0001
Bull 6	0.04	0.01	0.01	0.04	0.06	0.55
Bull 7	0.9	0.06	0.01	0.04	0.01	0.01
Bull 8	0.9	0.06	0.08	0.01	0.01	0.07
Bull 9	0.9	0.02	0.02	0.06	0.01	0.01
Bull 10	0.9	0.01	0.0003	0.02	0.01	0.72

Table 3. Prediction probability of *"Early morning"* with others

	App	Kitchen	Crocodile	Energy	Bull	Early morning
Early morning 1	0.9	0.0001	0.09	0.01	0.06	0.001
Early morning 2	0.8	0.0002	0.08	0.0001	0.06	0.01
Early morning 3	0.9	0.0002	0.04	0.0002	0.02	0.1
Early morning 4	0.01	0.03	0.01	0.06	0.02	0.0002
Early morning 5	0.9	0.03	0.01	0.06	0.06	0.0005
Early morning 6	0.9	0.06	0.03	0.01	0.06	0.001
Early morning 7	0.04	0.04	0.07	0.02	0.06	0.03
Early morning 8	0.9	0.05	0.04	0.02	0.06	0.0041
Early morning 9	0.9	0.0001	0.08	0.06	0.01	0.014
Early morning 10	0.9	0.06	0.08	0.02	0.06	0.01

Table 4. Prediction probability of *"Kitchen"* with others

	App	Bull	Early morning	Energy	Crocodile	Kitchen
Kitchen 1	0.9	0.02	0.06	0.01	0.01	0.02
Kitchen 2	0.9	0.02	0.04	0.02	0.03	0.06
Kitchen 3	0.02	0.02	0.04	0.07	0.06	0.02
Kitchen 4	0.9	0.02	0.09	0.02	0.03	0.01
Kitchen 5	0.9	0.02	0.07	0.01	0.02	0.06
Kitchen 6	0.9	0.02	0.06	0.06	0.06	0.01
Kitchen 7	0.9	0.02	0.06	0.04	0.01	0.06
Kitchen 8	0.9	0.02	0.01	0.02	0.01	0.03
Kitchen 9	0.9	0.01	0.05	0.02	0.01	0.09
Kitchen 10	0.9	0.02	0.06	0.02	0.02	0.06

Table 5. Prediction probability of *"Crocodile"* with others

	App	Kitchen	Early morning	Energy	Bull	Crocodile
Crocodile 1	0.9	0.0002	0.004	0.0002	0.02	0.03
Crocodile 2	0.9	0.06	0.04	0.02	0.02	0.06
Crocodile 3	0.9	0.02	0.02	0.02	0.02	0.03
Crocodile 4	0.01	0.07	0.05	0.05	0.07	0.58
Crocodile 5	0.9	0.06	0.09	0.02	0.01	0.01
Crocodile 6	0.9	0.04	0.07	0.06	0.02	0.09
Crocodile 7	0.04	0.01	0.07	0.07	0.04	0.58
Crocodile 8	0.9	0.06	0.05	0.02	0.09	0.06
Crocodile 9	0.9	0.06	0.03	0.07	0.09	0.07
Crocodile 10	0.9	0.06	0.08	0.02	0.06	0.01

Table 6. Prediction probability of *"Energy"* with others

	App	Kitchen	Early morning	Bull	Crocodile	Energy
Energy 1	0.9	0.02	0.0002	0.01	0.01	0.01
Energy 2	0.9	0.02	0.01	0.01	0.04	0.01
Energy 3	0.9	0.0001	0.0001	0.05	0.09	0.09
Energy 4	0.9	0.03	0.06	0.01	0.09	0.01
Energy 5	0.9	0.01	0.01	0.02	0.02	0.01
Energy 6	0.9	0.06	0.02	0.02	0.07	0.01
Energy 7	0.9	0.01	0.01	0.04	0.02	0.06
Energy 8	0.9	0.03	0.001	0.01	0.02	0.02
Energy 9	0.9	0.06	0.02	0.07	0.07	0.01

Hereby looking at the Table 1 and the graph we can conclude that the samples of app is having high accuracy of around 0.99, where as the prediction probability of test "app" with other words are too less. A table and a graph are drawn out of these values. Accuracy is calculated by,

Accuracy = Number of correctly classified words/Total number of words.

The Table 2 shows the prediction probability of word *"bull"* with other words, where as the Tables 3, 4, 5 and 6 shows the prediction probabilities of *"early morning"* , *"kitchen"*, *"crocodile"* and *"energy"*.

5 Conclusion

Here we proposed a deep learning based sign language recognition for isolated words by using the CNN based LSTM model. One more LSTM model is stacked inorder to increase the accuracy. CNN is used in the feature extraction and the output obtained will be directly passed on to the LSTM for the training and the testing. The accuracy obtained will be higher than other methods. In the future work we can include the sentences, so that we will be able to check whether the words will slide over other words in a sentence.

References

1. Koller, O., et al.: Deep sign: hybrid CNN-HMM for continuous sign language recognition. In: Proceedings of the British Machine Vision Conference (2016)
2. Cui, R., Liu, H., Zhang, C.: Recurrent convolutional neural networks for continuous sign language recognition by staged optimization. In: Proceedings of the IEEE Conference on Computer Vision and Pattern Recognition (2017)
3. Geetha, M., et al.: Gesture recognition for American sign language with polygon approximation. In: 2011 IEEE International Conference on Technology for Education. IEEE (2011)
4. Garcia, B., Viesca, S.A.: Real-time American sign language recognition with convolutional neural networks. In: Convolutional Neural Networks for Visual Recognition, vol. 2 (2016)
5. Tsironi, E., et al.: An analysis of convolutional long short-term memory recurrent neural networks for gesture recognition. Neurocomputing **268**, 76–86 (2017)
6. Li, C., et al.: Deep fisher discriminant learning for mobile hand gesture recognition. Pattern Recognit. **77**, 276–288 (2018)
7. Nunez, J.C., et al.: Convolutional neural networks and long short-term memory for skeleton-based human activity and hand gesture recognition. Pattern Recognit. **76**, 80–94 (2018)
8. Aloysius, N., Geetha, M.: A review on deep convolutional neural networks. In: 2017 International Conference on Communication and Signal Processing (ICCSP). IEEE (2017)
9. Bantupalli, K., Xie, Y.: American sign language recognition using deep learning and computer vision. In: 2018 IEEE International Conference on Big Data (Big Data). IEEE (2018)
10. Taskiran, M., Killioglu, M., Kahraman, N.: A real-time system for recognition of American sign language by using deep learning. In: 2018 41st International Conference on Telecommunications and Signal Processing (TSP). IEEE (2018)
11. Nguyen, H.B.D., Do, H.N.: Deep learning for American sign language fingerspelling recognition system. In: 2019 26th International Conference on Telecommunications (ICT). IEEE (2019)
12. Soodtoetong, N., Gedkhaw, E.: The efficiency of sign language recognition using 3D convolutional neural networks. In: 2018 15th International Conference on Electrical Engineering/Electronics, Computer, Telecommunications and Information Technology (ECTI-CON). IEEE (2018)

Air Quality Monitoring and Classification Using Machine Learning

Sami Tlais[1](✉), Hassan HajjHussein[1](✉), Fouad Sakr[2](✉), Mohamad Hallani[2](✉), Abdel-Mehsen Ahmad[2](✉), and Zouhair El-Bazzal[2](✉)

[1] Department of Biological and Chemical Sciences, School of Arts and Sciences, Lebanese International University, Beirut, Lebanon
{sami.tlais,hassan.hajjhussein}@liu.edu.lb
[2] Department of Computer Communications Engineering, School of Engineering, Lebanese International University, Bekaa Campus, Beirut, Lebanon
{81430563,81330301,abdelmehsen.ahmad,zouhair.bazzal}@liu.edu.lb

Abstract. Air pollution is considered one of the biggest health threats after it has become the fourth leading cause of death in the world. According to the Health Effect Institute (HEI), 95% of the world's population is currently breathing polluted air. This paper highlights the importance of using machine learning algorithms to classify and predict air pollution based on collected real-time environmental data. These algorithms would help decision makers and responsible authorities to take action to alleviate this critical situation. Machine learning algorithms will be evaluated with offline data and real-time data which will be collected through pollution sensors as a model study. The obtained results revealed that Artificial Neural Network had the best performance and the highest accuracy among KNN, SVM, and Naïve Bayes Classifier.

Keywords: Machine learning · Air pollution · Algorithms

1 Introduction

Air quality has major ramifications on the health and economy. In the past few years, air pollution in Lebanon has led to a huge increase in asthma cases, at least 50% higher than Europe and the United States. Studies done in Lebanon show a strong relationship between air pollution and emergency hospital admissions for respiratory and cardiovascular diseases. In 2008, the World Bank estimated an annual cost of pollution of 151 million dollars [1]. Air pollutants such as SO_x, NO_x, CO, CO_2, O_3, and particular matter ($PM_{2.5}$, PM_{10}) are considered harmful and dangerous to human health. These gases can be used to determine the air quality index (AQI) which is used by governmental agencies as a pollution indicator. There are different ways and equations to calculate AQI [2]. For this reason, ML (Machine Learning) is one of the tools which can evaluate air pollution in an accurate way and it can be used to predict its future by using algorithms. Posting these data on interactive websites will encourage the governmental and non-governmental institutes to push harder towards better air quality through

© Springer Nature Singapore Pte Ltd. 2020
S. M. Thampi et al. (Eds.): SoMMA 2019, CCIS 1203, pp. 135–143, 2020.
https://doi.org/10.1007/978-981-15-4301-2_11

the development and application of new legislations. There are many types of machine learning algorithms that can be used to classify air pollution, identify anomalies, and perform intelligent data analysis. The main contribution of this paper is to shed light on some specific machine learning algorithms like Artificial Neural Network, K-Nearest Neighbor, Support Vector Machine, and Naïve Bayes Classifier that would help to create valuable problem-solving platforms in identifying and warning affected areas.

2   Background and Related Work

Machine learning is one branch of artificial intelligence that provides computers with the ability to learn through the use of algorithms. The field of machine learning contains three main types [3]: supervised, unsupervised and reinforcement learning.

Supervised means to observe and direct the execution of a task, project, or activity. The basic idea for supervised learning is that the data provide examples of situations and for each example specifies an outcome (sometimes referred to as the "label" or "objective"), the machine then uses this training data to build a model which can predict the outcome of new data based on the past examples. Since the data in supervised learning has a known value for each example then the model can also be evaluated, this can be done by splitting the training data into two disjoint sets; the training set and the test set, the model can then be built on the training set and used to make a prediction for each instance in the test set. Since predictive values and initial values for every example in the test set are known, the performance of the model can be estimated at making predictions [3].

Unsupervised learning is letting the model work on its own to discover information and make correlations. The training data provides examples with no specific outcome because there is no label, so the machine instead tries to find interesting patterns in the data to draw conclusions. The main goal of this type of learning is to perform discovery rather than prediction. In comparison to supervised learning, unsupervised learning has a fewer tests and fewer models that can be used in order to ensure the outcome of the model is accurate, as such, unsupervised learning creates a less controllable environment as the machine is creating outcomes [3].

Reinforcement learning fills the gap between supervised and unsupervised learning. The algorithm knows if its answer is wrong but doesn't know, or is not told, how to correct it, so it's up to the algorithm to try and explore different strategies and possibilities until finding which works best [3].

The National Oceanic and Atmospheric Administration (NOAA) states that the U.S. spends billions of dollars to reduce air pollution [4]. Machine learning is a promising approach to solve the challenging task of providing accurate predictions of air quality. The work in [5] proposes a monitoring and prediction system that is built according to the four key layers in IoT (Internet of Things): application layer, perceptron layer, network layer, and physical layer. The first step in this design is measuring the most dangerous air pollutants like Carbone monoxide, Ozone, nitrogen dioxide, and sulfur dioxide using the MQ135-Gas Sensor, as well as measuring the temperature and humidity using DHT11 sensor. The collected data is then transmitted to the ESP8266 microcontroller which has the role of storing these data into the web server. A machine learning algorithm called

RNN (Recurrent Neural Network) composed of LTSM units (Long Short-Term Memory) is used to forecast the pollution rate. Contrary to traditional neural networks that have no memory, this algorithm has an internal loop by which it maintains information about the previous state which will be used for the prediction in the current state. Although RNN and LSTM reduce training cycle, RNN requires more resources to train.

The work in [6] focuses on ozone as a dangerous and harmful pollutant on human health, so a model is developed for smart cities to predict the level of ozone using deep learning and tested on big pollution and weather data in order to increase the accuracy of prediction. Deep learning is a class of machine learning technique that uses several processing layers of nonlinear information for the extraction and transfer of properties under supervision or without supervision, in addition to the analysis and classification of patterns. For better interaction with big data, a tool is used for data analysis called "In-Memory Computing", this technique has two main features which are parallel processing and Random-Access Memory (RAM) storage. The ozone and weather data were collected and prepared for training and prediction using the above technique of machine learning in Aarhus city. Although deep learning model offers training scalability, stability, and generalization with big data; it is extremely computationally expensive to train.

The work in [7] uses monitoring stations in Texas where special instruments are designed uniquely for each pollutant like ozone (O_3), sulfur dioxide (SO_2), nitrogen oxides (NO_x), carbon monoxide (CO), Lead (Pb), and particulate matter. As well as factors like wind speed and humidity were taken into consideration due to their effects on the concentration of particles in order to predict the future values of pollution concentration using neural network. This prediction was done using a large data for training the neural network. Furthermore, in this system, regression analysis is performed in order to examine the correlation between the actual and predicted results. This system uses advanced monitoring sites, but the used sites are expensive to establish and operate.

The work in [8] aims to predict the concentration of $PM_{2.5}$ among 52 cities in Japan. It involves the previous $PM_{2.5}$ concentrations along with other features such as wind speed and rain precipitations to compute $PM_{2.5}$ concentration levels in advance. The proposed system is based on a deep learning model that is pre-trained with a well-designed autoencoder for time series data and fine-tuned using RNN. The results proved that this system outperformed another prediction system developed by the National Institute for Environmental Studies in Japan.

The work in [9] consists of a DNN (deep neural network) with fusion components to predict the AQI, which is a metric that indicates the level of air pollution. A complex transformation component is used to find the spatial correlation between the influential factors in a distributed fusion network. The work in [10] consists of a Deep Air Learning approach to unify air quality feature selection, prediction and interpolation. The experiments performed on real world data showed excellent prediction results in the different zones of Beijing during the month of December 2015.

3 Proposed Model

To minimize the disadvantages of the published system, this paper presents a platform which is composed of four key layers that will be described below.

1. Sensing layer: comprises several sensing devices that deal with the environment. They are embedded to sense harmful gases in various regions and send feedback using the appropriate communication channel in the Network layer.
2. Networking layer: responsible for data transmission, it acts like a mediator between the two layers; sensing and middleware. This layer allows the collected data from sensors to be saved in the appropriate storage (Database).
3. Middleware layer: the collected data is processed using machine learning techniques to find the appropriate classification algorithm that gives the best results. The goal of this layer is to examine the ambient air in specific locations and determine whether it's polluted or not, and whether it affects people in the surrounding area.
4. Application layer: this layer provides a platform for users to monitor their air quality. This layer receives raw data from database that contains collected data from sensors and displays them on the web interface.

3.1 Implementation Tools

1. WEKA Software [11]: Waikato Environment for Knowledge Analysis is an open source machine learning software in Java developed by the University of Waikato, New Zealand. WEKA is a combination of machine learning algorithms, it is a powerful tool that supports various data mining tasks such as classification, clustering, regression, feature selection, and visualization.
2. XAMPP: free web server developed by Apache, it's an interpreter for scripts written in PHP language. In XAMPP software "PHP My Admin" is a control panel responsible for creation and management of the database [12].
3. Arduino Mega: it is a microcontroller board and the main processing unit that will be used to collect data from sensors using Arduino IDE provided by the Arduino website to develop the needed codes with C programing language.
4. Arduino Ethernet shield: this shield connects the Arduino to the internet in order to send data collected from sensors to the database.
5. MQ-135: high sensitivity sensor that detects the air quality including NH3, NO_x, alcohol, benzene, smoke, and CO2. This sensor is suitable for air quality monitoring as well it's a low-cost sensor.
6. MQ-7: a sensitive sensor to carbon monoxide and has several advantages such as long lifespan and low cost.
7. MQ-131: a sensitive sensor to ozone, compatible with Arduino used to detect the ozone concentration.

3.2 Offline Evaluation of ML Algorithms

Due to unavailability of monitoring stations in Lebanon that are specialized in collecting pollutants concentration and meteorological data using advanced and high-cost sensors, we were obliged to use an available dataset from Australia and apply our studies to it. This dataset contains information about the six major air pollutants which were mentioned above and composed of 157000 records. First, the data needs to be cleaned from null values, errors, and illogical data. In order to clean this dataset, 20000 records were taken from the original one and were modified using Excel to get rid of unrelated data.

Figure 1 shows thirteen columns, twelve of them represent the six major air pollutants concentration measures and their respective air quality index. However, to apply classification algorithms, a label in each row is needed, so the 13th column which indicates the overall AQI is changed to a label using a script to change all the values of the last column to 0, 1, 2, 3, where these numbers are replaced by good, moderate, poor and bad respectively in the Excel file.

NO2	O3_1hr	O3_4hr	CO	PM10	PM2.5	AQI_CO	AQI_NO2	AQI_O3_1	AQI_O3_4	AQI_PM1(	AQI_PM2.	AQI_Site
0.015	0	0	0.59	21.84	10.12	6	12	0	1	43	40	43
0.014	0.001	0.001	0.48	17.35	10.14	5	11	1	1	34	40	40
0.016	0	0.001	0.55	21.52	9.94	6	13	0	1	43	39	43
0.015	0.001	0.001	0.47	17.33	10.08	5	13	1	1	34	40	40
0.018	0.001	0.001	0.45	17.56	9.53	5	15	1	2	35	38	38
0.019	0.001	0.001	0.51	21.24	9.51	5	16	1	1	42	38	42
0.019	0.001	0.002	0.45	17.38	9.24	5	16	1	3	34	36	36
0.022	0.001	0.001	0.5	21	9.26	5	18	1	2	42	37	42
0.024	0.001	0.005	0.46	20.72	8.88	5	20	1	6	41	35	41
0.022	0.001	0.008	0.43	17.31	9.19	4	18	1	10	34	36	36
0.028	0.001	0.013	0.41	20.35	8.29	4	23	1	16	40	33	40
0.023	0.002	0.017	0.4	16.92	8.9	4	19	2	21	33	35	35
0.024	0.004	0.027	0.37	16.94	8.61	4	20	4	33	33	34	34
0.023	0.015	0.029	0.33	19.58	7.66	3	19	15	37	39	30	39
0.008	0.024	0.034	0.33	16.79	8.24	3	6	24	43	33	32	43
0.009	0.034	0.038	0.31	19.5	7.54	3	8	34	47	39	30	47
0.001	0.038	0.039	0.31	16.8	7.99	3	1	38	49	33	31	49
0	0.04	0.039	0.31	16.73	7.82	3	0	40	48	33	31	48
0.003	0.04	0.039	0.31	19.37	7.76	3	3	40	49	38	31	49

Fig. 1. Cleaned dataset

The values of the AQI site were labeled according to Australia State of the Environment [13], where each range of AQI indicates a specific category; Good (0–66), Moderate (67–99), Poor (100–149) and Bad ($\geq$150) (Table 1).

Table 1. AQI ranges and their respective category

AQI range	Category
0–66	Good
67–99	Moderate
100–149	Poor
$\geq$150	Bad

There are several classification algorithms that can be implemented in this study, four of them were used: K-Nearest Neighbor (KNN), Support Vector Machine (SVM), Multilayer Perceptron (MLP), and Naïve Bayes Classifier. However, in order to apply classification algorithms, train and test data using WEKA software, the CSV file is converted into ARFF format (Attribute-Relation File Format) as shown in Fig. 2.

```
@relation pollution

@attribute NO2 NUMERIC
@attribute O3_1hr NUMERIC
@attribute O3_4hr NUMERIC
@attribute CO NUMERIC
@attribute PM10 NUMERIC
@attribute PM2.5 NUMERIC
@attribute AQI_CO NUMERIC
@attribute AQI_NO2 NUMERIC
@attribute AQI_O3_1hr NUMERIC
@attribute AQI_O3_4hr NUMERIC
@attribute AQI_PM10 NUMERIC
@attribute AQI_PM2.5 NUMERIC


@attribute class {good, moderate, poor, bad}

@data
0.015   0       0       0.59    21.84   10.12   6       12      0       1       43      40      good
0.014   0.001   0.001   0.48    17.35   10.14   5       11      1       1       34      40      good
0.016   0       0.001   0.55    21.52   9.94    6       13      0       1       43      39      good
0.015   0.001   0.001   0.47    17.33   10.08   5       13      1       1       34      40      good
0.018   0.001   0.001   0.45    17.56   9.53    5       15      1       2       35      38      good
0.019   0.001   0.001   0.51    21.24   9.51    5       16      1       1       42      38      good
```

Fig. 2. ARFF file.

Afterwards, data is split into 80% training and 20% testing and all four algorithms are trained on the Australian dataset. The obtained models gave the results shown in Table 2. MLP gives the highest accuracy, where Naïve Bayes gives the lowest accuracy.

Table 2. Algorithms comparison

	KNN	Naïve Bayes classifier	MLP	SVM
Accuracy	98.77%	90.55%	99.10%	96.93%
Mean absolute error	0.0062	0.0484	0.0055	0.2527
Root mean squared error	0.0781	0.2027	0.0647	0.3162

New unseen data were tested on MLP model (the one with highest accuracy) were 39 out of 40 records were correctly classified (Fig. 3). In addition, this software allowed us to predict the value of any pollutant parameters.

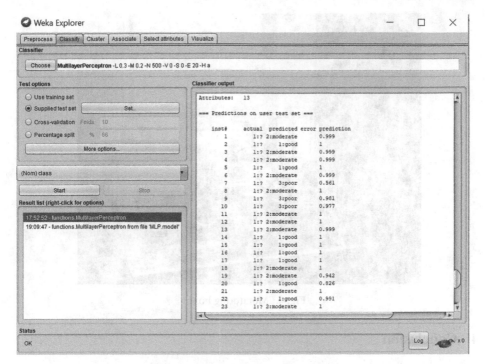

Fig. 3. Air quality classification

3.3 Online Evaluation of ML Algorithms

In order to create an interactive interface with the user, a website is developed to monitor the air quality. For this purpose, a box shown in Fig. 4 was assembled to collect weather and pollutants information from various sensors (MQ-135, MQ-131, MQ-7, DHT21) as a model. The web interface is composed of three major pages that have the following design: a home page, a map containing marker which indicates the location of monitoring, and a chart which shows the measured gases on a 24 h basis. A script code was written for data collection and transmission to the website.

The collected data are used to train a new MLP model that will help in predicting the pollution in various locations using WEKA. The obtained accuracy was above 98% which represents a good model that would help in predicting the class of new unseen data.

The classification algorithms used in our system show good results, where all of them have accuracy above 90%. Moreover, three of them: KNN, SVM, and Naïve Bayes are simple algorithms and need less training time. The fourth algorithm (ANN) needs more time to train data because it's much-complicated algorithm than the other three. Since in our system there is no need to implement any algorithm on hardware, ANN is the one used to classify new data since it has the best results. In addition, the web interface forms a good platform to inform people about their environmental information. This model will be developed further by adding extra sensors and recording data over longer period of time.

Fig. 4. Monitoring box

4 Conclusion

This paper sheds the light on the importance of artificial intelligence and machine learning technologies in all fields, especially in air pollution, which has become a worldwide problem over the past decades. Moreover, the system emphasizes the importance of selecting the most suitable supervised machine learning algorithms for air pollution data modeling. The obtained results revealed that Artificial Neural Network had the best performance measures on air pollution datasets, and highest accuracy among KNN, SVM, and Naïve Bayes Classifier. In addition, WEKA software offers variety of ML techniques and algorithms that helped in accomplishing our research. Finally, we aim that the presented system made a good use of experience and knowledge with intelligent technologies which represent the future of our world.

References

1. Chabarekh, C., Afif, C., Nagl, C., Mitri, G.: Lebanon's National Strategy for Air Quality Management for 2030, Department of Air Quality, Service of Environmental Technology, MoE (2017)
2. Bishoi, B., Prakash, A., Jain, V.K.: A comparative study of air quality index based on factor analysis and US-EPA methods for an urban environment. Aerosol Air Qual. Res. **9**, 1–17 (2009)
3. Sanjeevi, M.: Different types of machine learning and their types. Medium, 26 September 2017. https://medium.com/deep-math-machine-learning-ai/different-types-of-machine-learning-and-their-types-34760b9128a2
4. National Oceanic and Atmospheric Administration (NOAA): State of the science fact sheet, United States Department of Commerce, Washington, DC, Technical report (2016). https://nrc.noaa.gov/CouncilProducts/ScienceFactSheets.aspx

5. Ayele, T.W., Mehta, R.: Air pollution monitoring and prediction using IoT. In: International Conference on Inventive Communication and Computational Technologies (ICICCT 2018), Vadodara, India (2018)
6. Ghoneim, O.A., Doreswamy, Manjunatha, B.R.: Forecasting of ozone concentration in smart city using deep learning. Department of Computer Science, Mangalore University, Karnataka, India (2016)
7. Mbarak, A., Yetis, Y., Jamshidi, M.: Data-based pollution forecasting via machine: case of Northwest Texas. Department of Electrical and Computer Engineering University of Texas at San Antonio, San Antonio, Texas, USA
8. Ong, B.T., Sugiura, K., Zettsu, K.: Dynamically pre-trained deep recurrent neural networks using environmental monitoring data for predicting PM2.5. Neural Comput. Appl. **27**, 1553–1566 (2016). https://doi.org/10.1007/s00521-015-1955-3
9. Yi, X., Zhang, J., Wang, Z., Li, T., Zheng, Y.: Deep distributed fusion network for air quality prediction. In: Proceedings of the 24th SIGKDD International Conference on Knowledge Discovery Data Mining, pp. 965–973 (2018)
10. Wang, Z., Qi, T., Song, G., Hu, W., Li, X., Zhang, Z.M.: Deep air learning: interpolation, prediction, and feature analysis of fine-grained air quality. IEEE Trans. Knowl. Data Eng. **30**, 2285–2297 (2018)
11. T. U. o. W. (NZ). https://www.cs.waikato.ac.nz/ml/WEKA/
12. Apache Friends. https://www.apachefriends.org
13. Australia State of the Environment: Air quality index Abient air quality (2016). https://soe.environment.gov.au/theme/ambient-air-quality/topic/2016/air-quality-index

Facial Emotion Recognition
Using Shallow CNN

T. K. Sachin Saj$^{(\boxtimes)}$, Seshu Babu$^{(\boxtimes)}$, Vamsi Kiran Reddy, P. Gopika,
V. Sowmya, and K. P. Soman

Center for Computational Engineering and Networking (CEN),
Amrita School of Engineering, Amrita Vishwa Vidyapeetham,
Coimbatore, India
sachin96saj@gmail.com, seshuamrita123@gmail.com, v_sowmya@cb.amrita.edu

Abstract. Facial emotional recognition became an important task in
the modern day scenario to understand the state of emotions of a human
being by machines. With the development of computational power and
deep learning techniques, facial emotion recognition (FER) became feasible, which contributed to a wide range of applications in modern day
technology. In this paper, we propose a shallow convolutional neural network architecture with feature-based data, which can do this task more
effectively and attained the state-of-the-art accuracy with less computational complexity (in terms of learnable parameters). The proposed
architecture is shallow and gives comparable performance with all the
existing approaches for FER in deep learning.

Keywords: Deep learning · CNN · Facial emotion recognition

1 Introduction

Facial expressions render more information, which can be used to understand the
psychological state of a human being. The automatic facial emotion recognition
(FER) is very important and it's a challenging problem in the community of
computer vision [1]. This was successful in attracting attention in the modern
world due to its wide potential applications in areas such as robotics, autonomous
car, communication, health care etc. [2]. Convolutional neural network (CNN)
architectures in deep learning have achieved significant results in the field of
computer vision [3].

There exists many FER methods from past many years. In [2], the authors
have introduced two approaches for their FER method. One such method was
the use of auto-encoders but, it was unable to generate proper results and the
second method, CNN architecture with only 3 convolution layers, 3 max-pooling
layers and 2 fully connected layers. Through this architecture, they were successful in generating state-of-the-art accuracy with JAFFE dataset. In [4], the
authors proposed a method based on a weighted mixture deep neural network,

which process both grey scale facial emotion images as well as local binary pattern (LBP) facial images simultaneously. The weighted fusion techniques were used to improve the recognition ability. A partial VGG16 network is being constructed to extract features from the grey scale facial images and shallow CNN architecture is constructed to extract features from LBP facial images. They have done their evaluation on three benchmark dataset to verify the effectiveness of their proposed approach. Their approach was able to give better state-of-the-art accuracy and was compared with other existing approaches in FER.

Even though the computational complexity was high in [4], they were able to recognize the facial expression in few seconds and have high accuracy. In this paper, we propose a shallow CNN with feature-based data as the input in order to reduce the computational complexity (in terms of number of learnable parameters) of the architecture. The proposed architecture is experimented using JAFFE dataset, which attains comparable performance with all the existing FER approaches which use deep learning.

2   Proposed CNN Architecture

Based on previous publications and results, we understood the need to reduce the number of learnable parameters of the architecture without compromising the accuracy. So, we decided to design our own shallow CNN architecture from the scratch. Our proposed architecture is a 6-layer CNN with 3 convolution layers, 2 pooling layers and 1 fully connected layer. The proposed CNN architecture is shown in Fig. 1 and the details about the architecture is given in Table 1.

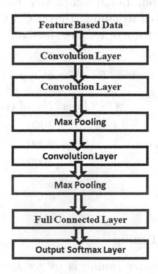

Fig. 1. Proposed shallow CNN architecture for Facial Emotional Recognition (FER)

Table 1. Details of the proposed shallow CNN architecture

Parameters	Conv2D	Conv2D	Max pooling	Conv2D	Max pooling
No. of filters	128	64	-	64	-
Size of the kernel	3×3	3×3	2×2	3×3	2×2
Strides	1	1	1	1	1
Padding	Same(1)	Valid(0)	-	Same(1)	-

3 Dataset Description

The dataset which we have used for facial emotion recognition is JAFFE dataset [2]. This dataset consists of 213 images of 10 different Japanese female posing for 7 different emotions such as happiness, sadness, surprise, anger, disgust, neutral and fear. The split of data is 70:30, where 70% of the data is used for training and 30% of the data is used for testing.

4 Results and Discussion

JAFFE dataset is given to our proposed shallow CNN architecture in three different ways: one as raw input without data augmentation, second as raw input with data augmentation and finally feature-based data is given, which is extracted using haar cascade package from OpenCV library. In this, only the features of the face are selected and the rest of the portions are deleted, thus helping in reducing the computational complexity. From Table 2, it is clear that, feature based data when given to sample 1-layer CNN architecture ran for 1000 epochs, outperformed other ways of feeding the data.

Table 2. Test accuracy for different types of data input

Data	CNN layer	No. of epochs	Test accuracy (%)
Raw input	1	1000	22.27
Raw input (data augmentation)	1	1000	50.32
Feature based data	1	1000	62.39

4.1 Hyper-Parameter Tuning

The reason for hyper-parameter tuning is to get the best combination of the number of filters in each layers, where the highest accuracy can be achieved. It is evident from the Table 2 that, with feature-based data given to 1-layer CNN, an accuracy of 62.39% is achieved. From Table 3, it is evident that the accuracy

Table 3. Hyper-Parameter tuning for no. of filters in each layer of convolution layer

No. of layers	No. of filters (each layers)	Batch size	Epochs	Test accuracy (%)
3	**128-64-64**	**20**	**3000**	**91.93**
3	128-64-64	20	2000	90.30
3	64-32-32	20	2000	87.09
3	256-128-128	20	2000	88.70
3	512-256-256	20	2000	88.70

increases with the number of CNN layers (from 1 layer to 3 layers) and epochs (1000 to 3000).

It is evident from the Table 3 that, 128-64-64 number of filter combinations in each layer gave the best result when it ran for 2000 epochs compared to all other combinations. Then all the combination was again ran for 1000 more epochs in which, only 128-64-64 combination was able to improve its accuracy from 90.30% to 91.93%. So, 3-layer CNN architecture with 128-64-64 number of the filter in each layer combination gave the best result. All the experiments were implemented by using keras [5] and scikit-learn [6] libraries.

4.2 Performance Measure

The performance of the proposed architecture which gave better results compared to all other combinations is evaluated on test data set. The details of the result are shown in Table 4.

Table 4. The performance measures for the proposed architecture

Class	Precision	Recall	F1-score
Happiness	0.89	1.00	0.94
Sadness	1.00	0.90	0.95
Surprise	0.67	1.00	0.80
Anger	1.00	1.00	1.00
Disgust	0.88	1.00	0.93
Neutral	1.00	0.69	0.82
Fear	1.00	1.00	1.00

It is evident from the Table 4, four classes have achieved 100% in precision and five classes were able to achieve 100% in recall. The f1-score which is a weighted average of precision and recall, represents the accuracy of the classifier in classifying the images in that particular class compared to all other classes. Among the obtained result, two classes achieved 100% and the rest of the classes is above 80%.

4.3   Comparison with Existing Approaches

To determine the performance of the classifier, confusion matrix corresponding to our proposed architecture is being taken and it is compared with the confusion matrix [4]. This is shown in Tables 5 and 6.

Table 5. Confusion matrix of our proposed architecture

	Happiness	Sadness	Surprise	Anger	Disgust	Neutral	Fear
Happiness	**0.89**	0.00	0.00	0.00	0.00	0.11	0.00
Sadness	0.00	**1.00**	0.00	0.00	0.00	0.00	0.00
Surprise	0.00	0.00	**0.67**	0.00	0.00	0.33	0.00
Anger	0.00	0.00	0.00	**1.00**	0.00	0.00	0.00
Disgust	0.00	0.12	0.00	0.00	**0.88**	0.00	0.00
Neutral	0.00	0.00	0.00	0.00	0.00	**1.00**	0.00
Fear	0.00	0.00	0.00	0.00	0.00	0.00	**1.00**

True label / Predicted label

In [4], the authors proposed an architecture considered only six facial emotions such as anger, disgust, fear, happiness, sadness and surprise and was able to achieve an accuracy of 92.2%. In present work, we considered all the seven facial emotions including neutral emotion and we were able to achieve the comparable result of 91.93% with [4]. In our proposed architecture, we were able to get 100% classification accuracy in four classes such as sadness, anger, neutral and fear. Only in surprise class, misclassification of 33% with a neutral class occurs. Whereas in [4], the proposed architecture was able to obtain more than 89% classification accuracy in all the classes. So, in our proposed architecture, even though we considered one more extra facial expression we were able to achieve the comparable result (91.93%).

Table 6. Confusion matrix of benchmark paper [4]

	Anger	Disgust	Fear	Happiness	Sadness	Surprise
Anger	**0.95**	0.02	0.01	0.00	0.02	0.00
Disgust	0.02	**0.89**	0.06	0.00	0.03	0.00
Fear	0.03	0.04	**0.90**	0.00	0.03	0.00
Happiness	0.01	0.00	0.02	**0.94**	0.00	0.03
Sadness	0.00	0.05	0.03	0.00	**0.91**	0.01
Surprise	0.02	0.00	0.02	0.03	0.00	**0.93**

True label / Predicted label

The Table 7 shows the comparsion of the proposed architecture with some of the existing facial emotion recognition methods in deep learning.

Table 7. Comparison of proposed architecture with the existing approaches in FER

Existing approaches	Testing accuracy (%)
Aly et al. [7]	87.32
Rivera et al. [8]	88.75
Prudhvi [2]	86.38
Zhang et al. [9]	91.48
Yank et al. [4]	92.21
Proposed architecture	91.93

It is evident from the Table 7, our proposed architecture was able to outperform many existing approaches in FER.

The Table 8, shows the number of learnable parameters of our proposed architecture compared with learnable parameters of the existing approaches.

Table 8. Comparison of learnable parameter of proposed architecture with the existing approaches

Approaches	Learnable parameters
Yang et al. [4]	58,482,062 (approx.)
Prudhvi [2]	440,167
Proposed architecture	18,990,471

The work proposed by Yank et al., is considered as the benchmark paper and the work proposed by Prudhvi, is considered as the base paper. It is evident from the Table 7, our architecture was able to give better accuracy than the results obtained in [2], and was able to achieve comparable accuracy with Yang et al. From Table 8, it is clear that the number of learnable parameters in [2] is very less and our proposed architecture have more learnable parameters than of [2], but we were able to increase the accuracy. When compared with, the learnable parameter in that architecture proposed in [4] is about 58,482,062 and ours is 18,990,471. We were successful in reducing the number of learnable parameters three times of the benchmark paper and still we were able to achieve the comparable accuracy with [4]. Hence, we have reduced the complexity (in terms of number of learnable parameters) to a larger extent without compromise on accuracy by using the feature based approach on JAFFE dataset [2].

5   Conclusion

This study proposes a method which uses shallow CNN architecture with feature-based data of JAFFE dataset. The proposed method is able to achieve state-of-the-art-accuracy with reduced number of learnable parameters compared to existing approaches based on deep learning for Facial Emotion Recognition. The performance of the proposed shallow CNN for Facial Emotional Recognition is mainly due to the haar cascade features extracted from the images are given as input to the proposed architecture. The future scope on the present work is to extend the analysis of feature based shallow CNN for the classification problems in other domains such as bio-medical and image based cyber security applications.

References

1. Lopes, A.T., De Aguiar, E., Oliveira-Santos, T.: A facial expression recognition system using convolutional networks. In: 2015 28th SIBGRAPI Conference on Graphics, Patterns and Images, pp. 273–280. IEEE (2015)
2. Dachapally, P.R.: Facial emotion detection using convolutional neural networks and representational autoencoder units. arXiv preprint arXiv:1706.01509 (2017)
3. Vinayakumar, R., Soman, K.P., Poornachandran, P.: Applying convolutional neural network for network intrusion detection. In: 2017 International Conference on Advances in Computing, Communications and Informatics (ICACCI), pp. 1222–1228. IEEE (2017)
4. Yang, B., Cao, J., Ni, R., Zhang, Y.: Facial expression recognition using weighted mixture deep neural network based on double-channel facial images. IEEE Access **6**, 4630–4640 (2018)
5. Gulli, A., Pal, S.: Deep Learning with Keras. Packt Publishing Ltd., Birmingham (2017)
6. Pedregosa, F., et al.: Scikit-learn: machine learning in python. J. Mach. Learn. Res. **12**(Oct), 2825–2830 (2011)
7. Aly, S., Abbott, A.L., Torki, M.: A multi-modal feature fusion framework for kinect-based facial expression recognition using dual kernel discriminant analysis (DKDA). In: 2016 IEEE Winter Conference on Applications of Computer Vision (WACV), pp. 1–10. IEEE (2016)
8. Rivera, A.R., Castillo, J.R., Chae, O.O.: Local directional number pattern for face analysis: face and expression recognition. IEEE Trans. Image Process. **22**(5), 1740–1752 (2013)
9. Zhang, W., Zhang, Y., Ma, L., Guan, J., Gong, S.: Multimodal learning for facial expression recognition. Pattern Recogn. **48**(10), 3191–3202 (2015)

Lead Artist Identification from Music Videos Using Auto-encoders

Prajwal Chandrashekaraiah$^{(\boxtimes)}$, Pranav H Kashyap, Sriharsha Hatwar, and Srinivasa Murthy

Department of Computer Science, PES University, Bengaluru, India
praji.1996@gmail.com, pranavkashyap39@gmail.com,
sriharsha02hatwar@gmail.com, hvsrinivasamurthy@pes.edu

Abstract. Music videos are now widely popular due to internet applications like YouTube and Facebook. Identifying lead artist from a music video is important in several scenarios including video classification, recommendation, etc. The proposed architecture involves using several image processing and machine learning techniques to identify the lead artist in the video. Firstly, selective frames are extracted from the video. Next, using DLib (a Deep Learning Library in C++) and YOLO (You Only Look Once) all the faces and corresponding human bodies are extracted from these frames. Auto Encoders are then used to encode and compare the facial features. Finally, the lead artist is selected by ranking the faces in order of frequency of occurrence in the video. Tests were performed on several music videos that were downloaded from the internet and the lead artist was identified successfully in most of them with an overall accuracy of the system being approximately 70% .

Keywords: Autoencoders · YOLO · DLib · Recall · Face-dictionary · Image processing

1 Introduction

With the widespread availability of internet applications like YouTube, Facebook, etc., music videos are widely circulated. Identifying the lead artist/singer from a music video is extremely important and useful in several circumstances like music video classification and music recommendation system. Many techniques have been applied that extract the audio features of the lead artist/singer and then match the features with existing lead artist/singer features. No exhaustive work has been done on the lines of lead artist identification using visual features. In this research project, we aim to identify a lead artist/singer based on visual features extracted from the video in a unique way. Specifically, using both image processing and machine learning techniques, we show how a lead artist can be identified. This visual identification technique is useful in several situations. Such visual features of the lead artist/singer can be combined with the

© Springer Nature Singapore Pte Ltd. 2020
S. M. Thampi et al. (Eds.): SoMMA 2019, CCIS 1203, pp. 151–161, 2020.
https://doi.org/10.1007/978-981-15-4301-2_13

audio features to perform lead artist/singer identification more robustly. This can also be used in enforcing copyright protection of the music videos. If the lead artist/singer is promoting a specific clothing or fashion, with further image processing, the same can be extracted. Finally, techniques mentioned here can also be applied to extract human actors from movies, surveillance and other videos.

2 Related Work

In this section we discuss research work that is related to this problem.

Brezeale and Cook [1] list a number of audio, text and visual features that are used for video classification. The visual features include colour-based features (texture, colour), object-based features (face, text), shot and motion-based features.

Schindler and Rauber [2] combine classifiers that are based on audio features and face recognition to identify an artist from a music video. Final predictions are based on weighted majority voting using bagging. It is observed that visual information provided by music videos improve the precision of artist identification. The average precision, recall and F1-score of the identification are 0.47, 0.38 and 0.37 respectively.

Face Recognition System (FRS) for images and videos is a popular research area. Stallkamp et al. [3] apply face recognition algorithms to real-time videos. Local appearance-based techniques first classify faces. By progressively combining the confidence scores from each classification, the face identity of the entire sequence is detected. They use distance-to-model, distance-to-second closest and their combination as measures to weigh the contribution of each frame to the overall classification decision.

Hashmat et al. [4] describes a technique of first detecting faces in a video, followed by verification against a set of preknown database of faces using the concept of skin like regions. The first step involves skin like regions detected in the CIELUV (CIE 1976 L*, u*, v*) colour space [5]. The second step involves the facial detection, trying to come up with a bounding box around faces based on these skins like detected regions, contour detection and geometrical properties like face shape, etc. The third step involves facial verification against a set of known faces using techniques like variance and skin to non-skin percentage in each facial feature.

Zheng et al. [6] leverage the two popular convolutional neural network models to achieve the task of person re-identification. These two models being the verification and identification models. The paper describes on how to combine the two models to learn more discriminative person descriptors. It proposes a network called as the Siamese network that simultaneously computes the identification loss and verification loss. So, as a result, the network predicts the identities of two input images as to whether they belong to the same identity or not. This is an alternative approach to face reidentification which just involves comparison of the faces, but here it involves comparison of the more generalized human descriptors/signatures. The problem of re-identification of human faces in a video surveillance system is addressed in [7]. In surveillance scenarios, face is not always in a frontal posture and may involve all kinds of postures. The re identification uses some of the features like hair, skin, and clothes. The 'Feret dataset' which has frontal gallery images is used for training and side probe images for testing.

The proposed algorithm analyses the colour and texture of the three patches and identifies the intensity correlation between those images to identify the similar ones. This analysis is further followed by the construction of a single, stronger classifier that combines the above measures to re-identify the person from his or her profile.

The authors of [8] propose a method for simultaneously learning features and a corresponding similarity metric for person reidentification. It explains about a deep neural network architecture that is specifically designed for the task of reidentification purpose at hand. Input for the system is a pair of images and the output is whether they belong to the same person or not. The architecture includes a layer that helps in capturing the similarity by computing cross-input neighborhood differences which internally captures local relationships between two images based on mid-level features from each input image. A high-level summary of the functionality of the layer is that the output of the layer is computed by a layer of patch summary features which are then spatially integrated into subsequent layers. The method proposed outperforms the state of the art on both large datasets (CUHK03, CUHK01) [9] and resistant to overfitting. Using CUHK03 dataset the model gave an accuracy of 40.5% and after 210K iterations it increased to 47.5%. The VIPeR dataset gave an accuracy of 34.18% when model was trained using CUHK03 and CUHK01.

3 YOLO – You Only Look Once

You Only Look Once (YOLO) [10–12] a state-of-the-art, real-time object detection system developed by Facebook AI Research. The basic idea of the algorithm is to identify and detect objects by looking at the image only once in an efficient way. Detection is a more complex problem than classification, which can also recognize objects but does not tell exactly where the object is located in the image — and it will not work for images that contain more than one object. YOLO divides up the image into a n * n grid (typically 7×7). For each grid it predicts B bounding boxes of arbitrary size. A bounding box is a rectangular box that encloses the object. If the threshold (hyper-parameter) is very high, then only objects that are completely enclosed by the box are considered. YOLO also outputs a confidence score that tells us how certain it is that the predicted bounding box encloses some object. This score doesn't say anything about what kind of object is in the box, just if the shape of the box is any good for each bounding box, the cell also predicts a class. This works just like a classifier: it gives a probability distribution over all the possible classes. The confidence score for the bounding box and the class prediction are combined into one final score that tells the probability that this bounding box contains a specific type of object. At 67 FPS, YOLOv2 gets 76.8 mAP (mean Average Precision) on VOC 2007 dataset [13].

4 Autoencoders

Autoencoders is a type of neural network which fits an identity function for a given input. It mainly involves two parts (Encoders and Decoders). Encoders convert the high dimensional data to lower dimensional representation (latent space). Decoders covert the concise representation of encoder output back to the original data. Encoder is a convolutional neural network, whereas decoder is a deconvolutional neural network. The goal is to compress the input data with the encoder, then decompress this encoded data with the decoder such that the output is a good/perfect reconstruction of the original input data. Since brute force comparison of faces (i.e. pixel-wise) for building a face dictionary is intractable, autoencoders is an efficient comparison mechanism as it preserves the low-level vital features and significantly reduces the dimensionality [14–16]. We are using auto-encoders for comparing faces extracted from the video. We have trained the auto-encoders model with a custom created dataset (called Lead-net - 10,000 coloured face images (100 * 100 pixels) of lead artists and co artists extracted by our pipeline from various video songs). We are using this custom trained model to encode any face image extracted from a given video to its corresponding auto encoded face vectors.

5 Implementation

We have applied basic image processing techniques using OpenCV and machine learning techniques for different tasks like video processing, human detection, face detection, face encoding and lead artist identification. The overall design and steps involved in the lead artist extraction is shown in Fig. 1. The reference made to a video in the later part of this section is that of Shakira's Waka-Waka song, for which we discuss and illustrate the results in a later section.

5.1 Frames Extraction

Given an input video, we break it into frames at 15 fps. We have assumed that the resolution of the input video must be 720p or higher. For a 5 min video (mp4 format) sampling at 15fps there will be 4500 frames. Getting more frames, will help in getting good quality frames for subsequent processing. This extraction can be done for multiple video formats and fps rating. We used the "videocap" method of cv2 module to extract the frames. The sample videos that were tested were downloaded from Youtube. Once extracted, the frames were saved as individual images. The naming convention of the images which are extracted will be saved according to the sequential order of its extraction. For example, the first frame which gets extracted is named as "frame1.jpg", the second as "frame2.jpg" and so on.

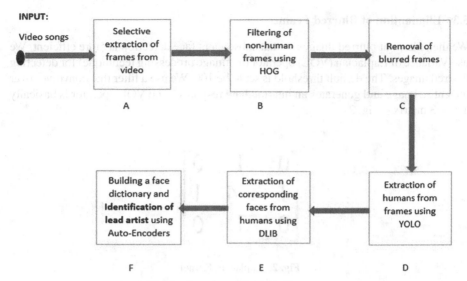

Fig. 1. System architecture diagram

5.2 Identification of Frames Containing Humans

From the extracted frames, we filter out frames that do not contain any humans. This was treated as a classification task where frames are classified into two classes viz. frames containing humans and other frames. We detect human frames using Histogram of Oriented Gradients (HOG descriptor/SVM detector) from OpenCV. HOG is a type of feature descriptor that depicts human objects as close as possible. Initially it has a sliding window which computes a feature vector of the entire image which is then provided to the SVM's (Support Vector machines) "GetDefaultPeopleDetector" method in OpenCV.

$$G_x(y, x) = Y(y, x + 1) - Y(y, x - 1). \tag{1}$$

$$G_y(y, x) = Y(y + 1, x) - Y(y - 1, x). \tag{2}$$

$Y(y, x)$ is the pixel intensity at coordinates x and y. $G_x(y, x)$ is the horizontal gradient, and $G_y(y, x)$ is the vertical gradient. The magnitude and phase of the gradient are determined as.

$$G(y, x) = \sqrt{\left(G_x(y, x)^2 + G_y(y, x)^2\right)}, \ \theta(y, x) = \arctan\left(G_y(y, x)/G_x(y, x)\right). \tag{3}$$

The SVM model is trained on human images and determines presence of human in the image. If the frame does not contain humans, the frame is discarded. After this step, approximately 30% to slightly greater than 50% of the frames were discarded from the original count. This may result in some false positives (~0.1%). For Shakira's waka-waka video, out of 1440 images which has been classified as human containing frames, there are around 15 frames which doesn't contain any humans in it. This results in a precision of about 98.95% and the error rate of the HOG-SVM detector comes to about 0.0104 for the same video.

5.3   Elimination of Blurred Frames

We then filter out blurred images so that subsequent face detection is more efficient. We use Variance of Laplacian (VOL) operator (an image processing technique) for detecting blurred images. The default threshold is set to be 100. We use a filter that convolves over the entire image and generates an intermediate response. The VOL operator is basically a 3×3 matrix – Fig. 2.

$$\begin{bmatrix} 0 & 1 & 0 \\ 1 & -4 & 1 \\ 0 & 1 & 0 \end{bmatrix}$$

Fig. 2. Laplacian Kernel

This filter is applied through an image and the variation of a pixel with its four neighbors is counted, summed up and averaged over the image. If the variance of the intermediate response is less than the threshold (meaning it is blurred), the image is discarded, or else it will be retained. After the convolving step the OpenCV's function would go over the entire image to calculate the difference between the value and the mean of the intermediate response at each point, then it would be summed up and is divided by the total number of elements in the intermediate response. If it is less than a threshold it means that the image is a blurred one. The number of blurred images discarded depends on the video. We found the range to be 50% to 65% of the number of frames obtained in previous step. The results until this step are illustrated in Fig. 3.

Fig. 3. The first set of frames (starting left) shows a sample of the extracted frames, followed by the filtering out of non-human frames in the second set of frames (middle) and filtering out of blurred frames in the third set of frames (right)

5.4 Human Extraction Using YOLO

Now all the frames contain crisp images of humans. We now extract humans along with their faces separately in each frame. YOLO is a pre-trained and a prebuilt architecture which has become the state of the art in segmentation and identification. It has been implemented in C. YOLO (You Only Look Once) is a CNN network implementation for classification. Localised Segmentation is an add-on to it. It is a real time state of the art object detection system. It has high mAP (Mean Average Precision) for extraction of humans and 20 other classes.

We used a python wrapper to call the pre-trained YOLO for object recognition. We loaded weights of PASCAL-VOC dataset (20 layers in Darknet) and the corresponding configuration files. We only considered human class and ignored the others. It predicts P bounding boxes by dividing the image into an x * y grid. It outputs the confidence and probability for each detection. Confidence specifies the extent to which an object is enclosed in the bounding box predicted and the corresponding mapping to the nearest class with the aid of probability measure. Threshold hyper-parameter of the model can be adjusted accordingly for stringent and perfect classification. False positives detected here can disrupt the results in the successive stages of the pipeline and hence this step is crucial.

5.5 Facial Extraction

For face extraction from human images, we have used a python module which is built using Dlib's (a Deep Learning Library in C++) state-of-the-art "face recognition" module. Its underlying architecture is a Convolution Neural Network which has an accuracy of 99.38% on "Labelled Faces in the WILD Benchmark (LFWB)" dataset.

The extracted faces are mapped to the corresponding human frames. The next step is to encode the faces and identify the lead artist. We assume that lead artist's face appears most often in the video and use this logic to identify the lead artist(s).

5.6 Building a Face Dictionary and Identification of Lead Artist

We used an existing architecture of deep auto-encoders and trained it on Lead-Net with KL regularization (Kullback – Leibler divergence). The network for vectorizing/encoding extracted faces to face vectors had an error of 0.098. The error signifies the loss between the original image and the reconstructed image. As the error is very low, identification of lead artist is performed with high confidence and recall.

$$D_{KL}(p\|q) = \sum_{i=1}^{N} p(x_i) \cdot log \frac{p(x_i)}{q(x_i)}. \tag{4}$$

KL Divergence, p - Original Distribution, q - Approximating Distribution.

We created a face dictionary with face (encoded vector) as key and frequency of its appearance in the video as value. Typically, we get thousands of faces from a 5 min video. We then consider the face with highest occurrence in the video as the face of the lead artist. As we already have the mapping to human bodies from the previous stage, we can then retrieve the human bodies of the lead artist. We have used scikit-learn Nearest Neighbors algorithm with its distance metric for finding the matches between faces. Each face is compared to all the other faces and its face count will be number of other faces that are 99.95% similar (threshold of 0.9995). The lead artist identification algorithm essentially outputs an $N \times N$ matrix, N being the total number of faces detected. A sample matrix is as shown in Fig. 4. Here the order of the rows represents the ranking of faces based on the face count and the order of columns represent the ranking based on the similarity score. For example, in the matrix shown, face F_1 has the highest face count, followed by F_2, F_3, and so on. Now faces F_{12}, F_{13}, F_{14} and so on are arranged in decreasing similarity with F_1 and so is the case with the other faces.

Ranking of faces based on similarity scores

Ranking of faces based on face count

F_1	F_{12}	F_{13}	F_{14}	F_{15}	F_{16}	F_{17}	F_{18}
F_2	F_{22}	F_{23}	F_{24}	F_{25}	F_{26}	F_{27}	F_{28}
F_3	F_{32}	F_{33}	F_{34}	F_{35}	F_{36}	F_{37}	F_{38}
F_4	F_{42}	F_{43}	F_{44}	F_{45}	F_{46}	F_{47}	F_{48}
F_5	F_{52}	F_{53}	F_{54}	F_{55}	F_{56}	F_{57}	F_{58}
F_6	F_{62}	F_{63}	F_{64}	F_{65}	F_{66}	F_{67}	F_{68}
F_7	F_{72}	F_{73}	F_{74}	F_{75}	F_{76}	F_{77}	F_{78}
F_8	F_{82}	F_{83}	F_{84}	F_{85}	F_{86}	F_{87}	F_{88}

Fig. 4. Face matrix showing the ranking based on face count (decreasing from top to bottom) and similarity scores (decreasing from left to right).

The faces in the first five rows and first five columns (5×5) would now essentially belong to the lead artist. The reason we are taking a subset here is to be able to capture the variations in the pose, attire, etc. of the lead artist. The results from steps 5.4 to 5.6 are illustrated in Fig. 5.

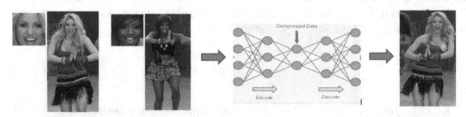

Fig. 5. Steps 5.4, 5.5 (left) which shows the faces and corresponding bodies (showing a sample of two images here) extracted from different frames, which are then provided as input to autoencoders (middle) for identification of lead artist (right) in step 5.6 (showing a sample of one image of the lead artist identified here)

6 Results and Discussion

The system was tested for 25 videos and achieved a recall of 70%. Positive results mean that the top 25 faces that were retrieved from the Lead Artist Identification Algorithm were all of the expected lead artist. The system failed to identify the lead artist in a few cases. Firstly, if the video had the lead artist appear in different attires, for example sometimes with spectacles and without. Secondly if the video had many artists on screen at the same time along with the actual lead artist. These are limitations of the current system and further work is needed to address these caveats.

The results have been tabulated for a subset of the input videos, as shown in Table 1.

Table 1. Results showing outcome for different videos and few performance metrics of the algorithm for each video.

Input video	Execution parameters					Outcome
	Length of video (in min)	No of frames (post pre-processing)	No of faces detected	Pre-processing time (in min)	Lead artist identification time (in min)	
Waka- Waka	3.500	643	742	16.833	9.167	Positively identified Shakira as the lead artist
Sorry	3.417	665	1148	13.833	10.583	Positively identified the lead artist
Despacito	4.683	866	695	21.167	12.583	Failed to identify the expected lead artist
Blank Space	4.533	246	83	20.667	3.000	Positively identified Taylor Swift as the lead artist
Gangnam Style	4.200	1,626	847	18.433	20.733	Failed to identify the expected lead artist
Kaala Chasma	2.883	2,195	1866	12.833	28.250	Positively identified Siddharth Malhotra as the lead artist
Swag Se Swagat	2.817	1,633	115	11.417	1.600	Positively identified Salman Khan as the lead artist

(continued)

Table 1. (*continued*)

Input video	Execution parameters					
	Length of video (in min)	No of frames (post pre-processing)	No of faces detected	Pre-processing time (in min)	Lead artist identification time (in min)	Outcome
Kush Kush	4.000	179	23	14.750	3.000	Positively identified Ganesh as the lead artist
Yeno Agide	4.667	332	61	28.000	4.500	Failed to identify the expected lead artist
Lungi Dance	3.500	2528	6425	30.000	58.250	Positively identified Shahrukh Khan as the lead artist

7 Conclusion

Identification of lead artist in a video has several important use cases like extraction of metadata of a video, extraction of fashionable items of the lead artist, and can also be used to support indexing of lead artist in the video. In this research project imaging and machine learning techniques are used to identify the lead artist. By using YOLO to detect faces and auto-encoders to encode the facial features, the problem has been reduced to that of facial vector matching to rank faces according to frequency of appearance. It is a new and a novel approach to tackle the problem using visual features especially with autoencoders. Experimental results show successful identification of lead artists. Our study suggests that a system using a neural architecture (rather than traditional algorithms) helps in distinguishing minute facial features which is utilized in similarity matching for lead artist identification. However, further work is needed to process videos that are lengthy, having multiple artists or where faces are not clearly visible.

Acknowledgment. The authors would like to acknowledge S Natarajan at PES University for his constant encouragement and support.

References

1. Brezeale, D., Cook, D.J.: Automatic video classification: a survey of the literature. IEEE Trans. Syst. Man Cybern. Part C (Appl. Rev.) **38**(3), 416–430 (2008)
2. Schindler, A., Rauber, A.: A music video information retrieval approach to artist identification. In: 10th Symposium on Computer Music Multidisciplinary Research (CMMR 2013) (2013)
3. Stallkamp, J., Ekenel, H.K., Stiefelhagen, R.: Video-based face recognition on real-world data. In: 2007 IEEE 11th International Conference on Computer Vision, ICCV 2007. IEEE (2007)

4. Heshmat, M., et al.: Face identification system in video. In: 2016 11th International Conference on Computer Engineering & Systems (ICCES). IEEE (2016)
5. Fedorovskaya, E.A.: Perceptual quality of color images of natural scenes transformed in CIELUV color space (1997)
6. Zheng, Z., Zheng, L., Yang, Y.: A discriminatively learned CNN embedding for person re identification. ACM Trans. Multimedia Comput. Commun. Appl. (TOMM) **14**(1), 13 (2017)
7. Dantcheva, A., Dugelay, J.-L.: Frontal-to-side face reidentification based on hair, skin and clothes patches. In: 2011 8th IEEE International Conference on Advanced Video and Signal-Based Surveillance (AVSS). IEEE (2011)
8. Ahmed, E., Jones, M., Marks, T.K.: An improved deep learning architecture for person re-identification. In: Proceedings of the IEEE Conference on Computer Vision and Pattern Recognition (2015)
9. CUHK person re-identification datasets. https://www.ee.cuhk.edu.hk/~xgwang/CUHK_identification.html
10. Redmon, J., et al.: You only look once: unified, real-time object detection. In: Proceedings of the IEEE Conference on Computer Vision and Pattern Recognition (2016)
11. Sistu, G.: Real-time joint object detection and semantic segmentation network for automated driving (2019)
12. Redmon, J., Farhadi, A.: YOLO9000: better, faster, stronger. arXiv preprint (2017)
13. The PASCAL visual object classes challenge (2007)
14. Berthelot, D.: Understanding and improving interpolation in autoencoders via an adversarial regularizer (2019). Google Brain
15. Le, Q.V.: A tutorial on deep learning Part 2: autoencoders convolutional neural networks and recurrent neural networks (2015). https://cs.stanford.edu/~quocle/tutorial2.pdf
16. Usman, M., Latif, S., Qadir, J.: Using deep autoencoders for facial expression recognition. In: 2017 13th International Conference on Emerging Technologies (ICET). IEEE (2017)

Enhanced Differential Evolution-Based EEG Channel Selection

Shireen Fathima[1(✉)] and Sheela Kiran Kore[2]

[1] Department of Electronics and Communication Engineering,
HKBK College of Engineering, Bengaluru, India
shireen.fathima6@gmail.com
[2] Department of Electronics and Communication Engineering,
KLE Dr. M. S. Sheshagiri College of Engineering and Technology, Belagavi, India
kle.ec.sheelakore@gmail.com

Abstract. Basically brain-computer interfaces (BCIs) make use of multichannel electroencephalogram (EEG) devices. Motor imagery tasks are at the core of BCIs and their performance in real-time systems need analysis of huge amounts of signal data coming from multiple channels. The process can be enhanced by selecting a subset of EEG channels to get away with noisy and irrelevant channels. Usage of lesser channels makes the system more convenient to be used in real time applications. This paper deals with the problem of optimal EEG channel selection using enhanced version of differential evolutionary (DE) algorithm. It is straightforward to use the task-specific channels pertaining to the stimulus like C_3, C_Z and C_4 in case of motor imagery. However, our findings show that the classification performance improves by selecting the optimal channels over the task-specific channels. Also, the performance of the optimal channels is compared with the performance achieved by using all the channels and it is seen that the proposed enhanced variant of DE is beneficial in this regard.

Keywords: EEG · Differential evolution · Optimization · Channel selection

1 Introduction

Brain computer interfaces (BCIs) are means of device control in a non-muscular form using brain signals. This is done by measuring, analyzing and decoding the signals acquired from brain using Electroencephalogram (EEG) device [1,2]. People with severe motor disabilities can make exclusive usage of BCIs for device control and communication [3]. Like EEG, there are many other physiological sensing modalities like pupillometry [4,5], Galvanic Skin Response (GSR) [6] and PPG [7], gaze tracking for device control [8] and cognitive assessments [9] and so on. However, they cannot be deployed in BCI scenarios as the signals are not as spontaneous and direct like brain waves acquired from EEGs. Apart from BCIs, brain waves have been used in a variety of applications like random

© Springer Nature Singapore Pte Ltd. 2020
S. M. Thampi et al. (Eds.): SoMMA 2019, CCIS 1203, pp. 162–174, 2020.
https://doi.org/10.1007/978-981-15-4301-2_14

number generation [10], cognitive states estimation like cognitive load [11], flow, boredom and anxiety [6]; training and assessment purposes [12] and so on.

BCIs make use of signals acquired from multiple scalp sites for achieving good results [13]. The main issue with this analogy is the redundancy and the noisy signals that become prevalent when large number of channels are used resulting in degraded performance of BCI [14,15]. Large number of channels results in large data and thus adds to the preparation and analysis time making the BCI application inconvenient to use. Hence, a subset of channels can improve performance as well as the user experience owing to the less preparation time. The task of selecting the optimal channels is not straightforward. Merely selection of channels manually based on the domain knowledge may not necessarily guarantee better results in comparison to using all the available channels [13].

There has been a lot of work carried on in the field of selecting the optimal EEG channels for a given BCI task, however, the solution to this problem is still in its phase of infancy [16]. This paper deals with selecting a subset of optimal channels that are subject dependent. The term, "all channels" used throughout the paper, refers to the available EEG channels as per the 10–20 norms. The works in [17–19] have used the channels that are most relevant to motor imagery tasks, i.e. C_3, C_Z and C_4, for BCI-based applications. In this paper, we have shown the effect of using these three channels on the BCI performance against the utilization of optimal EEG channels.

The rest of the paper is divided into the following sections. The most closely relevant works pertaining to the target research problem is discussed in Sect. 2. Section 3 briefs the methodology deployed in the current implementation of BCI. The results of the proposed work along with the existing methods is discussed in Sect. 4. The concluding remarks and the future roadmap of this work are given in Sect. 5.

2   Related Work

2.1   Channel Selection Using Optimization

In [14,15,20,21] the channel selection constraint is fed into a classifier like a standard support vector machine (SVM) that would recursively do away with the least contributing channels while computing the overall classification accuracy. There have been various attempts in using meta-heuristic optimization algorithms like genetic algorithm (GA) [22], particle swarm optimization (PSO) [23], ant colony optimization (ACO) [24], differential evolution [25] and so on in the feature selection space. It is to be noted that unlike the conventional feature selection tools which usually search for the optimal number of features $z < Z$ number of total features, our work targets a channel selection problem in which the value of z is pre-specified. The reason is that in cases with thousands of features with optimal solution being a small subset of features, the unconstrained versions of PSO and GA suffer tremendously by selecting subsets having large dimensionality [25]. Another advantage of using a constrained feature selection technique is that it provides a means to analyze the effect of varying size of z

which may vary or is not feasible with the unconstrained versions of optimization. Moreover, the works of Khushaba et al. [25] have shown that the variant of DE for feature selection is better in performance than the equivalent versions of GA, PSO, ACO. This paper proposes an enhanced version of the approach specified in the works of [25] by using a gaussian kernel-based mutant operator for DE-based channel selection problem. Since the proposed technique is built upon the capabilities of DE, a detailed mathematical review of the DE algorithm is provided in the subsequent section to help in understanding the contribution of the current work better.

2.2   Mathematical Review of Differential Evolution Algorithm

The DE algorithm consists of the following operations,

Initialization

First, the DE searches for a solution (global optimum) in the M - dimensional space bearing population $x_i = [x_{i,1}, x_{i,2}, ..., x_{i,M}]$, with $i = 1, 2, ..., N$; where N is the size of the population. The initial population spans uniformly in the search space defined by the lower and upper bounds L and U.

Mutation

The mutation operation deals with creating the mutant vector m_i where $i = 1, 2, ..., D$ for every target vector x_i. D is the dimensionality of the search space. There have been various existing variants of the mutation operation, few of which are listed below,

(i) DE/rand/1

$$m_i = x_{a1} + F \times (x_{a2} - x_{a3}) \tag{1}$$

(ii) DE/best/1

$$m_i = x_{best} + F \times (x_{a1} - x_{a2}) \tag{2}$$

(iii) DE/current-to-best/1

$$m_i = x_i + F \times (x_{best} - x_{a1}) + F \times (x_{a2} - x_{a3}) \tag{3}$$

(iv) DE/best/2

$$m_i = x_{best} + F \times (x_{a1} - x_{a2}) + F \times (x_{a3} - x_{a4}) \tag{4}$$

(v) DE/rand/2

$$m_i = x_{a1} + F \times (x_{a2} - x_{a3}) + F \times (x_{a4} - x_{a5}) \tag{5}$$

wherein the indexes a_1 through a_5 are mutually exclusive random values taken from set $1, 2, ..., N$ and they are not equal to index i. x_{best} is the best individual available from the current population set. F is scaling factor which is a value (>0) being used to scale the difference vector. This work mainly deals with the enhancement of the scaling factor F for finding the global solution as explained in the subsequent sections.

Crossover

A binomial crossover operator is performed upon the mutant vector m_i and the target vector x_i, for generating a trial vector $y_i = [y_{i,1}, y_{i,2}, ..., y_{i,D}]$ as,

$$y_{i,j} = \begin{cases} v_{i,j}, & \text{if } (rand[0, 1] \leq CR \text{ or } j = j_{rand}) \\ x_{i,j}, & \text{otherwise.} \end{cases} \tag{6}$$

The crossover rate (CR) is basically a user-defined constant lying in the range $(0, 1)$ which is responsible for controlling the fraction of trial vectors that are inherited from mutant vector. j_{rand} is selected randomly from the set $1, 2, ..., D$ so that the trial vector consists of atleast a single entity which is different from the target vector.

Selection

The selection process is performed among the trial and the target vectors as per the fitness value $f()$. The solution which is better and analogous to "survival of the fittest" analogy in the living kingdom is carried forward to the next generation. The operation is performed as,

$$x_i = \begin{cases} u_i, & \text{if } f(u_i) \leq f(x_i) \\ x_i, & \text{otherwise.} \end{cases} \tag{7}$$

This step ensures that the population set either gets better or remains the same but never gets deteriorated in terms of its fitness status.

3 Methodology

The brief outlook of the proposed methods used is shown in Fig. 1. The EEG data collected is subject to feature extraction phase (step 2 in Fig. 1) followed by division of the data into training, validation and testing components. The optimization of channel selection problem is given in block 5 in the figure and the enhanced version of optimization schema is given in block 6. The optimum channels thus selected are subject to classification. The study basically deals with a four class classification problem.

3.1   Data Acquisition

For the current study, we have used the 4-class motor imagery dataset 2a from BCI Competition IV [26]. The dataset consists of EEG signals acquired from 22 Ag/AgCl electrodes placed at a distance of 3.5 cm apart as shown in Fig. 2. The right mastoid was used as ground while the left as reference. The sampling rate at which the data was collected is 250 Hz. The signals are bandpass filtered in the range of 0.5 to 100 Hz and the amplifier sensitivity is set to 100 μV. The line noise was suppressed using an additional 50 Hz notch filter.

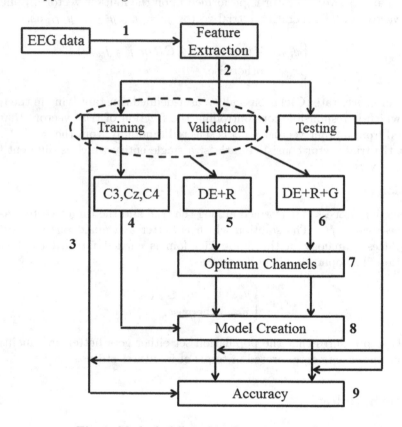

Fig. 1. Methods followed in the current study

3.2   Participants and Stimulus Used

The dataset comprised of nine participants. The participants were asked to sit on a comfortable armchair. The computer screen was placed right in their front. The BCI paradigm used for the data collection was mainly cue-based. It comprised of four motor imagery tasks, viz.,

– Imagining moving of left hand: $Class - 1$
– Imagining moving of right hand: $Class - 2$

- Imagining moving both the feet: $Class - 3$
- Imagining moving of the tongue: $Class - 4$

Two different sessions consisting of the above tasks was conducted on two different days for each subject and their corresponding EEG data was recorded. Each session comprised of 6 runs with short breaks in between wherein each run consisted of 48 trials having a balanced set of 12 trials per class of the above discussed motor imagery schemes. A total of 288 trials per session is provided. Figure 3 shows a sample EEG signal for four classes taken from location C_Z for a particular participant.

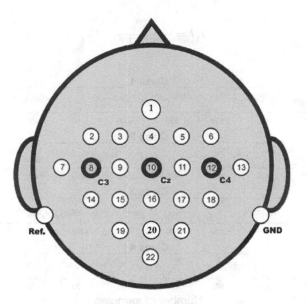

Fig. 2. Electrode placement

The stimulus used in this case is shown using the sequence diagram in Fig. 4. It comprised fixation cross ('+') on a black screen shown right at the beginning of the task. An acoustic warning tone was given. After two seconds, the cues in the form of arrows pointing to either left, right, top or bottom that corresponded to each of the four classes of motor imagery discussed previously were shown. These cues lasted for around 1.25 s on the screen. The participants were supposed to perform these tasks with full involvement until the fixation cross disappeared (time $t = 6$ s). This was followed by a quick short break which turned the screen black as the initial baseline screen.

3.3   Feature Extraction

The raw EEG from each channel is segmented into windows of length 3 s. The features extracted [6], *Feat* is given by,

$$Feat = \{E^\delta, E^\theta, E^{L\alpha}, E^{H\alpha}, E^{L\beta}, E^{H\beta}, E^{L\gamma}, E^{H\gamma}, EI, H^a, H^m, H^c\} \quad (8)$$

The first 8 features in *Feat* are the powers in bands with frequency ranges given by [27], delta (1–3 Hz), theta (4–7 Hz), low-alpha (8–9 Hz), high-alpha (10–12 Hz), low-beta (13–17 Hz), high-beta (18–30 Hz), low-gamma (31–40 Hz), high-gamma (41–50 Hz), respectively. Feature *EI* is the engagement index [28] given by,

$$EI = \frac{E^\beta}{E^\alpha + E^\theta} \quad (9)$$

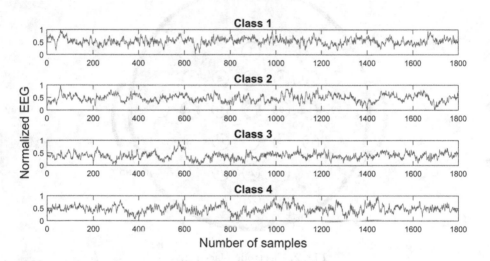

Fig. 3. Sample EEG data for the four classes taken from location C_Z for a particular participant

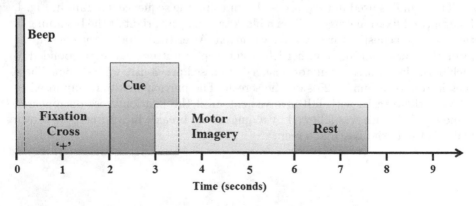

Fig. 4. Stimulus

The last three features are the Hjorth features [29] namely, Activity ($H^a =$ $var(x(t))$), Mobility ($H^m = \sqrt{\frac{H^a(\frac{dx(t)}{dt})}{H^a(x(t))}}$) and Complexity ($H^c = \sqrt{\frac{H^m(\frac{dx(t)}{dt})}{H^m(x(t))}}$), where $x(t)$ is the time domain signal representation for a given window length and $\frac{dx(t)}{dt}$ is the first order derivative of the signal. The details of the Hjorth parameters with respect to EEG analysis can be found in [30]. The features extracted $Feat$ are normalized as,

$$Feat_{normalized} = \frac{Feat - min(Feat)}{max(Feat) - min(Feat)} \tag{10}$$

We have further divided the data for each participant into training (75%), validation (15%) and testing (10%) samples.

3.4   Channel Selection

We have used the differential evolution based channel selection which is based on the usage of roulette wheel (DE + R) [25]. The method is further enhanced in this work by using a Gaussian Kernel (DE + R + G) as follows. Gaussian distribution is an important factor for the representation of the random variables given by $N(\mu, \sigma^2)$ with μ and σ being mean and standard deviation of the underlying distributions. We propose the updation of the scaling factor F (from mutation operation in DE-Sect. 2.2) in the (DE + R) algorithm as,

$$F = \exp \frac{-|dist(x_b, x_c)|}{\sigma^2} \tag{11}$$

where σ is a random number which plays a vital role in tuning the values of F and the cosine distance ($dist()$)between the 2 vectors x_b and x_c is given as,

$$dist(x_b, x_c) = cos(\theta) = \frac{x_b . x_c}{||x_b||||x_c||} \tag{12}$$

Lower values of σ results in increased values of F when the vectors x_b and x_c are similar. Larger values of σ results in relaxing the decision, i.e. though the points are well separated, they are considered to be similar. In this study, the farther points are considered similar as they belong to the entities of the same generation. As a result, σ values are generated uniformly in the range of 0.5 to 1 as given by,

$$\sigma = 0.5 \times (1 + rand(0, 1)) \tag{13}$$

where $rand(0, 1)$ is a random number in the range of 0 to 1 which is uniformly distributed. The mean value of σ is thus 0.75. This newly generated F using Eq. 11 generated as a result of gaussian kernel is used in the operations pertaining to the mutant operator of DE + R, thereby leading to the DE + R + G, with G being the acronym for gaussian kernel. The number of epochs or maximum function evaluations (or generations) set in each (DE + R) and (DE + R + G) is 50 and the population size is 50.

Table 1. Various pipelines used for the study

Method	Significance	Motivation
Path 1 $1 \rightarrow 2 \rightarrow 3 \rightarrow 9$	Direct classification	Baseline classification for comparison
Path 2 $1 \rightarrow 2 \rightarrow 4 \rightarrow 7 \rightarrow 8 \rightarrow 9$	Channels C_3, C_Z and C_4	Motor functions related channels
Path 3 $1 \rightarrow 2 \rightarrow 5 \rightarrow 7 \rightarrow 8 \rightarrow 9$	DE + R	Channel selection
Path 4 $1 \rightarrow 2 \rightarrow 6 \rightarrow 7 \rightarrow 8 \rightarrow 9$	DE + R + G	Modified channel selection

3.5 Task Classification

The classification of the dataset into 4 tasks is carried out using the four paths as shown in Fig. 1. The data is divided into training set (75%), validation set (15%) and testing set (10%). The features shown in Eq. 11 are extracted independently from each of the 22 channels. The DE + R and DE + R + G is used independently on the training and the validation to select the optimum channels (4 in our case). The selected optimum channels are used again in the training set to build the model and then it is tested against the testing dataset. kNN algorithm is used for the classification. The results of classification are presented in the results and discussion section.

3.6 Designed Algorithmic Chains

The overall study design can be formulated into four major algorithmic chains as briefed in Table 1. The Path 1 is direct baseline classification method devoid of any optimization in channel selection (it involves all the 22 channels EEG data). Path 2 refers to the selection of only three channels that are most relevant to motor imagery as suggested in [17–19]. The usage of differential evolution using roulette Wheel as suggested in [25] corresponds to Path 3 (DE + R). The proposed enhancement to the channel selection problem i.e. DE + R + G is referred to as Path 4.

4 Results and Discussions

Figure 5 shows the boxplot of accuracy values for the four algorithmic paths discussed in Table 1. It is to be noted that the proposed DE + R + G (Path 4) gives better accuracy over the baseline classification using all channels and the conventional approach of using only the task specific channels i.e., Path 2 (C_3, C_Z and C_4 for motor imagery).

Figure 6 shows the histogram of the occurrences of each channel as optimal using the proposed DE + R + G method. It is to be noted that no single channel

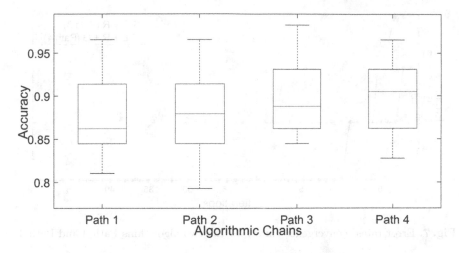

Fig. 5. Boxplot of accuracy values for the four algorithmic paths used in the study

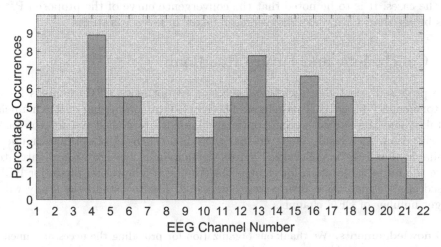

Fig. 6. Histogram of optimal channels as detected for the participants taken together using the proposed DE + R + G

is detected as optimal for a larger percentage (across all the participants). This is a pointer towards the argument that the creation of a generalized optimal channel model across participants is not a good idea as shown in the studies of [16], and our findings are in line with the hypothesis. This throws light on the fact that subject-dependent calibration for channel selection is a must for BCI-based applications.

We further evaluated the performance of DE + R (Path 3) against DE + R + G (Path 4) for their error rate's convergence curve. A sample plot of error rate is provided in Fig. 7 for one particular instance. Similar trend is observed in

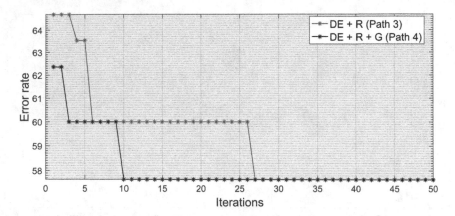

Fig. 7. Error rates (convergence curve) for the two algorithms Path 3 and Path 4

all the cases. It is to be noted that the convergence curve of the proposed Path 4 is better than Path 3 as it convergence faster in fewer iterations.

5   Conclusions and Future Roadmap

The proposed study deals with the selection of optimum EEG channels for a motor imagery-based BCI paradigm. The EEG data comprising of 22 channels is taken and the subject-specific optimal channels are considered for the task classification. As a result, it is seen that there is no such set of optimal channels available that can be generalized across participants. This creates an urge to have the initial calibration for channel selection and adaptation phase for BCI-based applications. As a future scope, we would like to extend the study with larger number of EEG channels.

Acknowledgements. We thank our organization for providing the necessary amenities for carrying out this research work.

References

1. Geeta, N., Gavas, R.D.: Enhanced learning with abacus and its analysis using BCI technology. Int. J. Mod. Educ. Comput. Sci. **6**(9), 22 (2014)
2. Sinha, A., et al.: Artifact removal from EEG signals recorded using low resolution Emotiv device. In: 2015 IEEE International Conference on Systems, Man, and Cybernetics, pp. 1445–1451. IEEE (2015)
3. McCane, L.M., et al.: P300-based brain-computer interface (BCI) event-related potentials (ERPs): people with amyotrophic lateral sclerosis (ALS) vs. age-matched controls. Clin. Neurophysiol. **126**(11), 2124–2131 (2015)
4. Gavas, R., et al.: Estimation of cognitive load based on the pupil size dilation. In: 2017 IEEE International Conference on Systems, Man, and Cybernetics (SMC), pp. 1499–1504. IEEE (2017)

5. Gavas, R.D., et al.: Cognitive load and metacognitive confidence extraction from pupillary response. Cogn. Syst. Res. **52**, 325–334 (2018)
6. Sinha, A., et al.: Dynamic assessment of learners' mental state for an improved learning experience. In: 2015 IEEE Frontiers in Education Conference (FIE), pp. 1–9. IEEE (2015)
7. Sinha, A., et al.: Physiological sensing based stress analysis during assessment. In: 2016 IEEE Frontiers in Education Conference (FIE), pp. 1–8. IEEE (2016)
8. Khasnobish, A., et al.: EyeAssist: a communication aid through gaze tracking for patients with neuro-motor disabilities. In: 2017 IEEE International Conference on Pervasive Computing and Communications Workshops (PerCom Workshops), pp. 382–387. IEEE (2017)
9. Chatterjee, D., et al.: Evaluating age-related variations of gaze behavior for a novel digitized-digit symbol substitution test (2019)
10. Gavas, R.D., Navalyal, G.U.: Fast and secure random number generation using low-cost EEG and pseudo random number generator. In: 2017 International Conference on Smart Technologies for Smart Nation (SmartTechCon), pp. 369–374. IEEE (2017)
11. Gavas, R., et al.: Inactive-state recognition from EEG signals and its application in cognitive load computation. In: 2016 IEEE International Conference on Systems, Man, and Cybernetics (SMC), pp. 003606–003611. IEEE (2016)
12. Navalyal, G.U., Gavas, R.D.: A dynamic attention assessment and enhancement tool using computer graphics. Hum.-Cent. Comput. Inform. Sci. **4**(1), 1–7 (2014). https://doi.org/10.1186/s13673-014-0011-0
13. Blankertz, B., et al.: The Berlin brain-computer interface: accurate performance from first-session in BCI-naive subjects. IEEE Trans. Biomed. Eng. **55**(10), 2452–2462 (2008)
14. Popescu, F., et al.: Single trial classification of motor imagination using 6 dry EEG electrodes. PLoS One **2**(7), e637 (2007)
15. Lal, T.N., et al.: Support vector channel selection in BCI. IEEE Trans. Biomed. Eng. **51**(6), 1003–1010 (2004)
16. Arvaneh, M., et al.: Optimizing the channel selection and classification accuracy in EEG-based BCI. IEEE Trans. Biomed. Eng. **58**(6), 1865–1873 (2011)
17. Leeb, R., et al.: Brain-computer communication: motivation, aim, and impact of exploring a virtual apartment. IEEE Trans. Neural Syst. Rehabil. Eng. **15**(4), 473–482 (2007)
18. Scherer, R., et al.: An asynchronously controlled EEG-based virtual keyboard: improvement of the spelling rate. IEEE Trans. Biomed. Eng. **51**(6), 979–984 (2004)
19. Pfurtscheller, G., et al.: EEG-based discrimination between imagination of right and left hand movement. Electroencephalogr. Clin. Neurophysiol. **103**(6), 642–651 (1997)
20. Sannelli, C., et al.: On optimal channel configurations for SMR-based brain-computer interfaces. Brain Topogr. **23**(2), 186–193 (2010)
21. Schröder, M., et al.: Robust EEG channel selection across subjects for brain-computer interfaces. EURASIP J. Appl. Sig. Process. **2005**, 3103–3112 (2005)
22. Yang, J., Honavar, V.: Feature subset selection using a genetic algorithm. In: Liu, H., Motoda, H. (eds.) Feature Extraction, Construction and Selection. The Springer International Series in Engineering and Computer Science, vol. 453, pp. 117–136. Springer, Boston (1998). https://doi.org/10.1007/978-1-4615-5725-8_8
23. Xue, B., et al.: Particle swarm optimization for feature selection in classification: a multi-objective approach. IEEE Trans. Cybern. **43**(6), 1656–1671 (2012)

24. Tabakhi, S., Moradi, P., Akhlaghian, F.: An unsupervised feature selection algorithm based on ant colony optimization. Eng. Appl. Artif. Intell. **32**, 112–123 (2014)
25. Khushaba, R.N., Al-Ani, A., Al-Jumaily, A.: Feature subset selection using differential evolution and a statistical repair mechanism. Expert Syst. Appl. **38**(9), 11515–11526 (2011)
26. Datasets - BNCI horizon 2020 (2019). http://www.bbci.de/competition/iv/# datasets
27. EEG-band-frequencies (2019). http://support.neurosky.com/kb/science/eeg-band-frequencies
28. McMahan, T., Parberry, I., Parsons, T.D.: Evaluating player task engagement and arousal using electroencephalography. Proc. Manuf. **3**, 2303–2310 (2015)
29. Vidaurre, C., et al.: Time domain parameters as a feature for EEG-based brain-computer interfaces. Neural Netw. **22**(9), 1313–1319 (2009)
30. Bose, R., Khasnobish, A., Bhaduri, S., Tibarewala, D.: Performance analysis of left and right lower limb movement classification from EEG. In: 2016 3rd International Conference on Signal Processing and Integrated Networks (SPIN), pp. 174–179. IEEE (2016)

An Efficient Word Embedded Click-Bait Classification of YouTube Titles Using SVM

K. V. Sankar Reddy$^{(\boxtimes)}$, K. Sai Nihith$^{(\boxtimes)}$, M. Sasank Chowdary$^{(\boxtimes)}$, and T. R. Krishna Prasad$^{(\boxtimes)}$

Department of Computer Science and Engineering, Amrita School of Engineering, Amrita Vishwa Vidyapeetham, Amritapuri, India
{sankarreddy,sainihith,sasankchowdary}@am.students.amrita.edu, krishnaprasadtr@am.amrita.edu

Abstract. Most of the online media outlets normally depend on the revenues generated from the clicks made by their viewers and due to presence of their outlets. To increase traffic onto their websites some people come with some misleading headlines as titles for their links. Such misleading headlines are known as Click-baits. These click-baits leave the user disappointed as the content of the address is very different from the headline or the title. The current work focuses on classification of YouTube titles into click-baits and non click-baits using tokenization and word embedding applied to SVM. Upon simulation of the algorithm we are able to increase the accuracy, compared to some of the other classification algorithms.

Keywords: Click-baits · Non click-baits · Classification · SVM · Word embedded · Comparison · Accuracy

1 Introduction

Now a days, every person in the society is hugely dependent on the news content. The online media, their content display forms shows very different choices that covers wide range of topic. Compared to the offline media, the online media give several choices as national or international on specific topics of interest. A lot of media outlets do not charge the users for subscription. Their major revenue earnings come from displaying advertisements on their pages [1,2]. With information moving more online, revenue generation also follows through. One of the duplicitous technique of drawing traffic is through click-baits. Click baits trick the user into clicking a link whose data the user finds is not what the description on the link provided, thus the user is unable to fulfill the space left vacant by curiosity [3] which may result in the user's decreasing proclivity to visit the same site again.

Classification of data is a field of major research interest. Some of the methods used in classification are CNN [4], MLP [5]. Amongst classification, Click-bait

© Springer Nature Singapore Pte Ltd. 2020
S. M. Thampi et al. (Eds.): SoMMA 2019, CCIS 1203, pp. 175–184, 2020.
https://doi.org/10.1007/978-981-15-4301-2_15

classification have gathered the attention of the researchers in the recent times with the advent of video streaming content. Some of the methods used to classify click baits have been Support Vector Machine(SVM), decision trees, random forest [6], neural networks [7], long short term memory [8].

SVM is a machine learning algorithm used for both classification and regression problems [9]. It can solve both linear and non-linear problems. The algorithm segregates the data into classes by creating a line or a hyperplane [10].

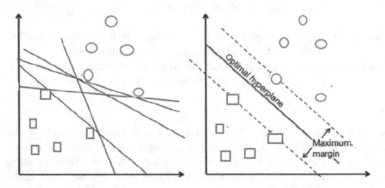

Fig. 1. An example of a SVM classification

Consider Fig. 1, In the first picture all planes are separating the data. Amongst the planes, the plane that maximises the distance between the two classes is to be selected. In Fig. 1 the picture on the right shows the plane, which delineates the two classes such that the distance between them is as maximum as possible.

Random forest [11] is an combination of decision tree such that each tree depends on the values of a random vector sampled independently and with the same distribution for all trees in the forest. Our classification accuracy have resulted from word embeddings of youtube titles in the form of ensemble of trees.

Decision Tree [12] is a structure of root, branches and leaf nodes and one of the classification algorithm in machine learning but sometimes we also uses for regression problems. It works for both categorical variables and continuous input and output variables. In our model we used categorical output. We used word embeddings on Decision Tree classifier to classify youtube titles into click-baits and non-clickbaits.

The proposed model uses Word Embedding on SVM algorithm on youtube data as it works with well with clear margin of separation. The proposed algorithm classifies the data set into click-baits and non-click-baits of youtube titles. The features that are used in the algorithm are titles of YouTube videos, number of views, number of likes , dislikes and number of subscribers. Upon simulation of the proposed algorithm, we are able to achieve a higher efficiency in classifying YouTube titles. The efficiency of the current algorithm is also compared with other algorithms such as decision trees and random forests which we got high accuracy on SVM as 97%.

2 Related Work

End-to-end Convolutional Neural Network (CNN) is used for click-bait detection. For classifier, they represent headlines as fixed-size, continuous and real-valued vectors. Their model supports all languages. Words are embedded into word vectors which are then used in the model. These vectors are provided as inputs to the CNN [13] for feature extraction. For classification, logistic regression is used.

Another method of classification of click-baits is using Natural language processing [14]. Both syntax and the semantics of the headlines are looked into and are manually classified whether they are click-baits or not. Supervised learning is used to train the model and this trained model is later used for classification. The dataset contains different types of headlines. The feature set is analyzed using sentiment analysis, readability of click-baits, mean word length and mean number of words.

A method for detecting and characterizing the click-bait on YouTube is given in [15], where a deep learning model based on encoders is used. The model depends on finite amount of labeled data to classify large unlabeled data. Firstly, YouTube thumbnail is processed to encoding part by Convolutional Neural Network (CNN). Then split the encoding part into two sub-encoders. To conclude, it is processed into decoding part.

An algorithm that works on detecting click-baits using Capsule Network is given [16]. In the first layer, they vectorize the text using word embeddings. The second layer is a Bi-directional GRU block [17]. The third layer is a text capsule layer which consists of primary capsule layer and convolutional capsule layer. Finally by using flatten layer and softmax prediction layer, we can get the desired output.

A technique of classification by analyzing the dwell time according to category is given in [18]. Dwell time means it says the how long user looked into a page. Dwell time is analyzed by category, Dwell time and length of news page, news content.

An algorithm that classifies click-baits and also a browser extension which alerts the user to click-baits is mentioned in [6]. Structure of the sentence, certain key words, parts of speech by using tags and n-gram are the some of the features used in this model to classify click-baits and non-clickbaits. SVM, decision trees and random forests were the algorithms used for classification of click-baits. We used only one technique that is word embeddings in SVM model with youtube data which detects automatically whether youtube title is click-bait or not in an easier way.

3 Proposed Model

A. Model Overview
Our proposed model is based on the Support Vector Machine (SVM), which predicts 1 if the YouTube video title is non-clickbait and 0 otherwise. Given below is a representative block diagram of the proposed model (Fig. 2).

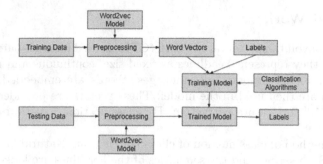

Fig. 2. Block diagram

B. Preprocessing

The first step in our proposed algorithm is Preprocessing. It involves formatting the data for the purpose of feeding it as input to the algorithm. In preprocessing we remove the stopwords, remove the double spaces, add spacing between numbers and alphabets, remove the words less than two characters in the youtube titles. We took 18000 samples from each datasets as two datasets are not balanced. After this tokenization is also one of the step in preprocessing. We divide the YouTube video titles into words. These words are called tokens. After tokenization we concate the two datasets, after concatenation we divide the data into train set and test set. As per our convenience the data set is divided into training and testing in the ratio of 80:20.

C. Word Embedding

Second step involves word embedding. To the best of our knowledge word embedding has not been tried to classify click-baits on YouTube links. In this phase, we embed the title into a vector representation by computing the mean vector of the title tokens from a Word2Vec model. Word2vec model is one of the model in Gensim [19] which is an open source library. In the case of the YouTube title vectors, each YouTube title vectors will have number of comments, number of likes, number of dislikes and number of views as features. If no token is present in the Word2Vec model, then the mean vector representation which is previously computed on the trained set is taken. To assign size of the input vectors, window size and number of iterations hyper parameters like size of vector, window, mincount, epoch are chosen as they have a direct affect on the accuracy on our model. We choose these parameters after iterating their values and observing the accuracy.

D. Logarithmic Computation

We applied logarithmic computations on our data which contains number of views, number of likes, number of dislikes, number of comments to get a normalized distribution. Logarithm of these numeric parameters are generally normalised to give better performance. The normalised distribution is represented in Figs. 3 and 4.

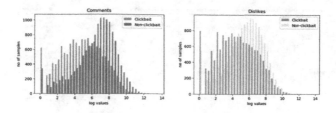

Fig. 3. Distribution of comments and dislikes

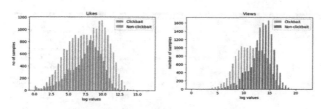

Fig. 4. Distribution of likes and views

E. Min-Max Scaling

SVM algorithm assumes that the input is within a finite range, typically from 0 to 1. Hence to ensure that the feature dimensions are within this range, min-max scaling is applied to bound the values between 0 to 1, else if one input dimension hugely varies from another it will skew results. The scaling is calculated as follows:

$$y_i = \frac{x_i - min(x)}{max(x) - min(x)} \tag{1}$$

where x_i is $(x_1, x_2, ..., x_n)$ and y_i is the ith normalised data which along with the title vectors are given as input to SVM algorithm. To best fit our data we train our model with SVM using Cross Validation with parameter tuning using grid search CV [20] by choosing best parameters C and Gamma. C and Gamma are used to avoid overfitting on the data.

4 Experimental Setup

A. Dataset

Two data sets are used for the purpose of simulation. One data set consists of click baits and the other data set consists of non click baits. Each data set consists of 18317 and 19080 rows and 11 columns. It's total size is 3.6 Mb. In datasets data is handpicked from some of the youtube clickbait and non-clickbait channels along with metadata. Alessioverti's who is a student provided to us upon request via mail. A sample of the training and testing data set is provided below (Figs. 5 and 6):

channel_name	channel_subscribers	channel_videos	channel_views	video_comments	video_dislikes	video_id	video_likes	video_title	video_views
Top List	0	193	143713154	131.0	183.0	hDcWfBq5bxM	1424.0	10 Amazing Places That Disappear During High Tide	380859.0
EG Mines	403931	658	119696149	1.0	7.0	D_wROW7u89Y	7.0	Simple Math Test in 59 Seconds - Genius Test	2483.0
TOP 10 INFORMATION -TTI	899318	199	271061831	0.0	0.0	S44UVG80-dY	7.0	5 World greatest unsolved mysteries	332.0
MrWolf	0	303	270690522	1215.0	535.0	V4l2Ivl-734	3380.0	5 SCP CREATURES CAUGHT ON CAMERA & SPOTTED IN	501277.0

Fig. 5. Click-bait data set

channel_name	channel_subscribers	channel_videos	channel_views	video_comments	video_dislikes	video_id	video_likes	video_title	video_views
The Tonight Show Starring Jimmy Fallon	17781648	4620	9678006744	2133.0	338.0	OF7H2fMdfqk	107154.0	Chris Evans Is Starting to Speak Like His Todd...	6260596.0
Nickelodeon	4501624	2967	2671265094	4178.0	1503.0	z71bRy2pY08	26516.0	JoJo Siwa, Jacob Sartorius & More On the Kids'...	2425378.0
minutephysics	4450206	225	379295736	12237.0	4029.0	XayNKY944lY	111238.0	Solution to the Grandfather Paradox	4767321.0
CBC News	289293	9882	178182807	688.0	106.0	5kW5K08wdvl	2145.0	Wayne Gretzky | Mixed Views on Modern Hockey	341167.0
The Tonight Show Starring Jimmy Fallon	17781648	4620	9678006744	4238.0	2410.0	N0mTsjpYhB8	111661.0	Phone Booth with Miley Cyrus	19758900.0

Fig. 6. Non Click-bait data set

B. Evaluation Metrics

(1) *Accuracy:* The overall accuracy [21] is the percentage of correctly classified instances. It is calculated using the number of correctly classified occurrence divided by the total number of classified cases. True Positive is given as TrPo and True Negative as TrNe (False Positive is depicted as FaPo and False negative as FaNe).

$$Accuracy = \frac{TrPo + TrNe}{TrPo + FaNe + FaPo + TrNe} \tag{2}$$

(2) *Precision:* The precision is the percentage of positive forecast retrieved that are actually positive cases. It is the number of true positives (TrPo) cleaved by the number of all regained positive results i.e. (true positives (TrPo), false positives (FaPo)) [22].

$$Precision = \frac{TrPo}{TrPo + FaPo} \tag{3}$$

(3) *Recall:* The recall is the percentage of correct predictions recovered from all positive cases. It is the number of true positives cleaved by the number of all positive cases i.e (true positives (TrPo), false negatives (FaNe))[22].

$$Recall = \frac{TrPo}{TrPo + FaNe} \tag{4}$$

(4) *F1 Score:* The F1 Score is the measure of harmonic mean of recall and precision. The harmonic mean is normally used when determining the average of rates [21].

$$F1Score = 2 * \frac{Precision * Recall}{Precision + Recall} \tag{5}$$

5 Results

Given below is the average recall and precision output (graph) for the proposed SVM model for the click-bait and non click-bait datasets.

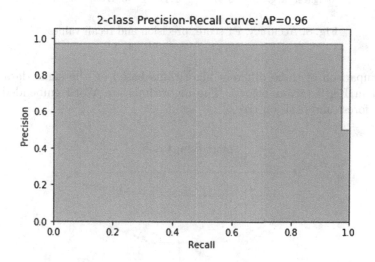

Fig. 7. Precision and recall

From the figure given above, it can be observed that the proposed model correctly classifies 96% of samples in the dataset.

The figure given below describes the output of the proposed SVM model after training. From Fig. 8, the observation can be made that 7200 samples were used for test dataset. Figure 8 also mentions the C and gamma values which are 3.66 and 5.0 respectively. It also mentions the harmonic mean of precision and recall values (F1 score) as 96%. The accuracy of the model is 97%. Figure 7 also describes the ROC value which is used in binary classification. In general, the closer a ROC curve is to the upper left corner, the better are the test results. From Fig. 8, we can observe that the ROC value is 97.04%.

```
SVM :
        C: 3.6666666666666665
        gamma: 5.0
        Best Score (F1): 0.9679794054920413
Performance on the test set (7200 samples):
        Accuracy Score: 0.9704166666666667
        Area under ROC curve: 0.9704298740772905
        Classification report (on the test set):
                precision    recall  f1-score   support

             0      0.97      0.97      0.97      3675
             1      0.97      0.97      0.97      3525

    micro avg      0.97      0.97      0.97      7200
    macro avg      0.97      0.97      0.97      7200
 weighted avg      0.97      0.97      0.97      7200
```

Fig. 8. Accuracy, F1 score, precision and recall values

A comparison of three different algorithms based on the same data sets is provided in Fig. 9 (given below). The algorithms are Word embedded SVM, Random forest and decision tree.

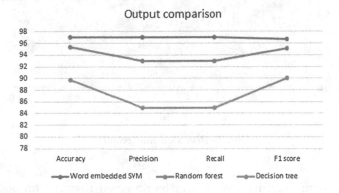

Fig. 9. Comparison of evaluation metrics for three algorithms

From the Fig. 9, we can observe that accuracies of Random forest and Decision tree are 95% and 89% which is comparatively lesser than SVM, So by comparing these accuracies we conclude that the word embedded SVM algorithm is more efficient in the classification of YouTube titles into click-baits or non click baits when compared to Random Forest and Decision tree.

6   Conclusion

Through simulation of word embedded algorithm, we can find that it is very efficient in the classification of YouTube titles into click-baits and non click-baits. As part of future work, we would like to modify the embedded word SVM model so that the classification can be achieved but with lesser time for the training model.

References

1. Galán, A.A., Cabañas, J.G., Cuevas, Á., Calderón, M., Rumin, R.C.: Large-scale analysis of user exposure to online advertising on facebook. IEEE Access **7**, 11:959–11:971 (2019)
2. Yang, K.-C., Yang, C., Huang, C.-H., Shih, P.-H., Yang, S.Y.: Consumer attitudes toward online video advertising: an empirical study on youtube as platform. In: 2014 IEEE International Conference on Industrial Engineering and Engineering Management. IEEE, pp. 1131–1135 (2014)
3. Loewenstein, G.: The psychology of curiosity: a review and reinterpretation. Psychol. Bull. **116**(1), 75 (1994)
4. Aloysius, N., Geetha, M.: A review on deep convolutional neural networks. In: 2017 International Conference on Communication and Signal Processing (ICCSP). IEEE, pp. 0588–0592 (2017)
5. Rajendran, G., Poornachandran, P., Chitturi, B.: Deep learning model on stance classification. In: 2017 International Conference on Advances in Computing, Communications and Informatics (ICACCI). IEEE, pp. 2407–2409 (2017)
6. Chakraborty, A., Paranjape, B., Kakarla, S., Ganguly, N.: Stop clickbait: detecting and preventing clickbaits in online news media. In: 2016 IEEE/ACM International Conference on Advances in Social Networks Analysis and Mining (ASONAM). IEEE, pp. 9–16 (2016)
7. Klairith, P., Tanachutiwat, S.: Thai clickbait detection algorithms using natural language processing with machine learning techniques. In: 2018 International Conference on Engineering, Applied Sciences, and Technology (ICEAST). IEEE, pp. 1–4 (2018)
8. Hochreiter, S., Schmidhuber, J.: Long short-term memory. Neural Comput. **9**(8), 1735–1780 (1997)
9. Nair, J.J., Mohan, N.: Alzheimer's disease diagnosis in mr images using statistical methods. In: 2017 International Conference on Communication and Signal Processing (ICCSP). IEEE, pp. 1232–1235 (2017)
10. Thara, S., Sidharth, S.: Aspect based sentiment classication: Svd features. In: 2017 International Conference on Advances in Computing, Communications and Informatics (ICACCI). IEEE, pp. 2370–2374 (2017)
11. Breiman, L.: Random forests. Machine Learn. **45**(1), 5–32 (2001). https://doi.org/10.1023/A:1010933404324
12. Vora, P., Khara, M., Kelkar, K.: Classification of tweets based on emotions using word embedding and random forest classifiers. Int. J. Comput. Appl. **178**(3), 1–7 (2017)
13. Fu, J., Liang, L., Zhou, X., Zheng, J.: A convolutional neural network for clickbait detection. In: 2017 4th International Conference on Information Science and Control Engineering (ICISCE), pp. 6–10, July 2017

14. Manjesh, S., Kanakagiri, T., Vaishak, P., Chettiar, V., Shobha, G.: Clickbait pattern detection and classification of news headlines using natural language processing. In: 2017 2nd International Conference on Computational Systems and Information Technology for Sustainable Solution (CSITSS), pp. 1–5, December 2017

15. Zannettou, S., Chatzis, S., Papadamou, K., Sirivianos, M.: The good, the bad and the bait: detecting and characterizing clickbait on youtube. In: 2018 IEEE Security and Privacy Workshops (SPW), pp. 63–69, May 2018

16. Bhattacharjee, U.: Capsule network on social media text: an application to automatic detection of clickbaits. In: 2019 11th International Conference on Communication Systems Networks (COMSNETS), pp. 473–476, January 2019

17. Tjandra, A., Sakti, S., Manurung, R., Adriani, M., Nakamura, S.: Gated recurrent neural tensor network. In: 2016 International Joint Conference on Neural Networks (IJCNN), pp. 448–455, July 2016

18. Seki, Y., Yoshida, M.: Analysis of user dwell time by category in news application. In: 2018 IEEE/WIC/ACM International Conference on Web Intelligence (WI), pp. 732–735, December 2018

19. Sultana Ritu, Z., Nowshin, N., Mahadi Hasan Nahid, M., Ismail, S.: Performance analysis of different word embedding models on Bangla language. In: 2018 International Conference on Bangla Speech and Language Processing (ICBSLP), pp. 1–5, September 2018

20. Jin, Z., Chaorong, W., Chengguang, H., Feng, W.: Parameter optimization algorithm of SVM for fault classification in traction converter. In: The 26th Chinese Control and Decision Conference (2014 CCDC), pp. 3786–3791, May 2014

21. Sokolova, M., Japkowicz, N., Szpakowicz, S.: Beyond accuracy, f-score and roc: a family of discriminant measures for performance evaluation. In: Sattar, A., Kang, B. (eds.) AI 2006. LNCS (LNAI), vol. 4304, pp. 1015–1021. Springer, Heidelberg (2006). https://doi.org/10.1007/11941439_114

22. Khan, S.A., Ali Rana, Z.: Evaluating performance of software defect prediction models using area under precision-recall curve (AUC-PR). In: 2019 2nd International Conference on Advancements in Computational Sciences (ICACS), pp. 1–6, February 2019

NSGA III for CNC End Milling Process Optimization

Tamal Ghosh$^{(\boxtimes)}$ and Kristian Martinsen

Department of Manufacturing and Civil Engineering, Norwegian University of Science
and Technology, 2815 Gjøvik, Norway
{tamal.ghosh,kristian.martinsen}@ntnu.no

Abstract. Computer Numerical Controlled (CNC) end milling processes require
very complex and expensive experimentations or simulations to measure the overall performance due to the involvement of many process parameters. Such problems are computationally expensive, which could be efficiently solved using surrogate driven evolutionary optimization algorithms. An attempt is made in this
paper to use such technique for the end milling process optimization of aluminium
block and solved using Non-dominated Sorting Genetic Algorithm (NSGA III).
The material removal rate, and surface roughness are considered as the crucial
performance criteria. It is shown that the regression driven NSGA III is efficient
and effective while obtaining improved process responses for the end milling.

Keywords: Parameter optimization · NSGA III · Regression · CNC end milling

1 Introduction

Metamodel or Surrogate function driven optimization has recently been emerged, which
exploits the cheap metamodel/surrogate functions as objective functions and eliminates
the requirement of complex mathematical functions or laboratory experiments. Traditional optimization methods could be used for these problems, such as, the exact methods,
evolutionary algorithms, and non-evolutionary methods as the solution methodologies.
Surrogate/black-box models are useful when less information exists on the problems
[1]. Surrogate based approaches can predict correlations among the process variables
depending on the data obtained through Design of Experiment (DOE) approaches [2].
Precision of the prediction model would be significant for the training of the models.
The Mean Square Error (MSE), Root Mean Square Error (RMSE) etc. are exploited
as performance metrics for the surrogate approaches. Once the training of the surrogate model is completed, a suitable optimization technique, such as Genetic Algorithms
(GA), Ant Colony Optimization (ACO), Bat Inspired Algorithm (BA), Particle Swarm
Optimization (PSO) etc. could be employed as an optimization technique to obtain Pareto
optimal front [3]. Surrogate models are substantially prompt and efficient. Therefore,
the surrogate-assisted optimization is not expensive in terms of computation.

DOE techniques, e.g. Latin Hypercube Sampling (LHS), Full Factorial Design
(FFD), Orthogonal Array Design (OAD) etc. are employed to design the experimental or trial sample points in the process design space. These could be employed as the

© Springer Nature Singapore Pte Ltd. 2020
S. M. Thampi et al. (Eds.): SoMMA 2019, CCIS 1203, pp. 185–195, 2020.
https://doi.org/10.1007/978-981-15-4301-2_16

training dataset for the surrogate/black-box models. The DOE techniques amplify the process information acquired from the experimental runs [4].

Some of the surrogate-based approaches are heavily practiced in literature. These could be Response Surface Models (RSM), radial basis functions (RBF), Support Vector Machines (SVM), Gaussian Process (GP), Artificial Neural Network (ANN) etc. [5].

Recently surrogate-assisted techniques are being practiced for manufacturing process optimization problems. Ref. [6] portrays a metamodel based process parameter optimisation. In Ref. [7], ANN coupled GA is used to find improved process parameters. Refs. [8, 9] introduced surrogate modeling for the optimisation of an injection molding process. Ref. [10] demonstrated the expected improvement, which could select the enhanced solutions in a surrogate-based optimization. Ref. [11] introduced a Model-Based Self-Optimisation (MBSO), which includes machines having the reasoning capabilities. Therefore, automatic parameters adaptation could be done by machines in uncertain conditions. In another work authors introduced surrogate-based optimisation to a composite textile draping process, which is a deep ANN and it could predict the shear angle of many textile elements [5]. It is shown to minimize the number of FEM simulations, which was needed to attain optimal level of parameters.

Computer Numerical Controlled (CNC) milling is an essential metal cutting technique among various machining processes in the modern era of manufacturing. CNC milling not only makes the milling process fully automated, but also enhances the machining time, reduces milling process variations, improves the quality of the machined parts, and enriches the overall productivity of the manufacturing companies [8]. For CNC milling, end mill is one of the most vital tools amongst various milling cutters due to its ability of high-speed cutting of metal with minimum surface roughness in a single pass [12]. CNC end milling is being practiced significantly in different manufacturing sectors, such as aerospace, automotive, electronics, jewellery, bioinstrumentation industries, etc. CNC end milling is used for making different geometrical shapes and holes in a metallic work-piece during milling, profiling, contouring, slotting, counter-boring, drilling, and reaming applications, etc. [13]. Aluminium alloy is mostly explored material for end milling, which has more than 90% pure Aluminium. It has high strength and ductility, corrosion resistance, weldability, machinability, and formability. It is used as an important material for vehicle bodies, refrigerated trucks, cold storage rooms, anti-skid flooring, manufacturing of mobile homes, residential siding, and rain carrying goods, etc. [14]. It is also used in sheet metal work. With optimum settings of end milling parameters, it is possible to achieve good surface quality and high Metal Removal Rate (MRR) for the aluminium alloy. For that matter, Tool Diameter (TD), Spindle Speed (SS), Feed Rate (FR), and Depth of Cut (DOC) could be the most important process variables. The Surface Roughness (Ra) is the primary machining attribute since most of the manufacturing companies try to maintain better surface quality for the machined parts. Therefore, Ra determines the manufacturing cost and quality of the engineered products [15]. Surface texture, fatigue resistance, and heat transmission of manufactured products are greatly influenced by Ra. Surface quality also depends on the abovementioned machining parameters of end milling. On the contrary, MRR is determined by the volume of removed metal and the machining time on the metal work-piece. MRR could affect the cost of manufacturing largely. When the combined effect of MRR and Ra is studied, the cutting process optimization becomes more complicated [16]. The solidity and life of the cutting tools could also be influenced by the cutting forces for the end milling process. Machining errors could be seen if the cutting forces are not considered while optimizing the process [17, 18]. The objective of this study is to determine the ideal parameter settings, which could yield high MRR and low Ra for the end milling of AA3105 alloy in desired range. Data-driven surrogate assisted optimization has rarely been used for machining process optimization [19], which is depicted in this work.

2   Material and Method

AA3105 alloy work-piece ($90 \times 140 \times 20$ mm^3) is used for the testing of end milling operation. AA3105 alloy is primarily used in sheet metal work and manufacture of mobile homes, residential siding, and rain carrying goods in sub-zero temperature. It is perfectly suitable for the climate of Nordic Europe. AA3105 portrays good machinability property. Percentages of weight in chemical composition of the AA5105 are Al - 98.56%, Mn - 0.716%, Fe - 0.38%, Zn - 0.128%, Cu - 0.118%, Cr - 0.081%, and Pb - 0.006%. The experimental set up is depicted in Fig. 1.

Fig. 1. End milling operation in laboratory

The experiments are carried out on Proxxon FF 500/BL 3-Axes CNC milling machine, manufactured by Proxxon, Germany. It has double roller bearing recirculating ball spindles at all 3-axes. The spindle speed varies in the range of 200-4000 rpm. It has large traverse area (X-290 mm, Y-100 mm, and Z-200 mm). Tools are based on the spiral design according to DIN 844 and made of the high-speed steel (HSS-Co5) 5% cobalt. To measure the surface quality of the machined work-pieces, a ZEISS Handysurf E-35B is used.

3   Surrogate Assisted Optimization Method

In this article a novel regression driven NSGA III algorithm is employed. The cutting process is modelled with a popular DOE tool namely, Taguchi's orthogonal design. For

Table 1. End milling parameters with their levels

Factors	Level 1	Level 2	Level 3	Level 4
	1	2	3	4
TD (mm)	6	7	8	10
SS (rpm)	1500	1750	2000	2250
FR (mm/s)	2	3	4	5
DOC (mm)	0.5	1.0	1.5	2.0

Table 2. Experimental design space using L_{16} orthogonal array

Ex#	TD	SS	FR	DOC	MRR (mm^3/s)	Ra (μm)
1	6	1500	2	0.5	5.263	0.08
2	6	1750	3	1	11.080	0.06
3	6	2000	4	1.5	18.100	0.06
4	6	2250	5	2	7.299	0.05
5	7	1500	3	1.5	6.652	0.29
6	7	1750	2	2	20.690	0.25
7	7	2000	5	0.5	5.848	0.05
8	7	2250	4	1	18.018	0.04
9	8	1500	4	2	41.379	0.18
10	8	1750	5	1.5	20.000	0.22
11	8	2000	2	1	13.043	0.29
12	8	2250	3	0.5	7.477	0.62
13	10	1500	5	1	25.641	0.075
14	10	1750	4	0.5	6.390	0.27
15	10	2000	3	2	40.000	0.89
16	10	2250	2	1.5	24.390	0.72

carrying out the basic experiments during the cutting of AA3105, the initial settings of the levels of the milling process parameters (Table 1). The responses are determined by conducting trials, which are portrayed in Table 2.

3.1 Regression Analysis

Multiple regression mode is obtained for MRR and Ra at 95% confidence level. Regression equations are depicted in Eqs. (1)–(2). These equations are used as the fitness functions for the NSGA III algorithm. Table 3 shows the p-values and R^2 values of the regression analysis, which states that the MRR is mostly dependent on the DOC and Ra is mostly dependent on the TD.

$$MRR = -18.6 + 3.60 * TD - 0.00464 * SS + 0.12 * FR + 12.73 * DOC \tag{1}$$

$$Ra = -0.885 + 0.1090 * TD + 0.000290 * SS - 0.1036 * FR + 0.0937 * DOC \tag{2}$$

Table 3. Regression models with P values and R^2 values

		P-value	R^2-value
P-values for regression models and parameters	Regression	0.015	0.002
	TD (mm)	0.022	0.001
	SS (rpm)	0.530	0.055
	FR (mm/s)	0.947	0.011
	DOC (mm)	0.005	0.193
R^2		64.69%	75.66%

3.2 NSGA III Technique

NSGA III is a recently published optimization technique developed in the Ref. [20]. NSGA III is extended based on the framework of previously published NSGA-II with a newer selection approach.

NSGA III works on an evenly distributed reference points in the state space. These are further updated using supervised learning technique. Algorithm 1 portrays NSGA III. It starts with a randomly generated initial population POP (size N). The set of reference points are assumed as Z^{ref}. The NSGA III runs for a fixed number of generations. The tournament selection, binary crossover, and polynomial mutation [21] are used for the NSGA III, which further produce N number of child solutions (e.g. POP_{new}).

NSGA III

1: **Create** the set of reference points Z^{ref} to put on hyper plane
2: **Create** random population POP
3: **Create** the Ideal points Z^{max}
4: **Calculate** fitness for the generated population
5: **Execute** non-dominated sorting on population
6: **for** i=1 to Iteration No. **do**
       7: **Compute** crossover with P_c probability
       8: **Compute** mutation with P_m probability
       9: **Add** new solutions to obtain NEWPOP = POP ∪ POP_{new}
       10: **Execute** non-dominated sorting on NEWPOP
       11: **Normalize** NEWPOP exploiting Z^{max}
       12: **Correlate** the NEWPOP solutions with the Z^{ref}
       13: **Compute** niche and **Execute** niche preservation
       14: **Send** niche obtained solutions to the next iteration
15: **end for**

The new population is combined with old population and the combined population of size $2N$ is achieved. Further the non-dominated sorting is performed [22], which clubs the solutions of combined population using some ranking method (F_i where $i=1, 2,..., n$). In the next iteration the population is acquired using this ranking method (e.g. initially F_1 members are picked, then F_2, F_3, etc.). Once the population size becomes N, this method stops. However, if the lth rank holders are being included in the next population as last set of members, then, rest of the members from $(l + 1)^{th}$ are discarded. This could mean that some of the members with F_l rank are counted (restriction of size N). To achieve such goal, reference point-driven selection technique is introduced. This method is different than the crowding distance technique of previous version of NSGA [23].

3.2.1 Reference Point Generation

A hyper-plane is defined as an inclined plane to the M-objective axes using $(M - 1)$-dimensional unit simplex. The technique suggested in Ref. [24] distributes the reference points on this normalized hyper-plane, where the Pareto solutions are mapped with the reference points. The number of segments of each of the objective axes decides the number of the reference points. For P segments, the number of reference points is computed using,

$$H = C_P^{M+P-1} \tag{3}$$

3.2.2 Normalization of Population

The normalization procedure proposed by [20] can recognize ideal points Z^{max}. This is done with solutions to the computationally expensive linear equations. The basic normalization technique is followed for that ease of computation. If $Z_j^{min} = (z_1^{min}, z_2^{min}, ..., z_M^{min})$ with the lowest fitness scores for j^{th} member $\forall\ j\ \in [1, N]$. z_i^{min} is the ith minimum fitness score $f_i\ \forall\ i\ \in [1, M]$. The $z_i^{max} \in Z^{max}$ is worst point for the ith objective. The normalized fitness score $f_i^*(x_j)$ is computed as,

$$f_i^*(x_j) = \frac{z_i^{max} - f_i(x_j)}{z_i^{max} - z_i^{min}} \quad \forall i \in [1, M] \ and \ \forall j \in [1, N] \tag{4}$$

3.2.3 Mapping the Population Members and Reference Points

After obtaining the normalized fitness scores, each solution is linked to a corresponding reference point. To facilitates that, reference lines are derived from reference points to hyper-plane origin and the perpendicular distance between each solution and each reference line is calculated. The solution is mapped to reference point based on this lowest perpendicular distance.

3.2.4 Niche Preservation

Niches are paired with reference points using the linked solution. Niche preservation is executed to decide, which candidates of rank F_l would be opted. First, the set of reference

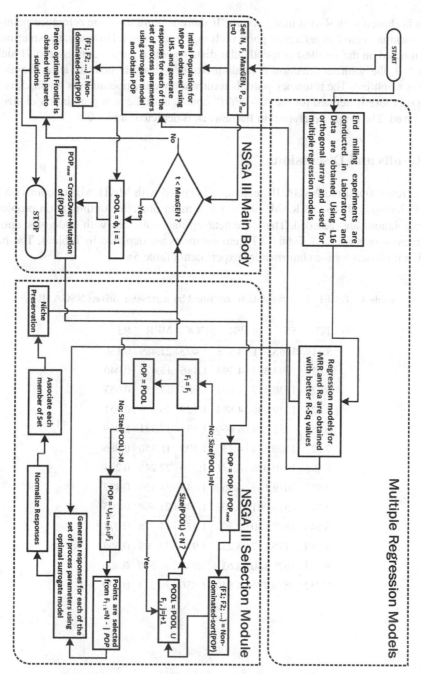

Fig. 2. Data-driven surrogate-assisted NSGA III framework

points is chosen with lowest niche counts. If there is more than one reference point in such situation, a random reference point is chosen from the set. However, the solution is chosen based on the smallest perpendicular distance when niche count is zero. If niche count ≥ 1, the solution selection is random from F_l front. In next iteration the niche count is amplified. The reference point is removed once the operation is finished for it. This procedure is iterated for the $N - |POP|$ counts until the new population of size N is achieved. The proposed algorithm framework is depicted in Fig. 2.

4   Results and Discussions

The regression-assisted NSGA III technique is coded with MATLAB functions on an Intel i7 laptop with 16 GB RAM. Since it is a multi-objective optimization problem, Pareto solutions are recorded. These are near-optimal solutions with trade-offs among the fitness scores (Fig. 3). Total 13 Pareto solutions are depicted in Table 4. The best solution is chosen for the confirmatory experiment (Table 5).

Table 4. Total 13 Pareto solutions obtained by regression driven NSGA III

TD	SS	FR	DOC	MRR	Ra
8.319	1565.011	4.548	1.403	22.489	0.136
6.077	1993.653	4.394	1.486	13.475	0.040
6.221	1829.457	4.095	1.685	17.252	0.057
8.323	1629.146	4.884	1.729	26.399	0.151
6.888	1835.224	4.660	1.531	17.731	0.059
7.527	1609.844	4.236	1.305	18.150	0.086
8.495	1580.086	4.131	1.736	27.245	0.234
9.813	2079.163	4.863	1.847	31.169	0.457
6.772	1519.991	3.408	1.749	21.404	0.105
6.543	1595.130	3.503	1.556	17.778	0.074
9.788	2176.137	3.233	1.970	32.009	0.663
9.481	1620.140	3.631	1.745	30.666	0.406
9.252	1874.775	4.840	1.856	30.213	0.340

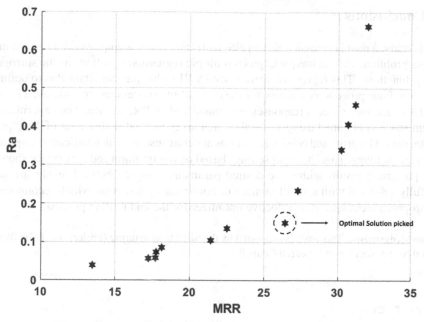

Fig. 3. Pareto solutions obtained by regression driven NSGA III

4.1 Confirmatory Test

Once the optimal levels of the control factors are identified, confirmatory test is performed. Total 10 experimental run are performed using the obtained set of parameters. The parameter values are rounded off to the nearest real values. The average MRR, and Ra scores are shown in Table 5. The confirmatory test results are compared with the model output, which are substantially close to each other with deviation of 10.66% and 3.22% for the Ra and MRR respectively, which are in the acceptable range. Therefore, the confirmatory test indicates that the selection of the optimal levels of the parameters could produce the best and accurate process responses for the end milling process.

Table 5. Confirmatory test result

End milling parameters	Predicted responses	Experimental responses	Errors
TD = 8, SS = 1629, FR = 4.88, DOC = 1.73	MRR = 26.4, Ra = 0.15	MRR = 27.25, Ra = 0.166	MRR = 3.22%, Ra = 10.66%

5 Conclusions

In this study, a novel regression driven NSGA III algorithm is employed for the end mill cutting problem. This technique exploits multiple regression equations as the surrogate fitness functions. This regression driven NSGA III technique can attain Pareto optimal solutions. Four process parameters for the end milling process are considered, TD, SS, FR, DOC and two process responses are considered, MRR, and Ra. The experimental design space is obtained using L_{16} orthogonal array method with a total of 16 experimental runs. The proposed NSGA III obtains accurate results, which indicate the optimal parameter settings. This choice of settings based on our intuition and experience showed very promising results within the desired parametric range. Obtained results are successfully validated with a small number of confirmatory test runs, which recommends the proposed technique as an effective optimizer for the end milling process.

Acknowledgement. This work is supported by the SFI Manufacturing (Project No. 237900) and funded by the Norwegian Research Council.

References

1. Alimam, H., Hinnawi, M., Pradhan, P., Alkassar, Y.: ANN & ANFIS models for prediction of abrasive wear of 3105 aluminium alloy with polyurethane coating. Tribol. Ind. **38**, 221–228 (2016)
2. An, Y., Lu, W., Cheng, W.: Surrogate model application to the identification of optimal groundwater exploitation scheme based on regression kriging method-a case study of Western Jilin Province. Int. J. Environ. Res. Public Health **12**, 8897–8918 (2015)
3. Chankong, V., Haimes, Y.: Multiobjective Decision Making Theory and Methodology. North-Holland, New York (1983)
4. Cook, D., Ragsdale, C., Major, R.: Combining a neural network with a genetic algorithm for process parameter optimization. Eng. Appl. Artif. Intell. **13**, 391–396 (2000)
5. Das, I., Dennis, J.E.: Normal-boundary intersection: a new method for generating the Pareto surface in nonlinear multicriteria optimization problems. SIAM J. Optim. **8**, 631–657 (1998)
6. Deb, K., Agrawal, R.: Simulated binary crossover for continuous search space. Complex Syst. **9**, 1–34 (1994)
7. Deb, K., Jain, H.: An evolutionary many-objective optimization algorithm using reference-point-based nondominated sorting approach, Part I: solving problems with box constraints. IEEE Trans. Evol. Comput. **18**, 577–601 (2014)
8. Dikshit, M.K., Puri, A.B., Maity, A., Banerjee, A.J.: Analysis of cutting forces and optimization of cutting parameters in high speed ball-end milling using response surface methodology and genetic algorithm. Procedia Mater. Sci. **5**, 1623–1632 (2014)
9. Giunta, A., Wojtkiewicz, S., Eldred, M.: Overview of modern design of experiments methods for computational simulations. In: 41st Aerospace Sciences Meeting and Exhibit, Aerospace Sciences Meetings, Reno, Nevada, USA (2003)
10. Hu, L.: CNC milling of complex aluminium parts. Thesis, Lehigh University (2017)
11. Kukkonen, S., Deb, K.: Improved pruning of non-dominated solutions based on crowding distance for bi-objective optimization problems. In: IEEE Congress on Evolutionary Computation (CEC), pp. 1179–1186 (2006)

12. Messac, A.: Optimization in Practice with MATLAB. Cambridge University Press, New York (2015)
13. Muñoz-Escalona, P., Maropoulos, P.G.: A geometrical model for surface roughness prediction when face milling Al 7075-T7351 with square insert tools. J. Manuf. Syst. **36**, 216–223 (2015)
14. Pfrommer, J., et al.: Optimisation of manufacturing process parameters using deep neural networks as surrogate models. Procedia CIRP **72**, 426–431 (2018)
15. Rajeswari, B., Amirthagadeswaran, K.S.: Experimental investigation of machinability characteristics and multi-response optimization of end milling in aluminium composites using RSM based grey relational analysis. Measurement **105**, 78–86 (2017)
16. Shen, C., Wang, L., Li, Q.: Optimization of injection molding process parameters using combination of artificial neural network and genetic algorithm method. J. Mater. Process. Technol. **183**, 412–418 (2007)
17. Shi, H., Gao, Y., Wang, X.: Optimization of injection molding process parameters using integrated artificial neural network model and expected improvement function method. Int. J. Adv. Manuf. Technol. **48**, 955–962 (2010)
18. Šibalija, T.V., Majstorović, V.D.: Advanced Multiresponse Process Optimisation. Springer, Cham (2016). https://doi.org/10.1007/978-3-319-19255-0
19. Ghosh, T., Martinsen, K.: CFNN-PSO: an iterative predictive model for generic parametric design of machining processes. Appl. Artif. Intell. **33**, 951–978 (2019)
20. Simpson, T., Toropov, V., Balabanov, V., Viana, F.: Design and analysis of computer experiments in multidisciplinary design optimization: a review of how far we have come - or not. In: 12th AIAA/ISSMO Multidisciplinary Analysis and Optimization Conference, Multidisciplinary Analysis Optimization Conferences, British Columbia (2008)
21. Tamiloli, N., Venkatesan, J., Ramnath, B.V.: A grey-fuzzy modeling for evaluating surface roughness and material removal rate of coated end milling insert. Measurement **84**, 68–82 (2016)
22. Thombansen, U., Schuttler, J., Auerbach, T., Beckers, M.: Model-based self-optimization for manufacturing systems. In: 17th International Conference on Concurrent Enterprising (2011)
23. Zhang, X., Ehmann, K.F., Yu, T., Wang, W.: Cutting forces in micro-end-milling processes. Int. J. Mach. Tools Manuf **107**, 21–40 (2016)
24. Zhao, P., Zhou, H., Li, Y., Li, D.: Process parameters optimization of injection molding using a fast strip analysis as a surrogate model. Int. J. Adv. Manuf. Technol. **49**, 949–959 (2010)

Steering Angle Estimation for Self-driving Car Using Deep Learning

Ajay Kumar and Suja Palaniswamy[✉]

Department of Computer Science and Engineering,
Amrita School of Engineering, Amrita Vishwa Vidyapeetham,
Bengaluru 560035, India
p_suja@blr.amrita.edu

Abstract. The contemporary age has seen a tremendous increase in the number of road accidents. Traffic accidents are commonly caused by driver error, mobile phone usage, in-car audio and video entertainment systems, and extensive traffic. The road accident in India causes one death every four minutes. Imagine if everyone can easily and safely get around while driving is not tired, drunk or distracted. Self-driving means of transport are those in which drivers are never required to drive the vehicle. In self-driving car, time spent on travel may well be time spent doing what one needs, because all driving is handled by the car. Also referred to as autonomous or "driverless" cars, they mix sensors and code to manage, navigate, and drive the vehicle. The self-driving cars have huge potential to alter the means of transportation. We have proposed an end-to-end method based on deep learning for estimating the steering angle and the accuracy obtained is 98.6%.

Keywords: Self-driving · End-to-end learning · Angle · Deep learning · Regression

1 Introduction

Imagine if everybody may get around simply and safely, while not tired, drunk or distracted while driving. Travel time spent may well be spent doing what one wishes because the automatic system handles all the needs of driving. Self-driving means of transportation are cars or trucks within which drivers are not needed to soundly operate the vehicle. Also referred to as autonomous or "driverless" cars, sensors are used, coded to manage, navigate, and drive the vehicle. The self-driving cars have huge potential to alter the means of transportation. Even with all types of sensors and intelligent systems on board, it remains a posh challenge to permit a vehicle to drive fully independently. Few of the challenges are listed as follows: Driving securely not withstanding hazy path markings, reliability of traffic signals that are not functioning sometimes, very often small objects detected on the road which must be avoided, the capability to react to spoken commands or hand gestures from traffic police, the control systems that can analyze sensory data in order to detect other vehicles and the road ahead accurately. In this work, we have proposed a method for estimating the steering angle using end-to-end learning based on deep learning.

© Springer Nature Singapore Pte Ltd. 2020
S. M. Thampi et al. (Eds.): SoMMA 2019, CCIS 1203, pp. 196–207, 2020.
https://doi.org/10.1007/978-981-15-4301-2_17

The sections of the paper are outlined as follows: Sect. 2 discusses related work, Sect. 3 elaborates proposed methodology, Sect. 4 briefs experimental setup, Sect. 5 narrates the training details, Sect. 6 illustrates experimental results and analysis, Sect. 7 provides the visualization of output and the final section summarizes conclusion and future work.

2 Related Work

This section discusses the work done in the advancement of self-driving cars. NVIDIA [1] built a self-driving car using end-to-end learning. NVIDIA used Convolution Neural Network (CNN) to map the raw pixels from the front-facing camera to the self-driving car steering instructions. This strong end-to-end strategy implies that the system learns to navigate on both local roads and highways with minimal human training data, with or without lane markings. In fields with uncertain visual guidance such as parking lots or unpaved highways, the system can also function. The advancement in the field of autonomous driving is depicted in Fig. 1.

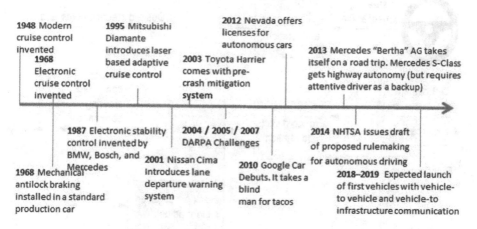

Fig. 1. Development in autonomous driving

The electric cruise was the beginning of the journey to develop self-driving cars in 1948–1968 [2]. In 1987, BMW, Bosch and Mercedes invented electronic stability control. Another big milestone achieved by Mercedes "Berth" AG takes itself on a road trip. Mercedes S-Class gets highway autonomy but it requires an attentive driver as a backup. DARPA funded by USA has contributed to this domain for American automatic vehicles [3].

DARPA challenges ended in 2015 which was a significant event in this field. A working model of self-driving car demonstrated using CNN [4] effectively reduces the complexity in developing the same. The developments in the autonomous vehicle which estimates road detection, lane detection, and traffic signal detection happened separately. It is followed by orchestration using a master algorithm which controls the self-driving car from the input received from these sub-systems. But an end-to-end learning model can outperform this complex system. We have considered [1] as a reference and developed our proposed model. We have implemented dropouts and performed hypermeter tuning to achieve maximum accuracy in addition to the work considered in reference [1]. The accuracy achieved is 98.6% which is significantly better than the result found in literature. This is our major contribution. The next section describes the proposed method.

3 Proposed Methodology

Figure 2 shows the general workflow of the proposed self-driving car using end-to-end learning. End-to-end model is a CNN structure that connects the front facing cameras directly to the steering instructions to assist in training a self-driving car to drive smarter and more independently.

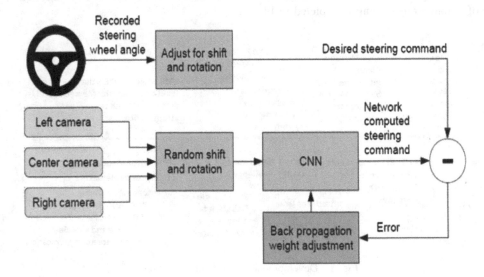

Fig. 2. Flowchart of an end-to-end learning system

The model proposed can see the driver's views (Images in dataset) and actions by using dashboard cameras i.e. adjusting steering angle. This idea has been used by the scheme to determine an ideal driving strategy for fully autonomous self-driving.

End-to-end learning model learns to emulate human driver conduct and can be implemented as an auto driver. End-to-end learning is taught using images of highway coupled with the steering angles produced by riding a data-collection vehicle. It stems from the information needed in domain knowledge. This eliminates the need for engineers to anticipate what is essential in an image and to predict all the laws needed for safe driving. Road studies have shown that end-to-end learning model can effectively maintain the lane in a broad range of riding circumstances, regardless of lane markings are present or not. We have implemented dropout [10] regularization to prevent overfitting. As this is a fully connected layer of neural network, we have implemented dropout as the network is densely connected. The key idea is to dropout some units randomly along with their connection from the neural network at the time of training. Dropout prevents unit from co-adapting too much, additionally, we have done hyperparameter tuning to achieve higher accuracy.

3.1 Visual Data Process by Convolution Neural Networks

CNN is a kind of neural network consisting of perceptron's that revolutionized the pattern recognition process. Prior to development of CNN features are extracted manually [4]. In this approach, first while driving, the network would generate a decision, compare it with the human driver's selection, then adjust itself and repeat the process.

The CNN model proposed in this work is depicted in Fig. 3. Images are captured from side cameras with random rotation because without this setting the driving direction is undesirably lean i.e., the vehicle could drive too close to the edge of the road. The model in Fig. 3 extracts any other objects present in the road and the steering angle could be predicted accordingly.

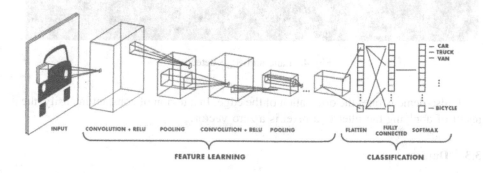

Fig. 3. Object classification and feature learning

3.2 Lane and Edge Detection of the Road

Edge and road boundary detection can be done using Lidar [5]. We have used Sobel filter in this work. It operates by calculating the image intensity gradient within the image at each pixel. It identifies the direction and rate of change of the highest intensity from light to dark. The outcome demonstrates sudden or smooth changes at each pixel, and the pixels that constitute an edge is depicted in Fig. 4.

Fig. 4. Lane and edge detection

It also demonstrates the orientation of the edge. In a region of constant intensity, the result of applying the filter to a pixel is a zero vector.

3.3   Dataset

Live video was recorded while driving and steering angle is captured for every moment. Video is converted into image frames such that one second video has 30 frames. Each image is synchronized with their respective steering angle. We have used 72 GB of data to train the system to achieve higher accuracy.

We have used one .csv file containing the image name and the steering angle with the time stamp and sample data is shown in Fig. 5. Figure 6 shows all the time-stamped image frames per second for the corresponding steering angle mentioned in Fig. 5.

```
24.jpg  0.000000,2018-07-01  17:09:46:67
25.jpg  0.000000,2018-07-01  17:09:46:137
26.jpg  0.000000,2018-07-01  17:09:46:166
27.jpg  0.000000,2018-07-01  17:09:46:233
28.jpg  0.000000,2018-07-01  17:09:46:293
29.jpg  0.000000,2018-07-01  17:09:46:330
30.jpg  0.000000,2018-07-01  17:09:46:398
31.jpg  0.000000,2018-07-01  17:09:46:426
32.jpg  -3.530000,2018-07-01  17:09:46:464
33.jpg  -3.930000,2018-07-01  17:09:46:493
34.jpg  -5.240000,2018-07-01  17:09:46:564
35.jpg  -5.340000,2018-07-01  17:09:46:621
36.jpg  -4.840000,2018-07-01  17:09:46:661
37.jpg  -3.530000,2018-07-01  17:09:46:727
38.jpg  -2.620000,2018-07-01  17:09:46:795
39.jpg  -2.320000,2018-07-01  17:09:46:856
40.jpg  -2.320000,2018-07-01  17:09:46:885
41.jpg  -2.320000,2018-07-01  17:09:46:924
42.jpg  -2.320000,2018-07-01  17:09:46:992
```

Fig. 5. Image with respective steering angles

Fig. 6. Image dataset

4   Experimental Setup

Each image size is 3 × 66 × 200 represented in RGB with each pixel value ranging from 0 to 255. The image is to be normalized and we have divided each pixel by 255. This normalization process makes each value ranging from 0 to 1. After normalization, we have performed convolution by using 5 convolution layers. The details of each convolution layer are depicted in Fig. 7. Initially, we have used fewer kernels in each convolution and as layer increases, we have increased the number of kernels. Extraction of the feature characteristics by the convolution layers is as follows: The first three layers use stride conversions with 5 × 5 kernels, the last two layers use non-stride convolutions with 3 × 3 kernel sizes. We have flattened the data after five convolution operations as mentioned in [6]. We have used arctan at the output layer.

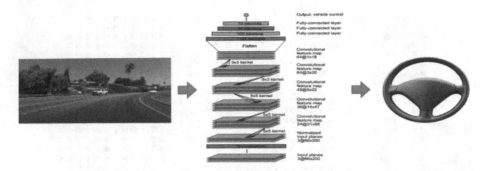

Fig. 7. Implementation overview

End-to-end learning aims to make the system automatically learn inner depictions of the needed processing steps such as identifying helpful street characteristics. End-to-end is relevant in such a manner that a model of machine learning can transform a piece of input information directly into an output forecast bypassing the intermediate steps in a traditional pipeline. The additional steps, such as data collection or auxiliary processes, cannot be part of the end-to-end model in this view unless the model can learn the intermediate processes with the data given.

5 Training of End-to-End Learning Model

In this work, to train the final model, we have used the following hyperparameter configuration:

- Optimizer: Adam optimizer with initial learning rate: 1e-4
- Batch size: 100
- Epochs: 30

The network has taken 30 epochs to train this model with a few dozen steps per epoch which are depicted in Fig. 8.

```
Epoch: 0, Step: 0, Loss: 6.7098
WARNING:tensorflow:************************************************
WARNING:tensorflow:TensorFlow's V1 checkpoint format has been deprecated.
WARNING:tensorflow:Consider switching to the more efficient V2 format:
WARNING:tensorflow:   `tf.train.Saver(write_version=tf.train.SaverDef.V2)`
WARNING:tensorflow:now on by default.
WARNING:tensorflow:************************************************
Epoch: 0, Step: 10, Loss: 6.43693
Epoch: 0, Step: 20, Loss: 6.1716
Epoch: 0, Step: 30, Loss: 6.41206
Epoch: 0, Step: 40, Loss: 6.23232
Epoch: 0, Step: 50, Loss: 6.08394
Epoch: 0, Step: 60, Loss: 6.18194
Epoch: 0, Step: 70, Loss: 5.97316
Epoch: 0, Step: 80, Loss: 6.04343
Epoch: 0, Step: 90, Loss: 5.9292
Epoch: 0, Step: 100, Loss: 5.87816
WARNING:tensorflow:************************************************
```

Fig. 8. Training phase

After hyperparameter tuning, a lower learning rate was obtained. It meant that the network could learn without much oscillation at a moderate pace. The "Loss" estimates the error of the model (or feature) in the Fig. 9. Conceptually, the real steering angle is likened to be the model's expected steering angle to calculate Loss. The bigger the difference, the higher is the loss [7]. Ultimately, the program utilizes the evaluation of loss and minimizing loss using Adam Optimizer in each iteration when training the model to decrease the loss through each iterative step.

6 Experimental Results and Analysis

6.1 Data Analysis on Steering Angle

The value of steering angles range between −2 to +2 and is depicted in Fig. 9. The Y-axis in the plot shows the frequency of change of steering angles. The Fig. 9 shows majority of steering angle are at zero, so steering is kept straight. The very first conclusion drawn from this exploratory data analysis that most of the time the steering was at zero degrees means the road is straight. The next section illustrates the test and visualization of output.

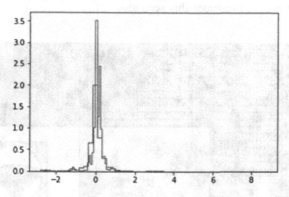

Fig. 9. Exploratory data analysis

7 Testing and Visualization

The proposed work has achieved 98.6% accuracy when compared to reference [1] which is 98% approximately. We can see that CNN detects the outline of the road as shown in Fig. 10. The best way to visualize the result of this system/model is by the turning of the steering angle predicted by the system along with the source image.

Fig. 10. Road outline detection

7.1 Almost Straight Road Scenario

The model output when the road is almost straight steering angle is at almost zero degree. Figure 11 shows illustrates this scenario.

Fig. 11. Almost straight road

7.2 Slightly Right Turn Scenario

When the road seems to be is slightly right turn the steering also moving towards the right direction that is evident in Fig. 12.

Fig. 12. Slightly right turn scenario

7.3 Sharp Right Turn Scenario

When the road seems to be curved right side then the previous scenario i.e. slight right turns the steering also moving more towards the right direction than the previous scenario that is evident in Fig. 13.

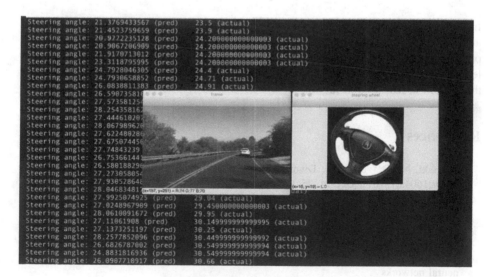

Fig. 13. Sharp right turn scenario

7.4   Slight Right Turn Scenario

When the road seems to be is slightly right turn the steering also moving towards the right direction that is shown in Fig. 14.

Fig. 14. Slight right scenario

8   Conclusion and Future Scope

In this work, we proposed an end-to-end model based on CNN to estimate the steering angle. The proposed work has achieved 98.6% accuracy. The CNN model can comprehend the highway's features. Without the need for particular road labels, the model learns from the sample to detect a road trait. Similar to [9] we will test the robustness of the system in real-time in future.

References

1. Bojarski, M., Del Testa, D., Dworakowski, D.: End-to-end learning for self-driving cars. arXiv:1604.07316v1 [cs.CV], 25 April 2016
2. Ioannou, P.A., Chien, C.C.: Autonomous intelligent cruise control. IEEE Trans. Veh. Technol. **42**, 657–672 (1993)
3. The DARPA LAGR program: goals, challenges, methodology, and phase I results. https://onlinelibrary.wiley.com/doi/abs/10.1002/rob.20161
4. Krizhevsky, A., Sutskever, I., Hinton, G.E.: ImageNet classification with deep convolutional neural networks
5. Wijesoma, W.S., Kodagoda, K.S., Balasuriya, A.P.: Road-boundary detection and tracking using ladar sensing. IEEE Trans. Robot. Autom. **20**(3), 456–464 (2004)
6. Sreedhar, P.B., Palaniswamy, S.: Robotic Grasper based on an end-to-end neural architecture using Raspberry Pi. In: Proceedings of Advance Computing and Communication Conference, September 2018

7. Pan, X., You, Y., Wang, Z., Lu, C.: Virtual to real reinforcement learning for autonomous driving. arXiv:1704.03952v4 [cs.AI], 26 September 2017

8. Jain, A.K.: Working model of self-driving car using convolutional neural network, Raspberry Pi and Arduino. In: 2018 Second International Conference on Electronics, Communication and Aerospace Technology (ICECA) (2018)

9. Dev, V.S., Variyar, V.V.S., Soman, K.P.: Steering angle estimation for autonomous vehicle. In: 2017 International Conference on Advances in Computing, Communications and Informatics (ICACCI 2017) (2017)

10. Wager, S., Wang, S., Liang, P.: Dropout training as adaptive regularization. In: Advances in Neural Information Processing Systems 26, pp. 351–359 (2013)

11. Dahl, G.E., Sainath, T.N., Hinton, G.E.: Improving deep neural networks for LVCSR using rectified linear units and dropout. In: 2013 IEEE International Conference (2013). ISBN 978-1-4799-0356-6

A Textural Feature Based Cytological Image Classification Using Artificial Neural Network

Pranaba K. Mishro[1], Sanjay Agrawal[1(✉)], and Shipra Sharma[2]

[1] VSS University of Technology, Burla, Odisha, India
mailpranaba@gmail.com, agrawals.72@gmail.com
[2] SUIIT, Sambalpur University, Burla, Odisha, India
sharmashipra167@gmail.com

Abstract. Cytological image classification is essential for the diagnosis and treatment planning of cancerous diseases. The accuracy of classification is determined from the set of extracted features. Thus, the selection of features is an important part in any supervised learning technique. In this paper, we suggest a texture based cytological image classification scheme utilizing artificial neural network (ANN). The training dataset is prepared from the gray level co-occurrence matrix (GLCM) based textural features obtained using Laws Texture Energy Measure (LTEM) algorithm. The textural features are further classified into desired benign-malignant tissue types. The proposed approach is experimented using cytological images from the NITRC: human imaging database. The result of the classification using the suggested model is compared with that of state-of-the-art schemes. It is observed that encouraging results are obtained with the proposed model.

Keywords: Cytological image classification · ANN classifier · GLCM · LTEM

1 Introduction

Cytological image classification is a routine challenge for the pathologist in the diagnosis of cancerous cells. Stability and accuracy are the main challenges for the diagnosis of benign and malignant tissues. The improvement in stability and accuracy is achieved by using computer aided diagnosis (CAD) process. Basically, the CAD systems are designed for the analysis of the cytological images. They are designed using the image processing and machine intelligence techniques for reporting more accurate information regarding the clinical images. This may support in augmenting the physician's capabilities and reducing human errors. In this paper, we propose a textural feature based ANN classifier for cytological image classification. ANN is widely used machine intelligence module in medical image classification.

In recent years, the researchers proposed a number of approaches for cytological image classifications, such as logistic regression method, fuzzy clustering based systems, radial basis network and neural networks [1–6]. In, Chou *et al.* [7], the authors proposed a 2-stage model based on multivariate adaptive regression splines for the diagnosis of breast cancer. The model uses an auxiliary predictor variable for designing the neural

© Springer Nature Singapore Pte Ltd. 2020
S. M. Thampi et al. (Eds.): SoMMA 2019, CCIS 1203, pp. 208–217, 2020.
https://doi.org/10.1007/978-981-15-4301-2_18

network. In, Alayon *et al.* [8], the authors suggested a pattern recognition technique using the fuzzy finite state machine for diagnosing the normal and the abnormal breast tissues. In, Jelen *et al.* [9], the authors suggested a feature based classifier using the support vector machine (SVM) for finding the malignancy in the abnormal breast regions. The method assigns a membership grade to the nuclei representation based on the segmentation results. The feature-based classifier classifies the structural parameters, such as area, perimeter, eccentricity and convexity used to generate the training dataset. In, Subashini *et al.* [10], the authors proposed a feature based SVM classifier to support the diagnosis of the malignant tissue regions in the cytological images. This method uses clinical attributes, such as differential cell size, nuclear pleomorphic, and frequency of cell mitosis for formulating the feature vectors.

In, Marcano *et al.* [11], the authors proposed a training algorithm for the neural network model based on biological meta-plasticity property. In the training phase, the artificial meta-plasticity multilayer perceptron (AMMLP) algorithm updates the relative weight of the activations of the meta-plasts present in the mammogram image. In, Pouliakis *et al.* [12], the authors proposed a back propagation ANN framework for classifying the normal and abnormal types of cell images based on their morphometric features. In, Burke *et al.* [13], the authors suggested a probabilistic neural network classification framework using learning vector quantization and SVM classifier. It is used to classify the cytological images for detecting the malignancy in the cell regions. The SVM classifier uses the structural features for detecting the malignancy regions in the cytological images. It is observed that most of the methods discussed above are silent about the textural features of the images. This affects the stability of the algorithms over a high range of input data. Further, the classification accuracy achieved using these methods is relatively low.

In this paper, we suggest a textural feature based ANN approach for cytological image classification. The textural features are extracted using the Laws texture energy measure (LTEM) algorithm [14]. As far as our knowledge is concerned, such an approach is new to the problem on hand. The textural features are used to generate the training dataset for the classification. The proposed approach is experimented with the cytological images obtained from the neuro-imaging tools and resources collaborator (NITRC): human imaging database [15]. The performance of the suggested approach is compared with the standard techniques (SVM, AMMLP, ANN and RBFNN). Further, it is validated utilizing the receiver operating characteristics (ROC) parameters [16].

The rest of the paper is organized as follows. In Sect. 2, the proposed framework is explained. The performance evaluation of the proposed model is discussed in Sect. 3. Section 3 shows the results and discussions. Section 4 draws the conclusion and future scope of the proposed approach.

2 Proposed Methodology

The proposed framework consists of the following stages, image pre-processing, feature extraction, image classification using ANN. Figure 1 shows the schematic block diagram of the proposed approach.

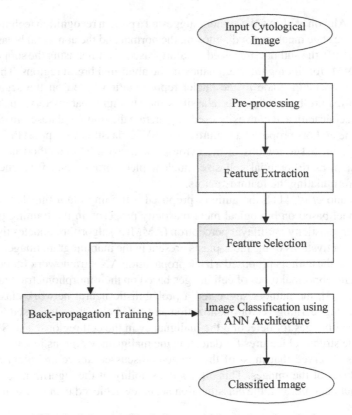

Fig. 1. Schematic block diagram of the proposed method.

Image Pre-processing

Image pre-processing is an essential requirement prior to the classification process. In general, region of interest (ROI) selection, contrast enhancement and denoising are carried out in this stage. The purpose of the ROI selection is to remove the irrelevant tissue regions from the cytological image. Further, the contrast enhancement and denoising are performed using standard approaches.

Feature Extraction

Designing a training dataset is an important pre-requisite in the image classification process using ANN. This dataset is prepared with the extracted features of the cytological images. In this paper, the feature extraction is carried out using the LTEM, a recent method of textural analysis. LTEM is a texture-energy approach that measures the amount of variations in a defined region window. A set of vectors are formed to describe the structural behaviors, such as the level, edge, spot and the ripple in an image. These vectors are reshaped to form a 5×5 convolution mask for computing the texture energy. Eighteen such masks are formed by combining these vectors and are used for computing the texture energy. The vectors representing the textural parameters are given as per the LTEM algorithm, as follows:

Table 1. Textural vector representation.

Texture	Vector
L5 (Level)	[1 4 6 4 1]
E5 (Edge)	[−1 −2 0 2 1]
S5 (Spot)	[−1 0 2 0 −1]
R5 (Ripple)	[1 −4 6 −4 1]

Each of the vectors represent a texture that can be focused in the image. These vectors are combined to form the convolution matrices which represents the joint probable textures. For example, the vector L5 is used to calculate the center-weighted local averaging window. Similarly, the vector E5 describes the edges, vector S5 represents the spots, and the vector R5 represents the ripples. A 2D convolution window is formed by combining the product pairs of the textural vectors. The combined masks, such as E5L5 is formed by the product of the vectors E5 and L5 (shown in Table 2). The resulting mask is shown as follows:

$$
\begin{bmatrix} -1 \\ -2 \\ 0 \\ 2 \\ 1 \end{bmatrix} \times \begin{bmatrix} 1 & 4 & 6 & 4 & 1 \end{bmatrix} = \begin{bmatrix} -1 & -4 & -6 & -4 & -1 \\ -2 & -8 & -12 & -8 & -2 \\ 0 & 0 & 0 & 0 & 0 \\ 2 & 8 & 12 & 8 & 2 \\ 1 & 4 & 6 & 4 & 1 \end{bmatrix} \tag{1}
$$

In LTEM algorithm, the textural parameters are formed using the texture vectors as given in Table 1 above. The illumination effects are reduced by spatial filtering the image using an averaging mask. The resulting image is then subtracted from the actual pixel intensity for each pixel.

Table 2. Combination of vectors

	L5	E5	S5	R5
L5	L5 L5	E5 L5	S5 L5	R5 L5
E5	L5 E5	E5 E5	S5 E5	R5 E5
S5	L5 S5	E5 S5	S5 S5	R5 S5
R5	L5 R5	E5 R5	S5 R5	R5 R5

In this paper, we formed eighteen energy masks for certain symmetric pairs such as L5 E5, L5 R5 etc. The combined masks are used to replace each pair with its average pixel intensity value. For example, E5 L5 mask for the horizontal edge content, and L5 E5 mask for the vertical edge content. In this paper, the cytological image is block transformed in to sub-images of size 16 × 16. Each sub-image is spatially filtered to determine the textural features of gray level co-occurrence matrix (GLCM) (such as: energy, entropy, contrast, homogeneity, correlation, shade, prominence) and statistical features (such as: mean, variance, standard deviation). These parameters are computed as follows:

$$\text{Energy} = \sum_{i,j=0}^{N-1} \left(P_{ij}\right)^2 \tag{2}$$

$$\text{Entropy} = \sum_{i,j=0}^{N-1} -P_{ij}\ln(P_{ij}) \tag{3}$$

$$\text{Contrast} = \sum_{i,j=0}^{N-1} P_{ij}(i-j)^2 \tag{4}$$

$$\text{Homogeneity} = \sum_{i,j=0}^{N-1} \frac{P_{ij}}{1+(i-j)^2} \tag{5}$$

$$\text{Correlation} = \sum_{i,j=0}^{N-1} P_{ij}\frac{(i-\mu)(j-\mu)}{\sigma^2} \tag{6}$$

$$\text{Shade} = \text{sgn}(A)|A|^{1/3} \tag{7}$$

$$\text{Prominance} = \text{sgn}(A)|A|^{1/4} \tag{8}$$

$$\text{Mean} = \frac{\sum_{w} neighboring\ pixels}{w} \tag{9}$$

$$\text{Variance} = \frac{\sum_{w} (neighboring\ pixels - mean)^2}{w} \tag{10}$$

$$\text{Standard Deviation} = \sqrt{\frac{\sum |x_j - \bar{x}|^2}{N}} \tag{11}$$

where,

P_{ij} is the normalized GLCM factor
N is the number of intensity levels
μ is the GLCM mean
σ^2 is the variance in the pixel
A is a real number derived from GLCM mean and correlation feature
$\bar{x}$ is the mean value of the pixels
W is size of the window

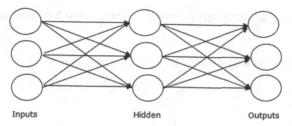

Fig. 2. ANN architecture

ANN Classifier

ANN is an automatic scheme used for image classification as a supervised classifier. This is applied to a variety of pattern recognition and classification task. From the literature, it is found that ANN is a promising solution to the complex classification problems, such as: cytological image classification (Fig. 2).

The feed-forward architecture of the neural network consists of three functional layers. The weights are updated by preceding the direction conjugate to its prior step by minimizing the error function. In general, ANN is initialized with random weights with each iteration. So, output is marginally varied at every run. This randomness is avoided using random seed, which generates same weights every time. In this paper, ANN architecture with ten input layer for ten features in the training dataset, one output layer to show the normal/abnormal and benign/malignant tissue regions is designed. This ANN architecture is experimented with multiple hidden layers. The training dataset is generated for eighteen textures (as shown in Table 2) with ten features: energy, entropy, contrast, homogeneity, correlation, shade, prominence, mean, variance and standard deviation.

3 Results and Discussion

The proposed model is implemented using MATLAB and compared with SVM, AMMLP, ANN and RBFNN classifiers for classifying the benign and malignant tissue regions in cytological images. The model is experimented using a selected volume of 200 abnormal cytological images from NITRC: human imaging database [9]. From this selected volume, 60% of the images are used to generate the training dataset. The rest 20% data is used for the testing and 20% data is used for validation purpose. The feature vectors are formed from the textural features using the LTEM algorithm. Further, these feature vectors are given as the input to the ANN classifier. The suggested approach is validated utilizing the ROC parameters, accuracy, specificity and sensitivity using Eqs. (12–14). The classification rate in abnormal cytological image is shown in Table 3.

From the table, it is observed that the classification rate reaches the maximum value with five hidden nodes, whereas, it reaches the minimum value with eleven hidden nodes. The corresponding graph is shown in Fig. 3 to represent the variation of the classification rate with different number of hidden nodes.

The response curve presented in Fig. 3 shows the accuracy in classification rate. The classification rate is obtained with 5 to 15 numbers of hidden nodes. This shows

Table 3. Classification rate for benign-malignant tissue regions with different numbers of hidden nodes.

Number of hidden nodes	Rate of classification (in %)	
	Normal-abnormal	Benign-malignant
5	85.82	90.51
6	78.53	76.20
7	75.28	60.12
8	78.44	72.35
9	76.63	48.45
10	76.17	74.63
11	75.36	42.49
12	79.41	76.54
13	77.50	75.44
14	79.65	78.80
15	78.22	73.14

the variation of classification rate by selecting different number of hidden nodes for classifying the normal-abnormal and benign-malignant tissue regions.

The performance evaluation of the proposed method is carried using 200 numbers of cytological images from NITRC: human imaging database [9]. An example clinical cytological images for malignancy identification using ANN is shown in Fig. 4. This shows the true benign and malignant cell type classified results from the given cytological image. The cytological images shown has discrete and overlapped cell structures. The diagnostic parameters such as: dysplasia and necrosis can be observed clearly in the classification results. The proposed method gives a better output in terms of classifying the tissue structures. The performance of the classifiers was evaluated by the percentage

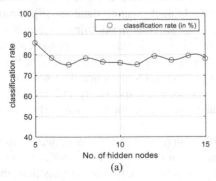 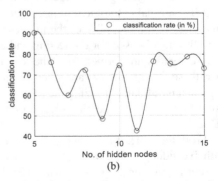

Fig. 3. Classification rate (in %), (a) normal-abnormal, (b) benign-malignant tissue regions for different number of hidden nodes.

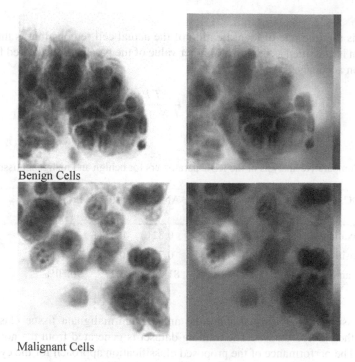

Benign Cells

Malignant Cells

Fig. 4. Classification results of benign-malignant tissue regions in cytological image.

of accurately classified benign-malignant tissue regions. The validation of the proposed model is performed using the ROC parameters. The parameters are obtained as follows:

Accuracy
This parameter indicates the accuracy in classification of the benign tissue regions in the abnormal cytological image. The higher value of accuracy indicates better performance of the classifier.

$$Accuracy(\%) = \frac{TP + TN}{TP + TN + FP + FN} \times 100 \qquad (12)$$

Specificity
This parameter indicates the true classification rate i.e. a non-malignant tissue classified as non-malignant. It is defined as:

$$Specificity(\%) = \frac{TN}{TN + FP} \times 100 \qquad (13)$$

Sensitivity
Sensitivity is the true rate of identification of the actual cell regions that is the benign tissue region is classified as benign. A higher value of the parameter is desired for better classification accuracy.

$$Sensitivity(\%) = \frac{TP}{FN + TP} \times 100 \qquad (14)$$

Table 4. Comparative analysis of the ROC parameters for benign and malignant tissue types.

ROC parameters	SVM	AMMLP	ANN	RBFNN	Proposed method
Specificity	0.7274	0.7624	0.8213	0.8341	**0.8666**
Sensitivity	0.7514	0.7436	0.7942	0.8054	**0.8967**
Accuracy	81.5%	78.11%	81.34%	83.27%	**90.50%**

The classification of normal-abnormal and benign-malignant tissue class is performed on the NITRC dataset. The training dataset is generated from the normal type of images. The performance of the proposed classification approach for the cytological images is presented in Table 4. This shows a comparison of the proposed approach with the SVM, AMMLP, ANN and RFBNN classifiers for cytological image classification.

4   Conclusion

In this paper, the LTEM algorithm is used as the textural feature descriptor for the cytological image classification. This describes the features more efficiently, which increases the classification accuracy significantly. In this framework, we used the ANN as the classifier for the classification of normal-abnormal and benign-malignant tissue regions. The combined framework provides accurate information for the critical analysis and treatment planning. The use of ANN enhances the performance of the cytological image classification in comparison to the SVM, AMMLP, ANN and RFBNN classifiers. The proposed model is evaluated using 200 numbers of cytological images. The performance evaluation for normal-abnormal and benign-malignant classification is validated using the ROC parameters: accuracy, specificity and sensitivity. It is observed that the performance of the proposed classifier is better in all the evaluation indices.

References

1. Saha, M., Mukherjee, R., Chakraborty, C.: Computer-aided diagnosis of breast cancer using cytological images: a systematic review. Tissue Cell **48**(5), 461–474 (2016)
2. Dey, P., Banerjee, N., Kaur, R.: Digital image classification with the help of artificial neural network by simple histogram. J. Cytol./Indian Acad. Cytol. **33**(2), 63–65 (2016)

3. Lantos, C., Kornblau, S.M., Qutub, A.A.: Quantitative-morphological and cytological analyses in Leukemia. In: Guenova, M., Balatzenko, G. (eds.) Hematology: Latest Research and Clinical Advances, pp. 95–113 (2018)
4. Hrebień, M., Steć, P., Nieczkowski, T., Obuchowicz, A.: Segmentation of breast cancer fine needle biopsy cytological images. Int. J. Appl. Math. Comput. Sci. **18**(2), 159–170 (2008)
5. Yang, Z., et al.: A new method of micro-calcifications detection in digitized mammograms based on improved simplified PCNN. Neurocomputing **218**, 79–90 (2016)
6. Jayasingh, E., Allwin, S.: Detection of cancer in pap smear cytological images using bag of texture features. IOS J. Comput. Eng. **11**(1), 01–07 (2013)
7. Chou, S.M., Lee, T.S., Shao, Y.E., Chen, I.F.: Mining the breast cancer pattern using artificial neural networks and multivariate adaptive regression splines. Expert Syst. Appl. **27**(1), 133–142 (2004)
8. Alayón, S., Estévez, J.I., Sigut, J., Sánchez, J.L., Toledo, P.: An evolutionary Michigan recurrent fuzzy system for nuclei classification in cytological images using nuclear chromatin distribution. J. Biomed. Inform. **39**(6), 573–588 (2006)
9. Jeleń, Ł., Fevens, T., Krzyżak, A.: Classification of breast cancer malignancy using cytological images of fine needle aspiration biopsies. Int. J. Appl. Math. Comput. Sci. **18**(1), 75–83 (2008)
10. Subashini, T.S., Ramalingam, V., Palanivel, S.: Breast mass classification based on cytological patterns using RBFNN and SVM. Expert Syst. Appl. **36**(3), 5284–5290 (2009)
11. Marcano-Cedeno, A., Marin-De-La-Barcena, A., Jiménez-Trillo, J., Pinuela, J.A., Andina, D.: Artificial metaplasticity neural network applied to credit scoring. Int. J. Neural Syst. **21**(04), 311–317 (2011)
12. Pouliakis, A., et al.: Artificial neural networks as decision support tools in cytopathology: past, present, and future. Biomed. Eng. Comput. Biol. **7**, 1–18 (2016). BECB-S31601
13. Burke, H.B., et al.: Artificial neural networks improve the accuracy of cancer survival prediction. Cancer **79**(4), 857–862 (1997)
14. Setiawan, A.S., Wesley, J., Purnama, Y.: Mammogram classification using law's texture energy measure and neural networks. Procedia Comput. Sci. **59**, 92–97 (2015)
15. NITRC Human imaging Database: https://www.nitrc.org/frs/group_id=82. Accessed Feb 2019
16. Streiner, D.L., Cairney, J.: What's under the ROC? An introduction to receiver operating characteristics curves. Can. J. Psychiatry **52**(2), 121–128 (2007)

Proposing Contextually Relevant Advertisements for Online Videos

Mankirat Singh[✉] and Rishab Lamba

Bharati Vidyapeeth's College of Engineering, Paschim Vihar, New Delhi 110063, India
mankirat.work@gmail.com

Abstract. Online videos are becoming a dominant part of the web. By 2022, it is predicted that online video will make up more than 82% of all consumer internet traffic, 15 times higher than it was in 2017. With the increasing consumption of Online Video Content, it is important for video platforms to understand videos and provide relevant advertisements. To improve viewer satisfaction and maximize advertisement revenue, a key factor needs to be taken into account, Ad applicability to video content. We present a solution that uses a combination of deep learning and natural language processing techniques to provide contextually relevant advertisement for a given input video.

Keywords: Online video · Advertisement · Natural language processing · Computer vision

1 Introduction

Nowadays, as more and more videos are uploaded on the social media sites like YouTube, Instagram, Facebook etc, the companies monetise these videos with relevant advertisement. Relevant Online advertisement is important not only for the growth of these services but also for user experience. Therefore, we propose a model which suggests contextually relevant advertisements for a given input video, thereby providing better meaningful advertisements.

The effectiveness of an online advertisement can be defined from two perspectives, advertiser and user. Advertiser perspective is usually measured online by performance metrics like click through rates or online polls. However, research has shown that the other perspective, user experience, can help explore the nature of negative impacts of advertising on users [8]. In further studies on the topic it has been shown that irrelevance of an advertisement has a considerably negative effect on user experience [4,5]. For instance, a video about a car crash should advertise car insurance or health insurance as opposed to a generic car advertisement, as the car in the advertisement can get negatively associated with the accident. Therefore, it is important to have ads based on semantic understanding of the video. Thus an effective online advertising platform must take relevance of advertisement into consideration.

© Springer Nature Singapore Pte Ltd. 2020
S. M. Thampi et al. (Eds.): SoMMA 2019, CCIS 1203, pp. 218–224, 2020.
https://doi.org/10.1007/978-981-15-4301-2_19

We find context in source video by semantic understanding of different events in the video through analysis of (a) Video frames (b) Text extracted from speech (c) Metadata of the source video. Through the above data we are able to understand three key factors (a) the central entity in the video clip (ex. Object, event, location) (b) event associated with the central entity (c) general theme of the video. Hence, using the above multi-modal information our system recommends relevant ads based on a semantic understanding of the source video.

Many approaches to context based ads have been proposed in the past. [6] proposed an ad recommendation framework which relied mainly on global textual relevance (title, tag, query etc) and local visual-aural features (color, motion, audio tempo etc). Similarly, [11] utilizes textual metadata to select a candidate list of relevant ads, then it selects the best ad based on visual salience. In another approach [9] proposed a method to identify appropriate ad insertion points, the neighboring video segments were then analysed for face, object detection to give logical cues for ad matching. Other notable approaches have used sentiments [10], past user history [1] and bidding's [12] to propose relevant advertisements.

A major limitation of previous work as evident is the lack of analysis of in video content to understand context. A majority of prior art relies on meta-data of source video or some visual/aural features. A logical understanding of source video through a multi-modal analysis of video, audio and metadata to insert the most relevant ads that will enhance the user experience and possibly generate a higher revenue for a platform.

To the best of our knowledge, this is the first work that features a multi-modal approach that uses the combination of a neural video captioning system together with an ad search system.

2   Research Methodology

The proposed solution is divided into 4 parts. In the first part, a source video is given as input, and outputs natural language captions of the video. In the second part text extracted from speech and video specific metadata are added to the caption to form a description. The third part of the algorithm takes the description generated above and forms a list of advertisements, which are relevant to the source video, using our advertisement database. The fourth step measures the similarity between the advertisement and the video, based on the video description generated in the second step. Finally, the most relevant advertisement is returned as the output for the source video. The architecture of the solution is shown in Fig. 1. Each step is explained in detail in the following subsections.

2.1   Generating Natural Language Description of Videos

In the first step of the algorithm, we do 2 steps. First, we divide the source video into meaningful chunks with standard scene detect python library pyscenedetect. Using this we extract key frames from each segment. Second, we build an end to end neural network that will be used to generate captions for the above frames.

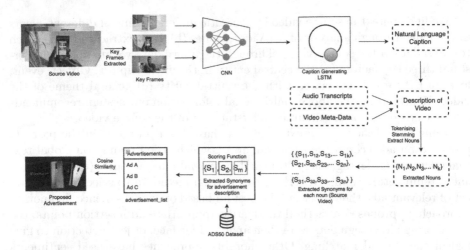

Fig. 1. Architecture of the proposed algorithm

Output from the penultimate layer of a pre trained InceptionV3 model was used to convert every image into a 2048 length vector. In the next step, the vector was fed sequentially to a captioning module consisting of a LSTM layer which used words and the current Image I as inputs and produces output one word at a time, taking into account the semantics of the image and the previous words of the caption generated $p(C_k|I, C_0, \ldots\ldots, C_{k-1})$. The model was trained on the Flickr8K Dataset [7] for 50 epochs with the learning rate at 0.001 and a batch size of 32 pictures. After 30 epochs, the learning rate was reduced to 0.0001 and batch size increased to 64. For each segment of the source video, we generated a caption. At the end all captions generated for each segment were concatenated and passed along to the second step.

2.2 Gathering of Speech and Meta-data Extraction

In this step, we extract the remaining information needed for our analysis. Speech inside the source video is extracted through python library Speech Recognition and the metadata corresponding to the source video is scrapped manually from the respective source network that hosted the source video. The speech and meta-data are then combined with the captions from the previous step, to form a combined description of the source video that will be used to predict relevant ads. The description is passed on to the third step.

2.3 Proposing Relevant Advertisement

The third step of the algorithm, a list of relevant ads is proposed. The relevant ads are picked from our ADS50 dataset, that includes 50 ads representing a variety of products and services. To make the list, a recursive comparison is made between two strings – the description of source video (fixed for all iterations) and the description of an ad from the database until all ads are compared.

Let $D = \{d_1, d_2, d_3, ...d_n\}$ and $A = \{a_1, a_2, a_3, ...a_n\}$ denote the description string of the source video and description string of an advertisement. First, both strings were tokenized followed by removal of stop words and stemming of the words. After the pre-processing, we are left with a bag of words, $bow = \{b_1, b_2..., b_n\}$, for each string. We then applied a part of speech tagger to extract the nouns from the bag of words.

Let Noun list be denoted as $N = \{n_1, n_2...n_k\}$, which are a set of nouns extracted from the step above for both strings. Therefore, we can further classify it into N_s which denoted noun list for the source video and N_a which denotes noun list for the ad. For each noun n_s in the video list and n_a in the ad list synonyms were extracted using PyDictionary package, and a list of list was created. We can denote this synonym list as S_d for the source video and S_a for the ad. Denoted by $S_d = \{\{d_{11}, d_{12}, ...d_{1x}\}, \{d_{21}, d_{22}, ...d_{2y}\}, ...\{d_{n1}, d_{n2}, ...d_{nz}\}\}$ and $S_a = \{\{a_{11}, a_{12}, ...a_{1x}\}, \{a_{21}, a_{22}, ...a_{2y}\}, ...\{a_{n1}, a_{n2}, ...a_{nz}\}\}$.

The relevancy score s_r, was calculated by searching if word d_{mn} in S_d was present in S_a, where d_{mn} is the nth word for the mth synonym in the synonym list. Once a match was found the score s_r was updated by one. An important feature in the algorithm was that once a word d_{mn} of the nth list in S_d found a match in the S_a, the iterator was increased to $(n+1)^{th}$ list and the rest of the nth list was skipped. Mathematically, for each ad description A_k, the score s_r was given by,

$$\forall n, m \quad If\ d_{mn}\ in\ S_a :$$
$$s_r = s_r + 1 \tag{1}$$
$$n = n + 1$$

A threshold of s_r equal to or greater than the length of N_s was set. Then, the ad descriptions with scores above the threshold, were listed as relevant advertisements, denoted by *advertisement_list*, which was passed to the fourth step of the algorithm.

$$If\ s_r >= len(N_s) :$$
$$advertisement\_list.append(s_r) \tag{2}$$

2.4 Semantic Comparison of Vectorized Advertisement Descriptions

In the final step of the algorithm each description in *advertisement_list*, obtained in the previous step, was encoded into a 8000 dimensional vector based on [2]. For this a similar approach to sentence encoding was done as [3]. The inclusive nature of the GRU based encoder provided a good match for our use case as it didn't limit our focus to a particular category or genre.

Let advertisement_list $= \{A_1, A_2, ...A_n\}$ in which A_i represents a description of an advertisement and n the total number of advertisements. Then the Vectorization is given by $A_i \rightarrow V(A_i)$ where $V(A_i)$ represents the vectorized form of A_i and $V(A_i) = [p_1, p_2, p_3, ...p_{8000}]$ where p_i is a floating point number. The video description obtained from the second step was also encoded to a vector using the same method, $D \rightarrow V(D)$ where D is the description of source video obtained in step 2.

Semantic similarity between D and A_i were found by using Cosine Similarity as a similarity measure, $C(x, y)$

$$C(x, y) = cos(V(A_i), V(D)) = \frac{V(A_i) \cdot V(D)}{||V(A_i)|| ||V(D)||} \tag{3}$$

Cosine similarity was chosen over other similarity measures such as Jaccard Similarity, Euclidean Distance, Manhattan Distance. Cosine similarity is a great fit when working with Natural Language Descriptions as our proposed solution does in the first step. This step further filters the list of candidate advertisements which are similar or relevant to the source video.

Finally, the most relevant ad was proposed from the *advertisement_list* having maximum similarity measure.

3   ADS50 Dataset

To test out solution we needed a database of video advertisements. Due to the specific nature of the requirements, as we needed video, audio and metadata, we chose to build a small advertisement dataset, ADS50. This data-set included 50 advertisements from various companies in a multitude of different domains ie. Technology, Travel, Education, Finance etc. All the 50 video advertisements were extracted from online video platform, YouTube. The final data-set prepared was in a folder format which contained 2 files – the video file and the metadata of the video ie. title, description of video, hashtags. The two files were then used as input in the system and their description was generated which was compared to that of the source videos. All advertisement videos were in English and had English descriptions and audio. The dataset can't be made public due to copyright restrictions.

4   Results and Discussions

A total of 50 videos from online platform Youtube were chosen to test out the system. The source videos were chosen independent of the advertisement videos to prevent bias. The videos chosen were from different categories which were relevant from an advertising point of view. Performance of the proposed solution was analyzed on the ADS50 dataset using both qualitative and quantitative approach.

Table 1. Examples of results obtained

Video Thumbnail with Title	Ad Thumbnail with Title	Similarity (in %)	Evaluation (User Study)
Title: Samsung Galaxy Note 10/10+ Impressions: A Great Duo!	Title: Introducing the OnePlus 7 Pro	74.2	+ 96%
Title: THE ULTIMATE HAWAII TRAVEL VLOG	Title: Expedia	68.7	+88%

4.1 Qualitative Analysis

The results of the proposed algorithm on two videos, out of a total of 50 test videos, are shown in Table 1. The first video in the table is a review of a recent smartphone, our algorithm accurately proposes an ad of a smartphone. In the second video we have a Vlog, in this our algorithm extracted themes such as "travel", "ocean", "mountain" from the source video and recommended an advertisement of a travel guide. Hence, as seen from the 2 examples above, the advertisement proposed for each of the videos display contextual coherency and therefore can be classified as context aware advertisements.

4.2 Quantitative Analysis (User Review)

To test our results, a user study of 50 users was conducted. To prevent any bias, the user group was selected from an age group of a range from 20 to 50 years. Each user was shown a source video and then the advertisement proposed by our system. The user was then presented with two choices "relevant advertisement" and "irrelevant advertisement". The experiment was performed using 50 YouTube videos and for each video, 50 users evaluated the advertisement proposed by our model. The overall accuracy obtained by our system was 82.2% which was calculated as the overall positive responses out of total responses.

5   Conclusion and Future Work

In this paper we have proposed a novel solution to propose relevant advertisement based on multi-modal analysis. The results were then evaluated using both qualitative and quantitative measures. In the future, we would like to combine our system into an optimized and automatic solution that will be able to recommend ads across a larger database of ads and videos.

References

1. De Bock, K., Van den Poel, D.: Predicting website audience demographics for web advertising targeting using multi-website clickstream data. Fundamenta Informaticae **98**, 49–70 (2010)
2. Hou, J., Kang, J., Qi, N.: On vocabulary size in bag-of-visual-words representation. In: Qiu, G., Lam, K.M., Kiya, H., Xue, X.-Y., Kuo, C.-C.J., Lew, M.S. (eds.) PCM 2010. LNCS, vol. 6297, pp. 414–424. Springer, Heidelberg (2010). https://doi.org/10.1007/978-3-642-15702-8_38
3. Kiros, R., et al.: Skip-thought vectors (2015)
4. Li, H., Edwards, S.M., Lee, J.H.: Measuring the intrusiveness of advertisements: scale development and validation. J. Advert. **31**(2), 37–47 (2002)
5. McCoy, S., Everard, A., Polak, P., Galletta, D.F.: The effects of online advertising. Commun. ACM **50**(3), 84–88 (2007)
6. Mei, T., Hua, X.S., Yang, L., Li, S.: VideoSense: towards effective online video advertising. In: Proceedings of the 15th ACM International Conference on Multimedia, MM 2007, pp. 1075–1084. ACM (2007)
7. Rashtchian, C., Young, P., Hodosh, M., Hockenmaier, J.: Collecting image annotations using Amazon's Mechanical Turk. In: Proceedings of the NAACL HLT 2010 Workshop on Creating Speech and Language Data with Amazon's Mechanical Turk, CSLDAMT 2010, pp. 139–147. Association for Computational Linguistics (2010)
8. Rohrer, C., Boyd, J.: The rise of intrusive online advertising and the response of user experience research at Yahoo! In: CHI 2004 Extended Abstracts on Human Factors in Computing Systems, CHI EA 2004, pp. 1085–1086. ACM (2004). https://doi.org/10.1145/985921.985992
9. Sengamedu, S.H., Sawant, N., Wadhwa, S.: vADeo: video advertising system. In: Proceedings of the 15th ACM International Conference on Multimedia, MM 2007, pp. 455–456. ACM (2007)
10. Vedula, N., et al.: Multimodal content analysis for effective advertisements on Youtube. In: 2017 IEEE International Conference on Data Mining (ICDM), November 2017
11. Xiang, C., Nguyen, T.V., Kankanhalli, M.: SalAd: a multimodal approach for contextual video advertising. In: 2015 IEEE International Symposium on Multimedia (ISM), pp. 211–216, December 2015
12. Zhang, W., Yuan, S., Wang, J.: Optimal real-time bidding for display advertising. In: Proceedings of the 20th ACM SIGKDD International Conference on Knowledge Discovery and Data Mining, KDD 2014, pp. 1077–1086. ACM (2014)

Comparison of Metaheuristics for the Allocation of Resources for an After-School Program in Remote Areas of India

Georg Gutjahr$^{(\boxtimes)}$, Radhika Menon, and Prema Nedungadi

Center for Research in Analytics and Technologies for Education,
Amrita Vishwa Vidyapeetham, Amritapuri, Kollam, India
georgcg@am.amrita.edu

Abstract. This paper describes an after-school education program in rural India. The program maintains 53 education centers in remote villages in 21 states of India. For the allocation of resources, we first describe the results of an multi-attribute utility assessment, where 130 teachers, coordinators, and people associated with the program specified their opinion on factors that are most important on running a successful after-school education center. We then formulate the problem of optimal resource allocating as a generalized assignment problem. To solve this problem, three different metaheuristics are compared: iterated hill climbing, tabu search, and simulated annealing. It is found that tabu search is giving the best performance.

Keywords: Generalized assignment problem · Multi-attribute utility assessment · Rural education · Metaheuristics · Iterated hill climbing · Tabu search · Simulated annealing

1 Introduction

RITE is a technology-aided rural education program that operates in 21 states of India. The purpose of the program is to enhance education and awareness in remote villages to ensure sustainable development. The program maintains education centers in 53 remote villages where local teachers train students in school subjects and give awareness training. The program is conducted 2.5 h every day for village students after their regular school timings. The program also offers value education and activity-based awareness classes on weekends.

RITE hires people from the local community in rural villages to teach. Studies have shown that community involvement is important for creating sustainable change and creating self-reliance [1]. Teachers receive pre-service and in-service trainings. The teacher conducts daily classes in English, mathematics, science, regional language and Hindi according to the school curriculum.

In rural India, the reasons for low literacy rate include poverty, technology and infrastructure barriers [2]. In order to overcome some of these barriers, the

© Springer Nature Singapore Pte Ltd. 2020
S. M. Thampi et al. (Eds.): SoMMA 2019, CCIS 1203, pp. 225–233, 2020.
https://doi.org/10.1007/978-981-15-4301-2_20

RITE program provides scholarships, tablets, and school supplies such as bags and books.

An estimate shows that 63 million girls of primary and secondary school age were out of school in 2013. Some of the reasons why girls drop out of school include child marriage, parental and social attitudes [3]. RITE conducts gender equality awareness programs to improve girls' education.

Since the 53 villages are distributed over a wide area, coordination of the program is a challenging task. The RITE program employs technology not only to manage the coordination, but also for teaching, for monitoring the progress of the children and the attendance of the teachers [4,5].

This article explores the idea of using information about the performance of the individual education centers to decide how to optimally allocate resources such as teaching material, hiring additional personal or sending teacher trainers to the village centers. Centers that do not perform well with respect to some factors should be given resources that will benefit them specifically. For example, teacher training will be most effective for centers with inexperienced teachers.

In order to quantify the benefit of teaching resources, the article elicits a utility function using a stated-preference survey. Once such an utility function has been obtained, the problem of allocating resources in an optimal way is formalized as a generalized assignment problem (GAP). Since this combinatorial problem is hard to solve exactly, three different metaheuristics will be compared.

The outline of the article is as following. Section 2 describes how the utility of allocating resources to centers was elicited. This utility function is then used in Sect. 3 to define and solve the generalized assignment problem. The article ends with a short conclusion in

2   Multi-attribute Utility Assessment

The RITE database is also used for administrative purposes such as keeping track of expenses of resources. Resources that need to be allocated between centers include material disbursement such technology aids and school supplies, and human resource such as hiring personal and sending teacher trainers to the village centers.

For quality education, properly trained teachers are required. Many of the teachers are from the local community and have little pedagogy training when they start. RITE provides teacher training in pedagogy, technology, classroom management and so on using audio-video, hands-on activities, computer and tablet labs and presentations.

RITE employs multiple teacher trainers who travel across the country to the rural education centers to provide pre-service and in-service training to the local teacher. RITE staff also coordinates material disbursement such as technology aids and school supplies.

Village visits are done in order of priority depending on the needs of the village education centers. Determining the priority of village visits can be a challenging task. The next section presents a solution based on the calculation of utilities of village visits.

We want to determine a utility function for providing interventions and allocating additional resources in the village centers. The utility should be higher if a program is not running well.

To determine which programs are performing well, we look at the following five factors that are regularly collected. for every village education centre:

1. *Daily attendance of students*
2. *Sunday program attendance*
3. *Assessments:* RITE conducts weekly and quarterly assessments to monitor student progress. Assessments follow the standardized method of Pratham [6].
4. *Teacher attendance:* Teacher attendance and student numbers are monitored daily with picture reports sent through Whatsapp.
5. *Regular reporting:* Zonal coordinators contact teachers if reports, such as student attendance and assessments, are not sent on time.

For each of the five factors, exponentially weighted moving averages are calculated. Based on these averages, three levels are assigned for each of the factor in each of the center according to Table 1. The distribution of the levels are shown in Fig. 1.

Table 1. Definition of the levels of the five factors for monitoring an education center.

	Low (per month)	Average (per month)	High (per month)
Student attendance	0 to 10 times	10 to 15 times	15 or more times
Teacher attendance	More than 3 missing	2 to 3 missing	At most 1 missing
Student performance	Less than 50%	50% to 75%	At least 75%
Regular reporting	More than 3 missing	2 to 3 missing	At most 1 missing
Weekend attendance	0 to 1 times	1 to 2 times	3 to 4 times

To decide on the relative importance of these factors and to combine them into a single utility value, we use a stated-preference utility assessment method introduced by Andrejszki et al. [7]. This method and the result of the assessment will be described next.

We surveyed 130 teachers, coordinates, and people associated with the program. We first asked what three factors the respondent thinks are the most important out of the five factors. Then we asks a series of questions, where in each question the respondent is asked to choose between three scenarios, where each scenario specifies levels for the three factors that the respondent thinks are most important. For example, one question might look like this:

The following describes three after-school centers. Which of the three do you think runs the most effective after-school program?

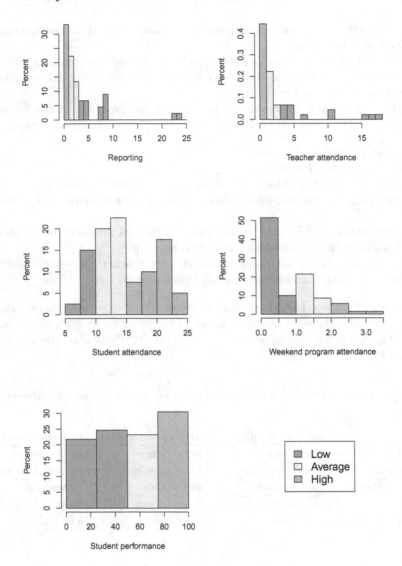

Fig. 1. Histogram of the distributions of the five factors in the 53 centers. Colors indicate the levels of the factors (low in red; average in yellow; high in green). The definitions of the factors and the levels can be found in Table 1 For reporting and teacher attendance, the colors are reversed since number of missing reports and days are measured. (Color figure online)

1. *Low student attendance, Low teachers attendance, High student performance*
2. *Average student attendance, Average teachers attendance, Average student performance*
3. *High student attendance, High teachers attendance, Low student performance*

The scenarios are such that the three scenarios contain all three levels for each of the three factors. This would give $3^3 \times 2^3 \times 1^3 = 216$ questions. But some of these questions contain the same options with different orders. Divided by the number of orderings leaves $216/3! = 36$ questions.

The number of questions can be further reduced by excluding trivial questions. By trivial question, we mean a question that contains a scenario where at least two factors are high and the third factor is either also high or average. By excluding these trivial questions, we are left with 20 questions.

After summarizing each quality, we find the square of the difference between the number of high and average answers. Let us write h_{ij}^2 for this squared distance for the i-th factor from the j-th respondent. We also find the square of the difference between the numbers of the low and the average answers, which we denote by ℓ_{ij}^2 for the i-th factor and the j-th respondent.

We then calculate, for the i-th factor and j-th respondent, an individual preference parameter $p_{ij} = (h_{ij}^2 + \ell_{ij}^2)/\sum_i(h_{ij}^2 + \ell_{ij}^2)$. Finally, the average preference parameter $\bar{p}_i$ for the i-th factor is taken as the mean of the individual preference parameters.

The utility for allocation resources to the k-th center is taken as

$$u_k = \exp(\bar{\mathbf{p}}^\mathsf{T}\mathbf{x}_k) - \exp(1), \tag{1}$$

where $\bar{\mathbf{p}} = (\bar{p}_1, \ldots, \bar{p}_5)^\mathsf{T}$ is the vector of average preference parameters for the 5 factors, and $\mathbf{x}_k$ is a vector of the 5 attributes of the k-th center, where levels of the factors are encoded by 3 for low, 2 for average, and 1 for high (centers with a low performance are give higher utility of an intervention).

The result of the utility assessment from the survey with the 130 teacher and village coordinates is shown in Fig. 2. The average preference parameters are 0.28 for student attendance, 0.16 for teachers attendance, 0.33 for student performance, 0.13 for regular reporting, and 0.10 for weekend program attendance.

3   Optimization Model

We will now formulate the problem of allocating resources to centers.

Assume there are m centers and n possible interventions, such as disbursement of teaching material, hiring additional personal or sending teacher trainers to the village centers.

Denote the decision variables by x_{jk} where $x_{jk} = 1$ if the j-th intervention is applied in the k-th center, and $x_{jk} = 0$ otherwise.

Write c_{jk} for the cost of applying the k-th intervention at the j-th center. Some of the interventions can only be applied to a limited number of centers; for example, teacher training per month will be restricted by the time of the teacher trainers. We will write w_j for the maximum number of number of interventions of the j-th type. we will write u_{jk} for the expected increase in the utility u_k— see Eq. (1)—when applying the j-th intervention at the k-th center. Finally, we assume that there is a total budget b for the interventions.

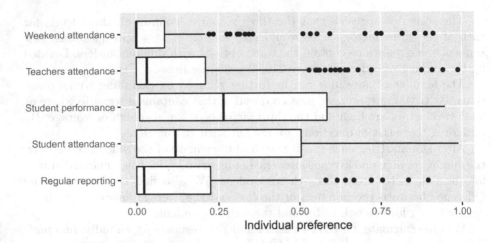

Fig. 2. Boxplots of the individual preference parameters for the five factors.

3.1 Objective Functions and Constraints

Corresponding to the above definitions and assumptions, we now give objective function to maximize the utility of the interventions:

$$\text{Maximize} \quad \sum_{j=1}^{m}\sum_{k=1}^{n} u_{jk}x_{jk}. \tag{2}$$

A feasible assignment must satisfy the constraint on the limited availability of interventions.

$$\sum_{k=1}^{m} x_{jk} \leq w_j \quad \text{for } j = 1, \ldots, m. \tag{3}$$

It also must stay within the total budget b:

$$\sum_{j=1}^{m}\sum_{k=1}^{n} c_{jk}x_{jk} \leq b \tag{4}$$

Equations (2)–(4) define a so-called generalized-assignment problem (GAP). The GAP was originally introduced by Ross and Soland in 1975 [8]. Various applications of the problem include assigning jobs to workers and packing items into bins [9].

3.2 Solving the Model

We consider the problem of assigning 10 different types of resources to the 53 centers.

The GAP is NP hard [10] and even the initial problem of finding a feasible solution is NP hard [11]. In order to obtain good solutions in a reasonable time, various heuristics and metaheuristics have been proposed. The performance of the heuristic solution methods depend on the particular features of the problem, in particular the form of the matrices u_{jk} and c_{jk}.

Here, we consider three different metaheuristics to solve the GAP: iterated hill climbing, tabu search, and simulated annealing.

Hill climbing is also known as greedy descent. It starts with an initial solution that itself is constructed by an heuristic. It then improves this initial solution by a local search procedure where in each step a new solution is picked from a neighborhood around the current solution. For combinatorial optimization problems, a neighborhood around a current solution may be defined as all the solutions that differ by a small, predefined number of values in the decision variables. Since this approach will find a local optima, but most likely not the global optimum, the procedure of selecting an initial solution and applying a local search is repeated a large number of time.

Tabu search is a modification of the iterative hill climbing algorithm described above. The goal is to avoid revisiting solutions that have already been explored. In particular, searches that lead to a previous local optima are avoided by identifying certain attributes of these solutions. In tabu search, these attributes are called tabu constraints. For the performance of the algorithm, the right type of storage of the tabu constraints is important.

Simulated annealing is motivated by an analogy with the technique of annealing in metallurgy: when a metal is heated, its atoms can move easily; as the metal cools, movement decreases and the atoms settle to a state of minimum energy when temperature is zero. Simulated annealing is an iterative procedure where in each step a new solution is picked at random from a large neighbourhood around the current solution. If the new solution is better than the previous solution, it is accepted as the current solution; if it is worse than the current solution, it is accepted as the current solution with a certain probability and rejected otherwise. The probability to accept a new solution decreases over time. In the beginning of the simulated annealing algorithm, steps are taken more or less at random. Later, only steps that improve the objective will be possible.

The three metaheuristics are implemented using GAPsolvers by Lorenzo Gatto [12]. Each metaheuristic was run 10 times for 5, 30, and 60 min. The results are compared against the best solution, which was obtained by running tabu search for 40 h. The results are shown in Table 2. While the performance of the metaheuristics is relatively close, tabu search obtained a small advantage for non-negligible runtimes. Even after 30 min some of the runs found the optimal solution obtained after 40 h. However, after 30 min, there was still a lot of variation in the results, with some runs ending up in a rather suboptimal local extrema.

Table 2. Average of the objectives obtained by different metaheuristics from ten runs relative to the best solution.

	Run-time (min)		
	5	30	60
Hill-climbing	0.68	0.87	0.91
Tabu search	0.66	0.89	0.93
Simulated annealing	0.62	0.87	0.88

4   Conclusion

This article has described an approach to decide how to distribute resources to 53 rural education centers that are part of the RITE program. The centers are distributed over a wide area and monitoring and distribution of resources is an important part to efficiently conduct the program.

The main idea of the article is to elicit an utility function to decide how to distribute the resources such as various forms of teaching material, hiring additional personal or sending teacher trainers to the village centers. Once such an utility function has been obtained, the distribution as resources can be formulated as a generalized assignment problem. Since such problems are hard to solve exactly, the article has compared three different metaheuristics to get sufficiently good solutions. It is found that running tabu search for 1 hour usually leads to a satisfying result.

We believe that the approach for resource allocation is applicable to other programs as well. For education programs the utility function may be used directly or modified according to the specific situation of the program. Also the type of available resources and their costs need to be specified in advance.

In the future, we hope to extend the resource allocation problem to include tour planning of the teacher trainers. We also hope to report on the results of the practical application of resource allocation method after an extended time of use.

References

1. Nedungadi, P., Raman, R., Menon, R., Mulki, K.: AmritaRITE: a holistic model for inclusive education in rural India. In: Battro, A.M., Léna, P., Sánchez Sorondo, M., von Braun, J. (eds.) Children and Sustainable Development, pp. 171–184. Springer, Cham (2017). https://doi.org/10.1007/978-3-319-47130-3_14
2. Nedungadi, P.P., Menon, R., Gutjahr, G., Erickson, L., Raman, R.: Towards an inclusive digital literacy framework for digital India. Educ. Training **60**(6), 516–528 (2018)
3. Nair, N.: Women's education in India: a situational analysis. IMJ **1**(4), 100–114 (2010)
4. Gutjahr, G., Nair, A.M., Menon, R., Nedungadi, P.: Technology for monitoring and coordinating an after-school program in remote areas of India. In: Internatioal Conference on ICT for Sustainable Development (2019)

5. Menon, R., Nedungdi, P., Raman, R.: Technology enabled teacher training for low-literate, remote and rural multi-grade education centers. In: 2017 International Conference on Advances in Computing, Communications and Informatics (ICACCI), pp. 1594–1599. IEEE (2017)
6. Rural India education. http://www.asercentre.org/p/289.html. Accessed 15 Apr 2019
7. Andrejszki, T., Torok, A., Csete, M.: Identifyingy the utility function of transport services from stated preferences. Transp. Telecommun. J. **16**(2), 138–144 (2015)
8. Ross, G.T., Soland, R.M.: A branch and bound algorithm for the generalized assignment problem. Math. Program. **8**(1), 91–103 (1975)
9. Öncan, T.: A survey of the generalized assignment problem and its applications. INFOR Inf. Syst. Oper. Res. **45**(3), 123–141 (2007)
10. Sahni, S., Gonzalez, T.: P-complete approximation problems. J. ACM (JACM) **23**(3), 555–565 (1976)
11. Fisher, M.L., Jaikumar, R.: A generalized assignment heuristic for vehicle routing. Networks **11**(2), 109–124 (1981)
12. Gatto, L.: Project title (2017). https://github.com/lorenzogatto/GAPsolvers

A C-LSTM with Attention Mechanism
for Question Categorization

J. Ashok Kumar[1(✉)], S. Abirami[1], Ashish Ghosh[2], and Tina Esther Trueman[1]

[1] Department of Information Science and Technology, Anna University, Chennai 600025,
Tamil Nadu, India
{jashokkumar83,abirami,tina_trueman}@auist.net
[2] Machine Intelligence Unit, Indian Statistical Institute, Kolkata 700108, West Bengal, India
ash@isical.ac.in

Abstract. Text categorization plays a vital role in text mining applications such as customer care service, business intelligence, and records management. Specifically, text categorization assigns content into a set of predefined aspects or categories. In this paper, we propose a convolutional long short-term memory (C-LSTM) with an attention mechanism for question categorization. The convolutional neural network (CNN) layer extracts higher-level feature representation on input data. These features fed into an LSTM network for creating a document or sentence context representation sequentially. Attention mechanism employed to pay selective attention to the output of C-LSTM. Also, a fully connected layer and output layer added on the top of the attention layer. We evaluate the proposed model on the question classification dataset. The results show that the proposed C-LSTM with attention mechanism outperforms.

Keywords: Deep learning · Attention mechanism · Convolutional neural networks · C-LSTM with attention · Long short-term memory

1 Introduction

The World Wide Web provides a large amount of information to the users based on specific queries, rules, and linguistic knowledge such as documents, hyperlinks, and uniform resource identifiers (URIs). Therefore, the need of a question answering (QA) plays a vital role in the field of information retrieval and dialogue systems. The question answering system meets the demand of users with a concise and accurate answer for the given questions in natural language processing (NLP). This kind of system saves users time and their difficulties in finding facts or events from a large textual database [1–3]. As part of QA, the question classification (QC) is an important step to answer users' questions. The main objective of QC is to map a question with a specific category from a set of predefined categories, also known as a taxonomy of possible answer types. This answer type taxonomy is categorized into flat taxonomies (one level of categories) and hierarchical taxonomies (super- and sub-categories). QC method directly influences the performance of the QA system for extracting and selecting an answer [4]. For instance, the given questions *"title What is the oldest profession?"* and *"individual Who created*

© Springer Nature Singapore Pte Ltd. 2020
S. M. Thampi et al. (Eds.): SoMMA 2019, CCIS 1203, pp. 234–244, 2020.
https://doi.org/10.1007/978-981-15-4301-2_21

Maudie Frickett?" are assigned to a category *human*. The sub-category answer type *"title"* and *"individual"* refers to the title of a person and an individual, respectively, and *"mountain Where is the highest point in Japan?"* is assigned to a category *location* [5]. This category directly influences the QA system to identify users' expected answers like WolframAlpha and IBM Waston QA systems. To maintain and upgrade the QA system, a set of manually defined rules is not sufficient to map a question to a category. Machine learning and deep learning architectures play a more important role in focusing on specific and higher-level feature representations [6].

In particular, the convolutional neural network (CNN) and long short-term memory (LSTM) networks remarkably achieve great success in the field of NLP and QA systems [7]. Recently, an attention mechanism has gained popularity for training neural network models [8]. Thus, we propose a hybrid model convolutional long short-term memory (C-LSTM) with an attention mechanism for QC. First, the model converts all text questions into sequences of word index with a fixed length and then prepared an embedding matrix to build on the top of 1D CNN. Second, the 1D CNN extracts higher-level features with filters sliding over an input sentence to produce new features. Third, the LSTM network is used to remember and discard information based on the context. Fourth, the attention mechanism is employed to focus on the key part of a question that is produced by the LSTM layer. Fifth, the output of the attention layer is passed to a fully connected layer. Finally, we flatten the feature representations to an output layer (also called the softmax layer) for predicting an output. The rest of this paper is organized as follows. Section 2 presents the related works in the field of question and text classification. Section 3 describes the proposed C-LSTM with attention model and evaluation metrics for question categorization. Section 4 presents the experimental results and analysis. The conclusion of this research paper is presented in Sect. 5.

2 Related Work

Deep learning techniques achieved great success in natural language processing tasks such as sentiment analysis [9–11], machine translation [12], question classification [13, 14], and many other tasks at the sentence level and document level. In neural network models, sentences are represented as input word sequence or syntactic parse tree [15]. This representation requires a little domain knowledge. However, convolutional neural networks (CNN) and recurrent neural networks (RNN) plays an important role in representation learning. Therefore, we describe the existing developments of CNN and RNN for sentence and question classification tasks as follows. Zhou et al. [1] improved the text classification accuracy by applying two-dimensional max pooling with bidirectional LSTM. Xia et al. [7] proposed the attention-based LSTM network for question classification. Kim et al. [9] proposed a CNN model on top of the pre-trained word vectors (word2vec) with several variants, namely, CNN-rand (randomly initialized all words), CNN-static (all words are kept as static and learned on other parameters), CNN-non-static (fine-tuned for each task), and CNN-multichannel (two word vectors with multiple filters). As a variant of CNN, Kalchbrenner et al. [11] proposed a dynamic convolutional neural network with k-max-pooling over linear sequences. In [13], the authors presented a rule-based question classification system. This system extracts the relevant words based on structure and then classifies questions based on the association between words and concepts. Silva et al. [14] presented a rule-based question classifier to directly mapping a category with a question using the question headword and WordNet. Zhou et al. [15] proposed a convolutional long short-term memory (C-LSTM) model for text categorization. The authors captured local and global features and sentence semantics.

Moreover, a self-adaptive hierarchical sentence approach was proposed to form a multi-scale hierarchical representation from phrases and sentences [16]. Also, Komninos et al. [17] studied the dependency-based word embeddings with three algorithms, namely, support vector machine (SVM), long short-term memory (LSTM), and CNN. This study indicated that dependency-based embeddings with CNN outperform for question type classification. Furthermore, a weight initialization method was presented with semantic features to improve the classification performance of CNN [18]. Ding et al. [19] proposed a densely connected bidirectional LSTM for the sentence classification task. This study indicated that the vanishing-gradient and overfitting problems solved with deep dozens of layers. In [20], the authors developed an attention-gated CNN (AGCNN) and NLReLU (Natural Logarithms rescaled Rectified Linear Unit) for sentence classification. The authors empirically demonstrated that AGCNN with NLReLU outperforms. In recent works, Guo et al. [21] empirically investigated the mix-up of sentence classification with CNN and LSTM. The authors indicated that the result significantly improves both CNN and LSTM. Zhang et al. [22] proposed a coordinated CNN-LSTM-Attention (CCLA) for sentiment classification. This study captures the local semantic features through CNN and long-distance features through LSTM on the same layer. Thus, in this paper, we present our C-LSTM with attention mechanism and including the fully connected layer and softmax layer over the attention layer.

3   The Proposed C-LSTM with Attention Mechanism

In this section, we present the proposed convolutional long short-term memory network with an attention mechanism (C-LSTM_Attn_FCL) for question categorization. The proposed C-LSTM with the attention model is shown in Fig. 1. This model mainly consists of three components, namely, convolutional neural network, long short-term memory, and attention mechanism. Each components is described as follows.

Fig. 1. The proposed C-LSTM with attention mechanism.

3.1   Convolutional Neural Network (CNN)

The one-dimensional (1D) convolutional layer defines a filter sliding over an input sequence to produce a new feature at different positions [9–11, 15, 22, 30]. Let $x_i \in \mathbb{R}^n$ denote the n-dimensional word vector for the corresponding word i in the sentence.

Let $x \in \mathbb{R}^{l \times n}$ be the input sequence with the length l. Let k denote the filter length, and the vector $m \in \mathbb{R}^{k \times n}$ represents the filter to produce a new feature in the convolution operation. A window vector w_j with v consecutive word vectors for each position j in the sentence is represented as follows in (1).

$$w_j = [x_j, x_{j+1}, \ldots, x_{j+v-1}] \tag{1}$$

Where the commas denote the concatenation of word vectors. A filter m generates a feature map $c \in \mathbb{R}^{l-v+1}$ at each position with the window vectors. A feature c_i is generated for window vector w_j as follows in (2).

$$c_j = f(w_j \otimes m + b) \tag{2}$$

Where $\otimes$ refers to the element-wise multiplication operation, $b \in \mathbb{R}$ denotes a bias, and f refers to the non-linear transformation function, namely, sigmoid, softmax, and hyperbolic tangent. In this model, we use rectified linear units (ReLU) as the non-linear transformation function. The proposed model uses multiple filters to produce multiple feature maps, as follows in (2).

$$W = (c_1; c_2; \ldots; c_n) \tag{3}$$

Where semicolons denote the concatenation of column vector, and c_i refers to the generated feature map with the i-th filter. Each row W_j of $W \in \mathbb{R}^{(l-v+1) \times n}$ refers to the generated new feature with n filters at different window position j. Then, a max-over-pooling operation applied over the feature map to select the most important feature value corresponding to the particular filter. These features are passed to the LSTM layer for long-term dependency.

3.2 Long Short-Term Memory (LSTM) Network

Recurrent neural networks (RNNs) use feedback connections to store the current information x_t in sequential order. The standard RNNs fails to learn long-term dependencies due to a large gap between two-time steps [10, 15, 22, 23]. To overcome this issue, an adaptive gating mechanism called long short-term memory (LSTM) network is introduced [23]. This network controls the write, read, and reset operations through input gate i_t, output gate o_t, and forget gate f_t. These gates update the recent memory cell c_t and the hidden state h_t. Therefore, the LSTM network achieves significant performance in machine translation. In this paper, we use the standard LSTM architecture [15, 23] for question classification. The computational transition functions for the LSTM network is defined as follows in (4)–(9).

$$i_t = \sigma(W_i \cdot [h_{t-1}, x_t] + b_i) \tag{4}$$

$$f_t = \sigma(W_f \cdot [h_{t-1}, x_t] + b_f) \tag{5}$$

$$q_t = \tanh(W_q \cdot [h_{t-1}, x_t] + b_q) \tag{6}$$

$$o_t = \sigma(W_o \cdot [h_{t-1}, x_t] + b_o) \tag{7}$$

$$c_t = f_t \otimes c_{t-1} + i_t \otimes q_t \tag{8}$$

$$h_t = o_t \otimes \tanh(c_t) \tag{9}$$

Where σ refers to the logistic sigmoid function, and it outputs in the range $[0, 1]$, *tanh* refers to the hyperbolic tangent, and it outputs in the range $[-1, 1]$, and $\otimes$ refers to the element-wise multiplication. Moreover, the LSTM network is precisely developed for time-series data to handle long-term dependencies. Therefore, we use the LSTM network upon the convolution layer to learn long-term dependencies in higher-level features.

3.3 Attention Mechanism

Attention mechanism has successfully demonstrated in the tasks of image classification, question answering, neural machine translations, image captioning, multimedia recommendations, and speech recognition [10, 12, 24, 25]. In particular, the attention mechanism pays selective attention to the key part of a sentence. Therefore, we propose an attention mechanism for the question classification task. Let $H \in \mathbb{R}^{d \times l}$ be the hidden vectors (or output vectors) $[h_1, h_2, ..., h_l]$ that are produced by the LSTM layer, where d denotes the size of the output layer, and l denotes the length of the input sequence. The attention mechanism produces an attention weight vector α and weighted output representation r, as in (10)–(12).

$$M = \tanh(H) \tag{10}$$

$$\alpha = \text{softmax}(w^l M) \tag{11}$$

$$r = H\alpha^T \tag{12}$$

Where, $M \in \mathbb{R}^{(d+d\alpha) \times l}$, $\alpha \in \mathbb{R}^l$, $r \in \mathbb{R}^d$, and $w \in \mathbb{R}^{d \times d}\alpha$ are projected parameters. We then obtain the final sentence representation as follows in (13).

$$h^* = \tanh(r) \tag{13}$$

3.4 Question Classification

The output of the attention layer is passed to a fully connected layer and then flattens the feature representations to a softmax layer for predicting an output. The softmax layer transforms sentence vectors to conditional probability distribution as in (14).

$$y = \text{softmax}(W_s h^* + b_s) \tag{14}$$

Where W_s and b_s denote the parameters for the output layer. Also, we applied the categorical cross-entropy as the loss function to compare the predicted values with true values [22].

3.5   Evaluation Metrics

In this section, we present the evaluation metrics for multiclass, namely, confusion matrix, precision, recall, F1-measure, accuracy, micro average, macro average, and weighted average [26]. The confusion matrix describes the classification performance of a model, as shown in Table 1.

Table 1. Confusion matrix

		Predicated class					
		A	B	C	D	E	F
Actual class	A	**tpA**	eAB	eAC	eAD	eAE	eAF
	B	eBA	**tpB**	eBC	eBD	eBE	eBF
	C	eCA	eCB	**tpC**	eCD	eCE	eCF
	D	eDA	eDB	eDC	**tpD**	eDE	eDF
	E	eEA	eEB	eEC	eED	**tpE**	eEF
	F	eFA	eFB	eFC	eFD	eFE	**tpF**

Where the diagonal values represent true positives for the classes A, B, C, D, E, and F, and the values except the diagonal values represent the false positives for the classes A, B, C, D, E, and F, respectively. The precision, recall, F1-measure, and accuracy are defined for the class A as follows in (15)–(18).

$$\text{Precision}(A) = \frac{tpA}{tpA + eBA + eCA + eDA + eEA + eFA} \quad (15)$$

$$\text{Recall}(A) = \frac{tpA}{tpA + eAB + eAC + eAD + eAE + eAF} \quad (16)$$

$$F1 - measure(A) = 2 \times \frac{\text{Precision}(A) \times \text{Recall}(A)}{\text{Precision}(A) + \text{Recall}(A)} \quad (17)$$

$$\text{Accuracy} = \frac{\text{Total number of true positive classes}}{\text{Total number of predicted classes}} \quad (18)$$

Similarly, the precision, recall, and F1-measure calculated for other classes. Let q be the number of classes. Then, the macro average, micro average, and weighted average calculated as follows in (19)–(25).

$$\text{Macro average precision} = \frac{1}{q} \sum_{i=1}^{q} \text{Precision}(i) \quad (19)$$

$$\text{Macro average recall} = \frac{1}{q} \sum_{i=i}^{q} \text{Recall}(i) \quad (20)$$

$$\text{Macro average f1 - measure} = \frac{1}{q} \sum_{i=1}^{q} \text{F1 - measure}(i) \tag{21}$$

$$\text{Micro average} = \frac{\sum_{i=1}^{q} tp(i)}{\sum_{i=1}^{q} tp(i) + \sum_{i=1}^{q} e(i)} \tag{22}$$

$$\text{Weighted average precison} = \frac{\sum_{i=1}^{q} (\text{precision of class } i \times \text{number of instances from class } i)}{\text{Total number of instances in data}} \tag{23}$$

$$\text{Weighted average recall} = \frac{\sum_{i=1}^{q} (\text{recall of class } i \times \text{number of instances from class } i)}{\text{Total number of instances in data}} \tag{24}$$

$$\text{Weighted average f1 - measure} = \frac{\sum_{i=1}^{q} (\text{f1 - measure of class } i \times \text{number of instances from class } i)}{\text{Total number of instances in data}} \tag{25}$$

4   Experimental Results

We evaluate the proposed model on the question classification (TREC) dataset [5]. This dataset consists of 5952-labeled questions, which are split into the train (5452) and test (500). All questions were divided into one of six categories, namely, location, description, numeric, human, abbreviation, and entity. Moreover, the labeled questions are imbalanced categories. We performed the proposed C-LSTM with the attention mechanism on this dataset. This model classifies a question into one of the predefined aspect types [27]. For instance, the question *"What does the abbreviation AIDS stand for?"* classifies into one specific category, namely, abbreviation. In the train set, we holdout 546 samples for dev set based on stratified sampling (also called proportional random sampling). The stratified sampling divides the whole samples into subgroups known as strata, which are formed based on shared characteristics. The hyperparameter search performed on the train and dev dataset.

In our experimental settings, we use the pre-trained Glove [28] embedding layer with 100 dimensions, one convolutional layer with 64-filter size, a max-pooling layer with size 4, one LSTM layer with 64 units, an attention layer with the softmax activation function, one fully connected layer with 32 units, and finally, an output layer with softmax activation. We also used the dropout layer with the probability of 0.1 in the word vector and fully connected layers. The proposed model achieves the best result using the Adagrad optimization algorithm [29]. Figure 2 shows the accuracy and loss for both training and validation and training and testing for 30 epochs. Tables 2 and 3 shows the confusion matrix for training, dev, and test. This model achieves the mean accuracy of 98.55% and 98.18% for training and validation, and 98.38% and 98.15% for training and testing in 30 epochs. In particular, we present the results of precision, recall, F1-measure, micro average, macro average, and weighted average in Table 4 for the multiclass imbalanced data. The proposed C-LSTM with attention mechanism achieves 98% F1-measure. Table 5 shows the comparison of this model with the previous works.

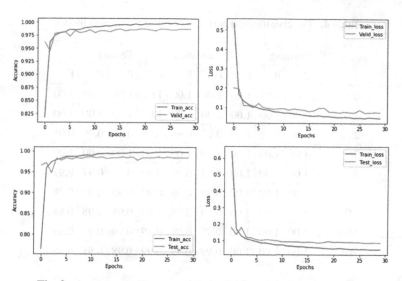

Fig. 2. Accuracy and loss curve for training, validation, and testing.

Table 2. Confusion matrix for training and validation.

Class	Training						Validation					
	0	1	2	3	4	5	0	1	2	3	4	5
0	78	0	0	0	0	0	9	0	0	0	0	0
1	0	1072	0	0	0	0	0	119	0	0	0	0
2	0	0	1108	0	0	0	0	0	121	0	1	1
3	0	1	0	1061	0	0	0	0	0	118	0	0
4	0	0	0	0	755	0	0	0	4	0	80	0
5	0	0	1	0	0	830	0	0	0	0	1	92

Table 3. Confusion matrix for training and test.

Class	Training						Testing					
	0	1	2	3	4	5	0	1	2	3	4	5
0	78	0	0	0	0	0	8	0	0	0	0	0
1	0	1072	0	0	0	0	0	109	0	0	0	0
2	0	0	1108	0	0	0	0	0	109	0	2	2
3	0	1	0	1061	0	0	0	0	0	108	0	0
4	0	0	0	0	755	0	0	0	2	0	75	0
5	0	0	1	0	0	830	0	0	2	0	0	83

Table 4. The classification performance of the proposed model.

	Training			Validation			Testing		
	P	R	F	P	R	F	P	R	F
0	1.00	1.00	1.00	1.00	1.00	1.00	1.00	1.00	1.00
1	1.00	1.00	1.00	1.00	1.00	1.00	1.00	1.00	1.00
2	1.00	1.00	1.00	0.97	0.98	0.98	0.96	0.96	0.96
3	1.00	1.00	1.00	1.00	1.00	1.00	1.00	1.00	1.00
4	1.00	1.00	1.00	0.98	0.95	0.96	0.97	0.97	0.97
5	1.00	1.00	1.00	0.99	0.99	0.99	0.98	0.98	0.98
MIC_A	1.00	1.00	1.00	0.99	0.99	0.99	0.98	0.98	0.98
MAC_A	1.00	1.00	1.00	0.99	0.99	0.99	0.99	0.99	0.99
WA	1.00	1.00	1.00	0.99	0.99	0.99	0.98	0.98	0.98

Table 5. Comparison of the proposed model with previous works.

Authors	Model	System accuracy
Silva et al. (2011)	SVM	95.0
Kim et al. (2014)	CNN-rand	91.2
	CNN-static	92.8
	CNN-non-static	93.6
	CNN-multichannel	92.2
Kalchbrenner et al. (2014)	DCNN	93.0
Zhao et al. (2015)	Paragraph vector	91.8
	Ada-CNN	92.4
Zhou et al. (2015)	LSTM	93.2
	Bi-LSTM	93.0
	C-LSTM	94.6
Komninos et al. (2016)	tree-CNN	96.0
Madabushi et al. (2016)	Rule-Based	97.2
Zhou et al. (2016)	BLSTM-2DCNN	96.1
Li et al. (2017)	CNN-non-static + BI	94.6
Ding et al. (2018)	DC-Bi-LSTM	95.6
Liu et al. (2018)	AGCNN-SELU-3-channel	95.3
	AGCNN-ReLU-static	94.5
Guo et al. (2019)	CNN + senMixup	94.8
Zhang et al. (2019)	CCLA (same layer) + Max-pooling	95.6
Proposed	C-LSTM_Attn_FCL	98.0

5 Conclusion

In this paper, we have presented the convolutional long short-term memory with an attention mechanism. The C-LSTM_Attn_FCL model learns features using the convolutional layer and then fed these learned features into an LSTM layer for long-term dependency. Moreover, an attention mechanism employed to pay selective attention to the outputs. The performance of the system is evaluated using confusion matrix, precision, recall, F1-score, micro average, macro average, and weighted average. The experimental result shows the proposed model outperforms. In the future, we intended to replace a simple attention mechanism with multiplicative attention and regularization for tree-structured convolutions.

References

1. Zhou, P., Qi, Z., Zheng, S., Xu, J., Bao, H., Xu, B.: Text classification improved by integrating bidirectional LSTM with two-dimensional max pooling. arXiv preprint arXiv:1611.06639 (2016)
2. Xin, L., Huang., H.-J., Wu, L.: Question classification using multiple classifiers. In: Proceedings of the Fifth Workshop on Asian Language Resources (ALR 2005) and First Symposium on Asian Language Resources Network (ALRN) (2005)
3. Aggarwal, G., Sharma, N.V.: Enhancing web search through question classifier. In: Somani, A., Srivastava, S., Mundra, A., Rawat, S. (eds.) Smart Innovation, Systems and Technologies, pp. 791–798. Springer, Singapore (2018). https://doi.org/10.1007/978-981-10-5828-8_75
4. Bae, K., Ko, Y.: Efficient question classification and retrieval using category information and word embedding on cQA services. J. Intell. Inf. Syst. 53, 1–23 (2019)
5. Li, X., Roth, D.: Learning question classifiers. In: Proceedings of the 19th International Conference on Computational Linguistics-Volume 1, pp. 1–7. Association for Computational Linguistics, August 2002
6. Huang, Z., Thint, M., Qin, Z.: Question classification using head words and their hypernyms. In: Proceedings of the Conference on Empirical Methods in Natural Language Processing, pp. 927–936. Association for Computational Linguistics, October 2008
7. Xia, W., Zhu, W., Liao, B., Chen, M., Cai, L., Huang, L.: Novel architecture for long short-term memory used in question classification. Neurocomputing 299, 20–31 (2018)
8. Luong, M.T., Pham, H., Manning, C.D.: Effective approaches to attention-based neural machine translation. arXiv preprint arXiv:1508.04025 (2015)
9. Kim, Y.: Convolutional neural networks for sentence classification. arXiv preprint arXiv: 1408.5882 (2014)
10. LeCun, Y., Bengio, Y., Hinton, G.: Deep learning. Nature 521(7553), 436 (2015)
11. Kalchbrenner, N., Grefenstette, E., Blunsom, P.: A convolutional neural network for modelling sentences. arXiv preprint arXiv:1404.2188 (2014)
12. Liu, Y., Zhang, J.: Deep learning in machine translation. In: Deng, L., Liu, Y. (eds.) Deep Learning in Natural Language Processing, pp. 147–183. Springer, Singapore (2018). https://doi.org/10.1007/978-981-10-5209-5_6
13. Madabushi, H.T., Lee, M.: High accuracy rule-based question classification using question syntax and semantics. In: Proceedings of COLING 2016, the 26th International Conference on Computational Linguistics: Technical Papers, pp. 1220–1230 (2016)
14. Silva, J., Coheur, L., Mendes, A.C., Wichert, A.: From symbolic to sub-symbolic information in question classification. Artif. Intell. Rev. 35(2), 137–154 (2011)

15. Zhou, C., Sun, C., Liu, Z., Lau, F.: A C-LSTM neural network for text classification. arXiv preprint arXiv:1511.08630 (2015)
16. Zhao, H., Lu, Z., Poupart, P.: Self-adaptive hierarchical sentence model. In: Twenty-Fourth International Joint Conference on Artificial Intelligence, June 2015
17. Komninos, A., Manandhar, S.: Dependency based embeddings for sentence classification tasks. In: Proceedings of the 2016 Conference of the North American Chapter of the Association for Computational Linguistics: Human Language Technologies, pp. 1490–1500, June 2016
18. Li, S., Zhao, Z., Liu, T., Hu, R., Du, X.: Initializing convolutional filters with semantic features for text classification. In: Proceedings of the 2017 Conference on Empirical Methods in Natural Language Processing, pp. 1884–1889, September 2017
19. Ding, Z., Xia, R., Yu, J., Li, X., Yang, J.: Densely connected bidirectional LSTM with applications to sentence classification. In: Zhang, M., Ng, V., Zhao, D., Li, S., Zan, H. (eds.) NLPCC 2018. LNCS (LNAI), vol. 11109, pp. 278–287. Springer, Cham (2018). https://doi.org/10.1007/978-3-319-99501-4_24
20. Liu, Y., Ji, L., Huang, R., Ming, T., Gao, C.: An attention-gated convolutional neural network for sentence classification. CoRR (2018)
21. Guo, H., Mao, Y., Zhang, R.: Augmenting data with mixup for sentence classification: an empirical study. arXiv preprint arXiv:1905.08941 (2019)
22. Zhang, Y., Zheng, J., Jiang, Y., Huang, G., Chen, R.: A text sentiment classification modeling method based on coordinated CNN-LSTM-attention model. Chin. J. Electron. 28(1), 120–126 (2019)
23. Hochreiter, S., Schmidhuber, J.: Long short-term memory. Neural Comput. 9(8), 1735–1780 (1997)
24. Zhou, P., et al.: Attention-based bidirectional long short-term memory networks for relation classification. In Proceedings of the 54th Annual Meeting of the Association for Computational Linguistics (Volume 2: Short Papers), pp. 207–212, August 2016
25. Wang, Y., Huang, M., Zhao, L.: Attention-based LSTM for aspect-level sentiment classification. In: Proceedings of the 2016 Conference on Empirical Methods in Natural Language Processing, pp. 606–615, November 2016
26. Kashef, S., Nezamabadi-pour, H., Nikpour, B.: Multilabel feature selection: a comprehensive review and guiding experiments. Wiley Interdisc. Rev. Data Min. Knowl. Discov. 8(2), e1240 (2018)
27. Dohaiha, H.H., Prasad, P.W.C., Maag, A., Alsadoon, A.: Deep learning for aspect-based sentiment analysis: a comparative review. Expert Syst. Appl. 118, 272–299 (2019)
28. Pennington, J., Socher, R., Manning, C.: GloVe: global vectors for word representation. In: Proceedings of the 2014 Conference on Empirical Methods in Natural Language Processing (EMNLP), pp. 1532–1543, October 2014
29. Duchi, J., Hazan, E., Singer, Y.: Adaptive subgradient methods for online learning and stochastic optimization. J. Mach. Learn. Res. 12, 2121–2159 (2011)
30. Zhou, Z., Zhu, X., He, Z., Qu, Y.: Question classification based on hybrid neural networks. In: 2016 4th International Conference on Electrical & Electronics Engineering and Computer Science (ICEEECS 2016). Atlantis Press, December 2016

QuicklyCook: A User-Friendly Recipe Recommender

Naila Bushra[✉] and Mehedi Hasan

Mississippi State University, Starkville, MS 39759, USA
{nb921,mh3092}@msstate.edu

Abstract. We present 'QuicklyCook', an instance-based recipe recommender system. It uses a recently developed database called 'Recipe 1M' which contains 1 million recipes for a variety of food items. The proposed system is developed by taking advantage of the fast execution of available python data types and libraries which greatly enhance the proposed model's performance. The system is built off the idea of a very popular algorithm i.e. K-nearest neighbor (KNN) where a new instance is classified based on the classes of already-seen instances. However, we have proposed a slightly different and unique way of calculating the similarity score of the new to-be-classified instance with the previous ones. The proposed system allows the user to input a unrestricted list of ingredients and finds the closest 'k' recipes containing preferably all of the input ingredients. Unlike many recipe recommender systems to date, our proposed system does not restrict the user to choose ingredients from an existing ingredient list thus providing more flexibility to the user. Performance-wise, its execution time is considerably faster as it does not require large feature vectors to be formed and compared for classification. Hence, QuicklyCook can be considered as a simple but powerful application.

Keywords: K-nearest neighbor · Recipe recommender · Sequence matching · Text comparison · Recipe 1M

1 Introduction

Food datasets are an interesting area that can be explored to extract a variety of information. The images of food are commonly used to recognize meal type, ingredients list, predict and learn food habits and the variability of food habits across cultures and places. Also, food recipes are used to predict the name of the food, ingredient list is used to predict the recipe, learn about food patterns of different countries, and so on.

We propose a recipe recommender system in this paper called **QuicklyCook** where given a list of ingredients as inputs, the system will suggest recipes based on those ingredients. The target users of this system are the ones who have necessary ingredients in their hands to make an appropriate meal but lacks references or ideas on how to do so. The main motivation for the proposed

© Springer Nature Singapore Pte Ltd. 2020
S. M. Thampi et al. (Eds.): SoMMA 2019, CCIS 1203, pp. 245–254, 2020.
https://doi.org/10.1007/978-981-15-4301-2_22

idea is to benefit people by reducing their valuable time and money as well. A lot of time is wasted on the internet to read recipes and watch cooking shows on media. People also spend a lot of their valuable time reading unnecessary detailed cookbooks claiming to contain 'all the recipes' of the world. Moreover, in addition to wasting time people when hungry run to restaurants or fast food shops to grab a quick bite that may not always be quick considering the travel and waiting time. Most of the time eating outside can be a negative factor for people who are trying to watch their health. In most of the cases mentioned here, there is a great possibility that these people already have enough ingredients in their kitchens to make a meal in a surprisingly quick amount of time. These people will then be able to save a good amount of time and money to do other things that are of more priority to them. Thus the proposed system can be proven to be very much useful for people who do not want to waste time or money on food. QuicklyCook applies the simplest ideas to suggest recipes to users based on the readily available ingredients they have in their kitchens.

The rest of the paper is organized as follows; Sect. 2 contains the discussion of different research work related to food dataset especially recipe recommendation systems. Section 3 contains the proposed idea in a nutshell and the list of features that our system has. Section 4 contains the overview of the resources that are used in the proposed system including the Recipe 1M dataset [10] followed by Sect. 5 that contains a detailed description of the methodology used to develop the system (data processing, model training, and prediction). Section 6 lists the results and performance analysis of the system. Section 7 describes the limitation of this paper and the possible future works to improve the current system.

2   Discussions

Before building our system we have explored existing web-based recipe recommender systems as well as the ones in the literature that provide similar service proposed by our system. A small list of several online websites that we have looked into is given in Appendix A.

The goals of the existing recipe recommender system are diverse. Each recommender system fulfills the specific needs of the user of the system. A lot of them emphasize on providing the user with healthy recommendation [2,4,7,11]. This type of recipe recommender ultimately helps with several health-related issues such as obesity. However, they do not provide the option for the user to selectively choose healthy ingredients of their preference.

Techniques such as folksonomy, similarity measures, ingredient tags, and latent factors computation, content-based, semantic understanding, etc. are widely uses to provide the user with the best experience with the recommender system [3,8,12]. Collaborative filtering is another popular technique used in a lot of popular recommender system that suggests products (in our case recipes) to users based on their similar preferences with other users [1,2]. The goal of QuicklyCook is more inclined towards giving the user more personalized, specific, and fewer number of recommendation as possible.

These existing websites mentioned above have a range of constraints that lie between a hungry user and his quickly cooked meal. The limitations of these services are given in the following subsections:

- **Restricted Ingredient List.** Most of the time, the ingredients that the user tries to enter have to be chosen from a list provided by the website. Sometimes, the desired ingredient may not even be on that list. E.g. recipeland.com.
- **Lengthy Steps.** Sometimes users have to search through a long list to find his/her desired ingredient. On most of the website, the user has to go through certain steps to define the type of ingredient, its amount and other unnecessary customization which delays the process by making it complex. E.g. ideas4recipes.com.
- **Too Many Results.** The list of suggested recipes is usually too long for the user to search thoroughly to find the one that the user really wants to cook at that time. E.g. bigoven.com.
- **Missing Essential Customization.** In relation to the previous limitation, on several websites that we have explored, there were no customization options like preparation time or cuisine type or food type. These filtering options are pretty essential for the user to limit the results to the most intended ones. E.g. recipekey.com.
- **Recipes With Additional Ingredients.** One of the reasons for their long result list is that they include recipes in the results which have a lot of additional ingredients that the user does not have and also did not give as inputs. If the user does not have the majority of the listed ingredients, he/she is most likely to avoid using that corresponding recipes. E.g. ideas4recipes.com.
- **Limitation of The Number of Input Ingredients.** The websites often limit the list of ingredients that is entered by the user from one to five which also limits the options for the user to try on more versatile recipes. E.g. ideas4recipes.com.

3 Proposed Idea

The proposed system is built off the idea used in the K-nearest neighbor (KNN) algorithm [6]. QuicklyCook is developed using python programming language and suggests recipes based on the ingredients that the user enters as inputs. This system uses the recently developed 'Recipe 1M' dataset [10] containing 1 million food items' recipe (categories shown in Fig. 2). 70% of this dataset (700,000 recipes) is used to train our model and the other 30% (300,000 recipes) is used to test the model. This 70:30 split ratio allows the model to be trained better and learn about the data pattern before it starts to classify the never-seen-before data items in the test set. If we choose less ratio of data items for training, the model maybe under-trained and if we choose more than it may over-fit the data and completely underperform on the test dataset. He training model forms a feature vector for each of the recipes. The features here are the ingredients of the recipe. The unlabeled list of input ingredients are compared with the feature vectors of the training data to output related recipes. The recipes that contain all the ingredients entered by the user are returned by the system and suggested to the user. If there are multiple recipes containing all the ingredients entered by the user then preference is given to the recipes that have 'fewer' additional ingredients. Several python libraries such as 'pandas' [5] and 'difflab' [9] have been used for faster manipulation of the dataset. The major features of the system are described in the following subsections:

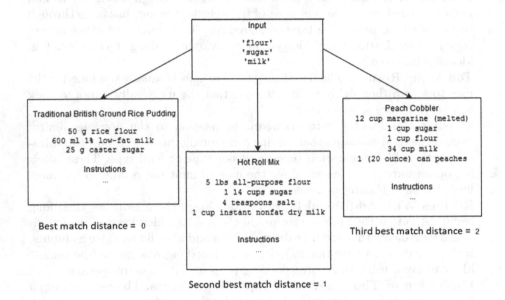

Fig. 1. Suggested recipes for $K = 3$

- **Unrestricted Ingredient List.** The user can enter as many ingredients as he/she wants according to their preference. The number of ingredients is not restricted and also the user does not have to choose the ingredients from an existing list. The user can also ask for recipes that only contain a subset of the entered ingredients.
- **Auto-fix Typos.** The system allows the user to make typos. In such cases, the system is still able to retrieve the recipe containing the corrected name of the input ingredient by finding the closest correct match to the misspelled word.
- **Differentiate Ingredients.** The system is able to understand the difference between tomato and tomato sauce, chili and chili powder and so on to find the appropriate recipe for the user.
- **Tune-able Similarity.** It is possible to set the threshold that will determine how similar two ingredients are. While in the default setting the match needs to be an exact one (banana should not match with bananas), these constraints can be relaxed to suit the scenario.

- **'K'-recipes.** Based on the user's preference, the system will result in 'K' nearest recipes that can be cooked with the input ingredient list. The result is increasingly ordered by the number of additional ingredients.
- **Food Sensitivity.** A large number of people have sensitivity for a certain type of food. For example, lactose intolerant consumers cannot consume food originated from dairy. Several have allergies of food like nuts, shrimp, eggplant, etc. The process flow of QuicklyCook allows filtering of food items not preferred by the user.

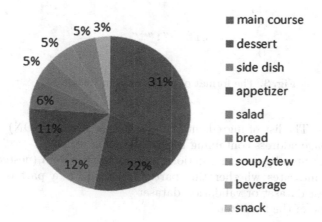

Fig. 2. Percentage of recipes based on categories in Recipe 1M

4   Data Sources

For the purpose of building our application, we have explored a range of available datasets of food recipes with ingredients and images of food as well. We have come across an outcome of pretty recent work by the researchers of the CSAIL lab of MIT where they have built up a database of various kinds of recipes from AllRecipes.com and Food.com websites. The database is called 'Recipe 1M' and contains 1 million recipes and 800,000 images of food [10].

The researchers who built this 'Recipe 1M' database have used Artificial Neural Network (ANN) to detect recipes from food images. For our research, we have used the recipe part of the dataset that is stored in a JSON file format (data stored as key-value pair). The size of this JSON file is around 1.3 GB. To reduce the memory load we have divided this JSON file into eleven smaller JSON files. Each of them having the size around 130 MB. Each of these smaller JSON files contains around 100,000 recipes. The key-value structure of the data is given in Fig. 3. This structure is maintained for each of the 1 million recipes.

```
            {
                "ingredients":"…"
            },
            {
                "url":"…"
            },
            {
                "instructions":"…"
            },
            {
                "partition":"…"
            },
            {
                "title":"…"
            }
```

Fig. 3. The format of recipe data in Recipe 1M

- Ingredients: The list of ingredients for the recipe (nested JSON)
- Url: Webpage address containing the detail of the recipe
- Instruction: Step by step instructions for cooking the item (nested JSON)
- Partition: indicates whether this particular recipe is a part of a training dataset, test dataset or validation dataset
- Title: Name of the food item.

5   Methodology

5.1   Data Pre-processing

In the data pre-processing stage, we have divided the large JSON file containing the 1 million recipes into eleven smaller JSON files. Each of them contains around 100,000 recipes. To reduce the data size we have initially removed the 'URL's (not used in QuicklyCook) from all the eleven input JSON data files and converted them to 'CSV's. This reduces each of the file sizes to 20% (from 130 MB to 106 MB). The 'CSV' files have the following headers: id, ingredients, instructions, partition, and title.

The eleven 'CSV' files are then read into 'pandas' dataFrame (python datatype) [5] and combined to form the unified train data containing 70% of the dataset (700,000 recipes). The process of combining the eleven files was done into two stages to avoid the memory outrun issue. In the first stage, five and six of the eleven files were combines separately to form two intermediate files. The sizes of these two files were 583 MB and 618 MB. Finally, these two files were combined to get the final one containing 1 million recipes with a size of about 1.17 GB. 70% of this 1 million recipes were then sent to the training model.

5.2   Formation of Feature Vector

5.3   K-Nearest Neighbor Algorithm

K-nearest neighbor is an instance-based learning algorithm. Here, the insta lie in an n-dimensional space. The training instances have their feature ve of n-length and these instances are already classified. These instances a recipes of our training data that already have their titles and details. Usu forming feature vector, a large set-based n-length feature vector is consid our case, that would be all possible n ingredients in the world (or at lea whole database). The training instances will fill in 1 or 0 in that lar vector depending on whether that particular ingredient is needed to recipe or not. When a new instance comes, it should form its own fe of length n. Then it is possible to compare these two vectors adopti of distance and similarity measures (i.e. Hamming distance, Euclic Cosine Similarity etc.). This also requires natural language proc extent.

As our problem cannot be totally classified as a classificat have avoided forming huge feature vectors for finding similarit and training ingredients which is described in the next section

5.4   Distance Measures

The ingredient list for 'Recipe 1M' dataset does not cont The list comes with the measurement as well (i.e. 1 cu we have split each of these ingredients into parts ('1', compare it with our input ingredient ('sugar'). The the library function that we have used for the pur flab.get_closer_match()) is not able to compare wher a string is present. Also, it is unable to find the ex and 'sugar' because of the cases. Therefore, we co the training dataset to lower case before computing distance measure.

Afterward, the system gives us a list of po 'sugur', 'sogar']) from the training dataset corre ('sugar'). Now, we can decide whether to let th or the closest match. This is measured by an Matcher.ratio()) and gives us 1.0 in case of a recipes that have exact matches for all the i are returned. This returned list of recipes is ordered by the lowest number of additional ingredient that is needed by the user (Fig. 1). Here, K determines how many closest match will be returned by the system.

6   Result and Performance

The execution time of several steps of the algorithm are given in Table 1. The experiments were performed in an Intel Core i7 (quad-core) 2.6 GHz computer.

Table 1. Pre-processing and execution time of different process (Environment: Intel Core i7. 6 GHz, 8 GB Ram, editor: pycharm, python: 3.6.2).

Processes	Time (in seconds)
Partitioning the 1.3 GB json file into 11 parts	3
Converting 11 JSON files to CSV	7 (avg)
Combining CSV File 1 to 5 into one (583 MB) - Pass 1	27
Combining CSV File 6 to 11 into one (618 MB) - Pass 2	38
Combining CSV files from pass 1 and 2 to one final CSV	73
Training Model using 1 Million dataset (1.3 GB)	129
Predicting using 1 Million dataset (1.3 GB)	695
Training using combined file from pass 1 (583 MB)	61
Predicting using combined file from pass 1 (583 MB)	435
Training using smaller CSV file (106 MB)	11
Predicting using smaller CSV file (106 MB)	84

As mentioned previously the proposed system cannot be totally a classification system. Therefore, the accuracy depends on the prediction not on training the model. The performance, however, is a great as the dataset that is used is quite large in size. A sample output for QuicklyCook is given in Fig. 4. The processing time compared to database is quite impressive after the initial run. However, it still for improvement.

```
Input ingredients: ['flour', 'sugar', 'milk']

matched_recipe_indexes = [28, 49, …, 69765, 69784]

OrderedDict([(0, 51586), (1, 50345), (2, 69029),
(3, 69648), (4, 69140), (5, 69749), (6, 69724),
(7, 69744), (8, 69519), (9, 69723), (10, 69765),
(11, 69784), (12, 69382), (13, 69066), (14,
69103), (15, 68111), (16, 68593), (17, 69473),
(18, 65528), (19, 65905), (20, 68463), (21,
66403), (22, 61850), (23, 51307), (24, 62925),
(25, 60688), (26, 25554), (27, 68166), (29,
38543), (30, 49304), (35, 68927), (37, 38427),
(40, 43439)])

You can make ->
Traditional British Ground Rice Pudding

Ingredients:
->   50 g rice flour
->   600 ml 1% low-fat milk
->   25 g caster sugar

Instructions:
->   Preheat oven to 200 Centigrade / 400
Fahrenheit / Gas Mark 6 and grease a bake-proof
dish.
->   Heat milk in a saucepan and sprinkle on the
Ground Rice.
->   Stirring continuously, heat on a low heat
bring to a boil until it thickens.
->   Simmer for a further 2-3 minutes.
->   Stir in the sugar (My mum would have probably
used a bit more than 25g - sweet tooth!)
->   Pour into greased bake-proof dish.
->   Bake for 25-30 minutes until lightly brown.
```

Fig. 4. Sample output of QuicklyCook

7   Conclusion and Future Work

This proposed system has a lot of scope for improvement in terms of adding more data (from various countries' cuisine) to enhance user experience. It is a work in progress with the plan to extend this system to a web-based service where the user can actually try out and get benefit from the system. More control to the user can be provided by letting users add filters based on meal (appetizer/dessert/entre) type, cuisine type, preparation time, etc. It may also contain options that will let the user mark an ingredient as 'must-be-present' in the resulted recipes.

Another crucial improvement that can greatly increase performance is completely removing unnecessary words in the ingredient list which do not play any part during the similarity calculation (i.e. '1', 'cup', 'of', 'teaspoon', 'ounces', symbols, etc.).

Appendix A

- http://www.supercook.com
- http://www.myfridgefood.com
- http://www.foodpair.com
- http://www.bigoven.com
- http://www.recipepuppy.com
- https://recipeland.com
- http://www.recipekey.com
- http://www.ideas4recipes.com
- https://foodcombo.com.

References

1. Berkovsky, S., Freyne, J.: Group-based recipe recommendations: analysis of data aggregation strategies. In: Proceedings of the Fourth ACM Conference on Recommender Systems, pp. 111–118. ACM (2010)
2. Freyne, J., Berkovsky, S.: Intelligent food planning: personalized recipe recommendation. In: Proceedings of the 15th International Conference on Intelligent User Interfaces, pp. 321–324. ACM (2010)
3. Ge, M., Elahi, M., Fernaández-Tobías, I., Ricci, F., Massimo, D.: Using tags and latent factors in a food recommender system. In: Proceedings of the 5th International Conference on Digital Health 2015, pp. 105–112. ACM (2015)
4. Ge, M., Ricci, F., Massimo, D.: Health-aware food recommender system. In: Proceedings of the 9th ACM Conference on Recommender Systems, pp. 333–334. ACM (2015)
5. McKinney, W.: pandas: a foundational python library for data analysis and statistics. Python High Perform. Sci. Comput. **14**, 1–9 (2011)
6. Michalski, R.S., Carbonell, J.G., Mitchell, T.M.: Machine Learning: An Artificial Intelligence Approach. Springer, Heidelberg (2013)
7. Mika, S.: Challenges for nutrition recommender systems. In: Proceedings of the 2nd Workshop on Context Aware Intel. Assistance, Berlin, Germany, pp. 25–33. Citeseer (2011)
8. van Pinxteren, Y., Geleijnse, G., Kamsteeg, P.: Deriving a recipe similarity measure for recommending healthful meals. In: Proceedings of the 16th International Conference on Intelligent User Interfaces, pp. 105–114. ACM (2011)
9. Rossum, G.: Python reference manual (1995)
10. Salvador, A., et al.: Learning cross-modal embeddings for cooking recipes and food images. In: 2017 IEEE Conference on Computer Vision and Pattern Recognition (CVPR), pp. 3068–3076. IEEE (2017)
11. Yang, L., et al.: Yum-Me: a personalized nutrient-based meal recommender system. ACM Trans. Inf. Syst. (TOIS) **36**(1), 7 (2017)
12. Yu, L., Li, Q., Xie, H., Cai, Y.: Exploring folksonomy and cooking procedures to boost cooking recipe recommendation. In: Du, X., Fan, W., Wang, J., Peng, Z., Sharaf, M.A. (eds.) APWeb 2011. LNCS, vol. 6612, pp. 119–130. Springer, Heidelberg (2011). https://doi.org/10.1007/978-3-642-20291-9_14

Early Detection of Suicidal Predilection on Instagram Social Networking Service

K. R. Rohini[1], Gayathri Rajendran[2], V. Arjun[2], and Prabaharan Poornachandran[2(✉)]

[1] Jyothi Engineering College, APJ Abdul Kalam Technological University,
Thrissur, Kerala, India
rohiniramachandran20@gmail.com
[2] Amrita School of Engineering, Amrita Vishwa Vidyapeetham, Amritapuri, Kerala, India
{gayathrir,arjunv,praba}@am.amrita.edu

Abstract. Social Networks has become the biggest medium of expression of one's thoughts and emotions. With more than one-third of the global population expressing their thoughts, opinions and events, these networks become rich with direct indicators about the subject. Multimedia based social networking services are gaining popularity than text-based ones. In this work, we analyze the data from Instagram, which is one of the largest image and video-based social networking service with more than one billion users. This paper analyzes the social media posts on Instagram with the goal of finding when the subject feels low that could potentially lead to a suicidal tendency in the initial stages. In this study, the Instagram posts were analysed using different features that are more inclined to exhibit suicidal behaviour. The best accuracy is achieved by J48 binary tree classifier with a classification accuracy of 87.68%.

Keywords: Suicidal predilection · J48 decision tree · Binary tree · Machine learning

1 Introduction

The advancement of social media plays an important role in the majority of youngsters on the web. They utilize such platforms mainly for communication and entertainment. The visible trend nowadays is communicating sentiments through social media. Most social media profiles look like a portrait of that user's life. The tendency of sharing every moment of their life instantly through different forms of social networks has grown, where Instagram holds the top rank within youngsters. Due to the popularity, impact and availability of data, we have chosen the Instagram platform for our study. The text-based analysis method we used for this research is facilitated by the availability of numerous public accounts and its associated public comments and hashtags related to them.

This study of social media helps us in understanding the views and emotions flowing through its users. Hence, such studies are heavily promoted to avoid any disastrous or unfavourable events bringing harm to individuality or society. One of the major problems encountered by youth generation is depression or emotional anxiety disorders. Being in depression or living in a black hole is a condition in which one undergoes through mental

S. M. Thampi et al. (Eds.): SoMMA 2019, CCIS 1203, pp. 255–263, 2020.
https://doi.org/10.1007/978-981-15-4301-2_23

disorder and imbalance leading from low to high criticality situations. The social media plays a very important role in identifying young generation undergoing such trauma. The individual tends to express such situations through various techniques while being active in social media. Most of the youngsters are using fake profiles or some public pages like quote page, to express their emotions and they are using many secret hashtags in their posts. The use of secret hashtags is increasing just because it helps to drape from the public and to get alleviation from their pain.

In our study, we are focusing on a special case of cyberbullying which is suicidal tendencies exhibition and its early detection from Instagram social media through various methodologies. Such individuals usually express their feelings either as extreme depression or extreme anger which can lead to suicidal tendencies, so we are trying to identify such tendencies exhibited from their posts, by considering the sentiment of the captions, hashtags used in the posts, activity frequency and the biography of the user. Hashtag based analysis can give an optimum result because they are more specific to the situation. The mood swings of users can be easily identified based on the emotions in captions. This research proceeds as a text-based approach using a J48 tree classifier model classification for the analysis.

2 Literature Survey

Various studies [2, 5–7, 9] deals with issues like cyberbullying and cyber grooming via social media. There are many works [1, 3, 4] related to text-based and image-based analysis using Twitter dataset. [1] is a study about the suicidal tendency of teens on Twitter using neural networks which adopts text feature set and emoji feature set and analysed with cross-validation and 70–30 split. The model achieved an accuracy of about 75%. [2] uses word distribution of hashtag in creating clusters of posts and represented in dendrogram format achieving preferable exactness over existing frameworks. Moise [3] proposed a system which uses the Twitter environment for analysing hashtags. The text is converted to a sequence file and vectors created and formatted by LDA. Using the CVB algorithm, they are improving the accuracy regarding design and implementation.

[4] made use of the Twitter hashtags utilizing fuzzy clustering approach, in which they use popularity analysis and change impact analysis. This exploration utilizes fuzzy logic to cluster information. [6] selected Instagram platform for analysis and is related to the automatic detection of cyberbullying using text-based analysis of comments as well as image-based analysis of posts. The combination of text, meta, and image data is analyzed using SVM classifier giving an accuracy of 85%.

[17] considered the objective words and intensifiers of informal textual communication through social media to detect the sentiments. This paper uses techniques like SVM, SentiWordNet lexical resource to improve the sentiment classification by enhancing the sentiment values. [22] proposed a system for sentiment analysis making use of deep learning technique CNN with k means. They use the analysis to obtain the review of the film, by using a combination of deep learning and unsupervised learning techniques. [5] adopted a system of unsupervised cyberbullying detection, which is based on a hybrid set of features with classical textual features and social features, and filtering process is taking place using syntactic and semantic analysis and NLP algorithms. [16] is an

article regarding rumours on social media, and proposes a system which is to isolate rumours by calculating the preparatory source. The system is mainly focusing on the identification of the root from which the common rumours are arriving.

3   Methods and Analysis

We analysed Instagram profiles and its associated posts for the suicidal tendencies detection. This section discusses data collection followed by filtering of relevant data, feature extraction, implementation and results.

3.1   Data Collection and Filtering

We are using Instagram data for analysis and the data was collected based on a set of keywords which includes suicide, self-harm, want to die, wish to die, depression, secret society etc. We chose these keywords by analysing different profiles and found that these are the most commonly used keywords. In this research, we also included negative hashtags and keywords and secret hashtags [23, 24], which are used to express their feelings while maintaining secrecy. The extracted fields of a profile from Instagram include the entire posts of the profile along with captions, hashtags, created time and the biography of the user. The biography has an important role in ease filtering of data i.e., if bio contains words like quotes, memes, awareness, motivation etc. then we can avoid those profiles in the initial stage. Also, these kinds of public pages will have more followers than followed by count. These points were used to filter the public pages like motivation pages or awareness pages etc. Secret hashtags used for the analyzed posts are commonly using noun phrases like Annie, Cat which is a replacement for self-harm, Deb instead of depression etc. When considering this aspect, the major problem was false positive profiles. Hence more precise filtering was done before feature extraction (Table 1).

Table 1. Dataset statistics.

	Type	Count
Profiles	Victim profiles	135
	Genuine profiles	155
Posts	Victim posts	1504
	Genuine posts	1666

For the study, we collected 290 different public profiles, in which 135 profiles belong to the case of suicidal victims and the remaining profiles are genuine profiles or public/motivation pages. The filtering of data into two different groups - public page and personal accounts are done based on their biography information and followed-following ration, as the ration will be much higher for the former group. The biography also contains details of the account being used as business account or not, which is also considered for filtering. From these filtered profiles, we collected their entire posts as well as their bio information and created a dataset which contains a total of 3170 posts along with captions, hashtags used, created time, number of likes, comments, etc.

3.2 Feature Extraction

Numerous features were analyzed and an abstract list was derived from them. Based on observation and experiments performed on each feature and a relevance score was assigned to each of them. The main features extracted from the collected data includes the sentiment of captions in each post, the negative and positive hashtags in post, the temporal posting pattern and bio information. The sentiments of captions are derived using pretrained Sentiwordnet [25] algorithm which is trained on a set of posts defined in each of the three classes - positive, neutral and negative. These classes are internally represented as a 0, 1, 2 for positive, neutral and negative respectively. We found a set of negative hashtags of about 1100 in number, which are closely related to such posts. This set was used to find the count of negative hashtags and the rest were included in positive hashtag count. These counts were also added as separate features. The post frequency plays a major role in determining the profile behavioural changes. The victim profile tends to deviate from the normal behavioural pattern and exhibit a rapid increased or decreased posting pattern. This factor is helpful to identify the activity of the user, with which we can infer whether the profile has deviations from the normal form. This tendency is analyzed by calculating the time delay in posting for five previous posts from the current post of the profile. The bio information feature is taken as positive if it contains any particular words indicating suicidal tendency like last-cut, depressive, etc. else will be marked as negative.

3.3 Implementation and Results

The dataset prepared with the features for each post was marked as 'yes' for suicidal victim post and 'no' for genuine profile posts for this binary classification problem. We experimented with different resampling techniques on the dataset like 10 fold cross-validation and applied on different machine learning algorithms. Another way we trained the dataset was by splitting the dataset into a train and test set in 5:1 ratio.

The prepared dataset is trained on various algorithms such as J48 decision tree, random forest, multiclass classifier, regression logistics and simple logistic classifier. The experimentation was performed using Weka [26] software which has a collection of machine learning algorithm for data analysis. The best accuracy was achieved for J48 tree classifier with a score of around 87.68% when the dataset was divided into train and test set but the same classifier showed less accuracy with 10 fold cross-validation of about 79.2%. The least accuracy was for random forest and simple logistics of around 82%. The accuracy was improved of about 3–6% when the 10 fold cross-validation resampling technique was replaced by train and test set procedure.

Table 2. Accuracy achieved for each algorithm.

	Algorithm	Accuracy
Training set and test set	J48 decision tree	87.68
	Multiclass classifier	83.33
	Regression logistics	83.33
	Random forest	82.85
	Simple logistics	82.14
10 fold cross validation	J48 decision tree	79.2
	Multiclass classifier	79.77
	Regression logistics	79.7
	Random forest	80.86
	Simple logistics	80.8

Table 3. Summary of algorithms

	Correctly classified instances	Incorrectly classified instances	Kappa statistic	Mean absolute error	Root mean squared error	Relative absolute error	Root relative squared error
J48 decision tree	224	66	.7507	.1684	.3151	33.77%	62.92%
Random forest	214	76	.6542	.1879	.3403	37.68%	67.96%
Multiclass classifier	215	75	.6632	.1819	.3273	36.47%	65.36%
Regression logistics	215	75	.6632	.1819	.3273	36.47%	65.36%
Simple logistics	215	75	.6632	.1819	.3273	36.47%	65.36%

So we finalized the features depending on different results obtained. In the studied profiles, the frequency of increase or decrease in activities could indicate tendencies such as personal issues or due to online attacks such as harassment and negative trolling. The negative-positive hashtag usage relation will be high in suicidal profiles and others having a low to medium ratio. If the bio information contains the selected keywords then the profile will fall under suicidal case. Out of the selected data set of 32 profiles, mentions in bio like last cut on a particular date, depressive, wand to die etc. depicted high case of suicidal tendencies. Also, the sentiment in captions having negative or neutral showed more suicidal tendencies when compared to positive motivational/quote profiles.

Table 4. Confusion matrix

	Algorithm	a = "yes" predicted	b = "no" predicted
Training set and test set	J48 decision tree	131	17
	Random forest	129	19
	Multiclass classifier	133	15
	Regression logistics	133	15
	Simple logistics	133	15
10 fold cross validation	J48 decision tree	49	93
	Random forest	57	85
	Multiclass classifier	60	82
	Regression logistics	60	82
	Simple logistics	60	82

Table 5. Detailed accuracy by class

	TP rate	FP rate	Precision	Recall	F-measure	MCC	ROC area	PRC area
J48 decision tree	0.981	0.235	0.815	0.981	0.891	0.768	0.979	0.978
	0.765	0.019	0.975	0.765	0.857	0.768	0.979	0.974
	0.876	0.130	0.893	0.876	0.874	0.768	0.979	0.976
Random forest	0.963	0.314	0.765	0.963	0.852	0.679	0.960	0.961
	0.686	0.037	0.946	0.686	0.795	0.679	0.960	0.951
	0.829	0.179	0.853	0.829	0.825	0.679	0.960	0.956
Multiclass classifier	1.000	0.343	0.755	1.000	0.861	0.704	0.975	0.977
	0.657	0.000	1.000	0.657	0.793	0.704	0.975	0.974
	0.833	0.176	0.874	0.833	0.828	0.704	0.975	0.976
Regression logistics	1.000	0.343	0.755	1.000	0.861	0.704	0.975	0.977
	0.657	0.000	1.000	0.657	0.793	0.704	0.975	0.974
	0.833	0.176	0.874	0.833	0.828	0.704	0.975	0.976
Simple logistics	1.000	0.343	0.755	1.000	0.861	0.704	0.978	0.980
	0.657	0.000	1.000	0.657	0.793	0.704	0.978	0.977
	0.833	0.176	0.874	0.833	0.828	0.704	0.978	0.978

From Table 2 it is clear that comparatively, J48 has higher accuracy, but in the case of 10 fold cross-validation random forest is having highest accuracy than J48. This indicates that the dataset used is enough for the classification and resampling techniques are not required. The training test set division method seems to understand the dataset and come with a better classification than 10 fold cross-validation. Table 3 is a comparison between different errors for each algorithm. Here also J48 have fewer errors, and the most error occurring algorithm is random forest. The confusion matrix represented in Table 4 is the relationship between the expected value and the actual predicted value. And the Table 5 is used to describe different evaluation criteria such as true positive rate, false positive

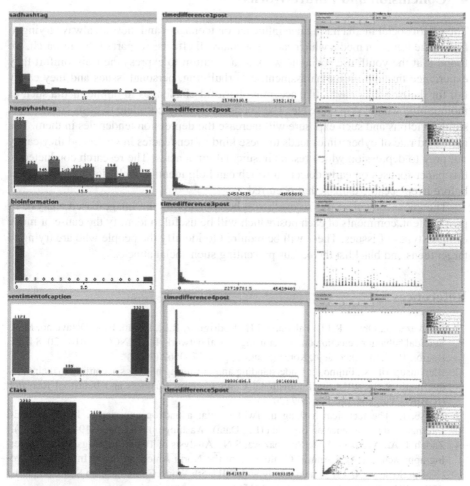

Fig. 1. Data distribution of the selected features.

Fig. 2. Data distribution of the selected features.

Fig. 3. Data visualization of instance spreading with attributes

rate, precision, recall, f-measure, etc., and all these are showing that J48 is the most suitable machine-learning algorithm for the prediction.

Figures 1and 2 shows the feature distribution in the data set under the "yes" and "no" classes in terms of an attribute, which depicts the feature contribution and interdependencies of the attribute per class. Also, the variations in attribute distribution reflect the variations in profile behaviour. In Fig. 3 the instance spreading is monitored. The figure indicates the dependency between two attributes with respect to the class.

4 Conclusion and Future Works

The use of social media has a huge influence on teenagers and they are always trying to follow the trends in media which can cause many ill effects. As part of this research, we found that the youth use social network as a medium to express their discomfort they experience through online harassment, cyberbullying, personal issues and they easily fall for the trends in media like accepting harmful challenges in online media such as momo, blue whale, skin erase etc. The youngsters easily correlate to posts from others similar victims and such exposure will increase the depression tendencies in them. The increased rate of cybercrimes leads to these kind of tendencies in youth and they easily fall prey to depression which results in suicidal tendencies. The research conducted in this paper focuses on early detection which can help identify such victims and recover before irreplaceable damage has occurred.

The enhancement of this research will be considering the image-based analysis of post content, comments of each post which will be useful to identify the cause or mode of these types of issues. These will be required to identify the people who are trying to target teens and blacklist them, thus preventing such social attacks.

References

1. Astoveza, G., Obias, R.J.P., Palcon, R.J.L., Rodriguez, R.L., Fabito, B.S., Octaviano, M.V.: Suicidal behavior detection on twitter using neural network. In: TENCON 2018 - 2018 IEEE Region 10 Conference, Jeju, Korea (South), pp. 0657–0662 (2018)
2. Bhakdisuparit, N., Fujino, I.: Understanding and clustering hashtags according to their word distributions. In: 2018 5th International Conference on Business and Industrial Research (ICBIR), Bangkok, pp. 204–209 (2018)
3. Moise, I.: The technical hashtag in Twitter data: a hadoop experience. In: 2016 IEEE International Conference on Big Data (Big Data), Washington, DC, pp. 3519–3528 (2016)
4. Zadeh, L.A., Abbasov, A.M., Shahbazova, S.N.: Analysis of Twitter hashtags: fuzzy clustering approach. In: 2015 Annual Conference of the North American Fuzzy Information Processing Society (NAFIPS) held jointly with 2015 5th World Conference on Soft Computing (WConSC), Redmond, WA, pp. 1–6 (2015)
5. Di Capua, M., Di Nardo, E., Petrosino, A.: Unsupervised cyberbullying detection in social networks. In: 2016 23rd International Conference on Pattern Recognition (ICPR), Cancun, pp. 432–437 (2016)
6. Hosseinmardi, H., Mattson, S.A., Rafiq, R.I., Han, R., Lv, Q., Mishra, S.: Prediction of Cyberbullying Incidents on the Instagram Social Network. arXiv, abs/1508.06257 (2015)
7. Noviantho, Isa, S.M., Ashianti, L.: Cyberbullying classification using text mining. In: 2017 1st International Conference on Informatics and Computational Sciences (ICICoS), Semarang, pp. 241–246 (2017)
8. Zois, D., Kapodistria, A., Yao, M., Chelmis, C.: Optimal online cyberbullying detection. In: 2018 IEEE International Conference on Acoustics, Speech and Signal Processing (ICASSP), Calgary, AB, pp. 2017–2021 (2018)
9. Sugandhi, R., Pande, A., Chawla, S., Agrawal, A., Bhagat, H.: Methods for detection of cyberbullying: a survey. In: 2015 15th International Conference on Intelligent Systems Design and Applications (ISDA), Marrakech, pp. 173–177 (2015)

10. Calderon-Vilca, H.D., Wun-Rafael, W.I., Miranda-Loarte, R.: Simulation of suicide tendency by using machine learning. In: 2017 36th International Conference of the Chilean Computer Science Society (SCCC), Arica, pp. 1–6 (2017)
11. Heathworldorganization-OMS.Suicide.   http://www.who.int/mediacentre/factsheets/fs398 /es/. Accessed 7 Aug 2017
12. Zhang, D., Tsai, J.J. (eds.): Machine Learning Applications in Software Engineering, vol. 16. World Scientific, Singapore (2005)
13. Tran, T., Phung, D., Luo, W., Harvey, R., Berk, M., Venkatesh, S.: An integrated framework for suicide risk prediction. In: Proceedings of the 19th ACM SIGKDD International Conference on Knowledge Discovery and Data Mining, pp. 1410–1418. ACM, August 2013
14. Reynolds, K., Kontostathis, A., Edwards, L.: Using machine learning to detect cyberbullying. In: 2011 10th International Conference on Machine Learning and Applications and Workshops, Honolulu, HI, pp. 241–244 (2011)
15. Rybnicek, M., Poisel, R., Tjoa, S.: Facebook watchdog: a research agenda for detecting online grooming and bullying activities. In: 2013 IEEE International Conference on Systems, Man, and Cybernetics, Manchester, pp. 2854–2859 (2013)
16. Krithika, R., Mohan, A.K., Sethumadhavan, M.: Jordan center segregation: rumors in social media networks. In: Thampi, S.M., Martínez Pérez, G., Westphall, C.B., Hu, J., Fan, C.I., Gómez Mármol, F. (eds.) SSCC 2017. CCIS, vol. 746, pp. 146–158. Springer, Singapore (2017). https://doi.org/10.1007/978-981-10-6898-0_12
17. Bhaskar, J., Sruthi, K., Nedungadi, P.: Enhanced sentiment analysis of informal textual communication in social media by considering objective words and intensifiers. In: International Conference on Recent Advances and Innovations in Engineering (ICRAIE-2014), Jaipur, pp. 1–6 (2014)
18. Kandasamy, K., Koroth, P.: An integrated approach to spam classification on Twitter using URL analysis, natural language processing and machine learning techniques. In: 2014 IEEE Students' Conference on Electrical, Electronics and Computer Science, SCEECS 2014, Bhopal (2014)
19. Raman, H.A., MuraliKrishnan, E., Abishek, M., SaiSandhesh, R., Vijaykanth, K., Harini, N.: Analysis of Twitter feeds using natural language processing and machine learning. Int. J. Appl. Eng. Res. **10**, 18911–18916 (2015)
20. Nair, B.B., Mohandas, V.P., Sakthivel, N.R.: A genetic algorithm optimized decision tree-SVM based stock market trend prediction system. Int. J. Comput. Sci. Eng. **2**(9), 2981–2988 (2010)
21. Pranavi, M.V.C., Yuganeshan, A.J., K, Y.V.S.S.N., Santhana, S.: Comparison of Naïve bayes using different feature selection techniques in twitter sentiment analysis. **9**, 12779–12786 (2014)
22. Lakshmi, S.B., Raj, P.S., Vikram, R.R.: Sentiment analysis using deep learning technique CNN with KMeans. Int. J. Pure Appl. Math. **114**, 47–57 (2017)
23. Brenneisen, N.: The Teens Using Instagram Hashtags to Glorify Suicide. VICE News, 18 January 2016. https://www.vice.com/en_us/article/9bg7w8/glorifying-mental-illness-on-ins tagram-876
24. Yandoli, K.L.: Inside the Secret World of Teen Suicide Hashtags. Buzzfeed News, 7 September 2014. www.buzzfeednews.com/article/krystieyandoli/how-teens-are-using-social-media-to-t alk-about-suicide
25. Baccianella, S., Esuli, A., Sebastiani, F.: Sentiwordnet 3.0: an enhanced lexical resource for sentiment analysis and opinion mining. In: LREC, vol. 10, no. 2010 (2010)
26. Frank, E., Hall, M.A., Witten, I.H.: The WEKA Workbench. Online Appendix for "Data Mining: Practical Machine Learning Tools and Techniques", 4th edn. Morgan Kaufmann, Burlington (2016)

Author Index